COUNSELLING SKILLS FOR WORKING WITH TRAUMA

Healing From Child Sexual Abuse, Sexual Violence and Domestic Abuse

CHRISTIANE SANDERSON

Jessica Kingsley *Publishers*
London and Philadelphia

First published in 2013
by Jessica Kingsley Publishers
73 Collier Street
London N1 9BE, UK

and

400 Market Street, Suite 400
Philadelphia, PA 19106, USA

www.jkp.com

Library of Congress Cataloging in Publication Data
Sanderson, Christiane.
Counselling skills for working with trauma : healing from child sexual abuse, sexual violence and
domestic abuse / Christiane Sanderson.
pages cm
Includes bibliographical references and index.
ISBN 978-1-84905-326-6
1. Sexual abuse victims--Mental health. 2. Sexual abuse victims--Counseling of. 3. Victims of family
violence--Mental health. 4. Victims of family violence--Counseling of. 5. Post-traumatic stress disorder--
Treatment. I. Title.
RC560.S44S26 2014
616.85'83690651--dc23
                                                        2013019206

British Library Cataloguing in Publication Data
A CIP catalogue record for this book is available from the British Library

ISBN 978 1 84905 326 6
eISBN 978 0 85700 743 8

Printed and bound in Great Britain by Bell and Bain Ltd., Glasgow

For James and Max

CONTENTS

Part 4 Post-traumatic Growth

Part 5 Professional Issues

ACKNOWLEDGEMENTS

I would like to thank all the survivors who have entrusted me with their experiences. They have been an inspiration and taught me about resilience and what it means to be human. I would also like to thank the many students, trainees, fellow counsellors and colleagues, in particular Michael, Linda Dominguez and all the staff at One in Four UK, Paul Glynn, Tony Evans, Matthew Trustman, Jo Cruywagen, Jean O'Callaghan, Marcia Worrall, Diane Bray, and Elwyn Taylor. A huge thank you to Jessica Kingsley, Stephen Jones, Allison Walker, Sarah Hull and Maureen Cox at Jessica Kingsley for supporting this handbook. Finally to James and Max who through their constancy, support and love continue to embolden me.

INTRODUCTION

Sexual violence and sexual abuse can no longer be ignored. Every week reports of rape, child sexual abuse (CSA), sexual trafficking and systematic abuse feature in both national and international media. Most recently the press in the UK has been dominated by allegations of sexual abuse against Jimmy Savile and other celebrities, reports of CSA in children's homes, the sexual trafficking of children and CSA by faith leaders, especially in the Roman Catholic Church. In addition, there has been an increase in reports of sexual violence and rape globally, most prominently in India, South Africa, and in war-torn countries. This has resulted in a climate change in how systematic sexual violence against women, children and men is viewed and tolerated.

The various inquiries into Jimmy Savile in the UK have led to proposed changes in how victims of sexual violence are dealt with by both the criminal justice system and mental health practitioners. As we learn more about how sexual abusers operate, how they not only groom children but other adults around them – and in the case of Jimmy Savile, a whole nation – we can identify how such abuse impacts on victims and survivors. In acknowledging how widespread sexual violence is and how hard it is to disclose to authorities, especially if the abuser is in a position of power and authority, survivors are more likely to be believed and offered appropriate support.

This means that there needs to be an increase in awareness of the impact of sexual violence and CSA and provision of appropriate therapeutic interventions. In the wake of the Jimmy Savile allegations, many of the specialist charities and volunteer agencies such as One in Four UK, National Association for People Abused as Children (NAPAC) and the NSPCC reported a huge increase in calls from survivors seeking therapeutic help. Due to reduced funding to such agencies and the high demand most of these survivors had to be put onto waiting lists with no guarantee when they would be allocated therapeutic support, which exacerbated their distress (Sanderson, 2012).

What is clear is that there needs to be an increase in the provision of psychotherapy and counselling for survivors of sexual violence and complex trauma. Many survivors who sought counselling support prior to the Jimmy Savile allegations report being disappointed by the lack of service provision for them. Most commonly they report a lack of specialist counsellors who have the expertise or training in sexual violence or complex trauma with waiting lists up to 12 months. When they are finally allocated a counsellor, they are dismayed to discover that they are only offered short term therapeutic support of between 6 and 12 sessions, which does not permit sufficient time to fully explore the impact of complex trauma, systematic sexual violence or CSA. In addition, they are usually only offered evidence based therapy such as cognitive behavioural therapy (CBT), which does not always incorporate full exploration of the dynamics in complex trauma. Due to these limitations many survivors are not able to recover, let alone fully heal from complex trauma, which reinforces their sense of failure and shame and confirms their fear that they are so damaged they may never recover.

As victims and survivors come forward with a greater than ever chance of being believed and responded to they need to be assured that they will be able to access the type of therapy that will not re-traumatise or shame them. Thus it is important that counsellors and practitioners have a good understanding of the complex dynamics of complex trauma, sexual violence and CSA and are able to provide the appropriate therapeutic intervention. It is with this in mind that this skills manual came into being.

The aim of the manual is to provide knowledge and understanding of the neurobiological as well as the psychosocial impact of complex trauma and how to manage the core symptoms associated with it. It is designed to support whichever therapeutic model the practitioner already uses and offers tried and tested therapeutic techniques that they can use with survivors. Many of these techniques and skills can easily be added onto or incorporated into the practitioner's preferred therapeutic model and enhance their practice with survivors of a range of complex trauma through systematic sexual or domestic abuse.

STRUCTURE OF THE BOOK

The book is divided into five parts with Part 1 focusing on understanding complex trauma and post-traumatic stress disorder (PTSD), dissociation and common trauma reactions, the role of attachment and relational worth, as well as the importance of assessment and the range of treatment interventions. Part 2 explores how practitioners can work most effectively with complex trauma by introducing the fundamental principles of working trauma including the need for safety and control, identifying the therapeutic challenges, building and maintaining a therapeutic relationship and the process of recovery and healing, including obstacles to healing.

Part 3 presents a range of skills to manage complex trauma such as how to establish safety and restore control to the survivor, skills to improve daily life and promote self-care and how to manage sensations and feelings through grounding skills. Skills to help manage flashbacks, panic attacks, nightmares and dissociation, negative thoughts, fragmented memories, shame and guilt and self-harm are also explored. How to restore boundaries and relationships skills to help the survivor set boundaries and how to manage relationships are introduced, alongside skills to manage sexuality and the process of loss, grief and mourning. In Part 4 the focus is on post-traumatic growth and skills to restore reality, relapse prevention and how to reconnect to self and others, while Part 5 explores the importance of counsellor self-care to minimise vicarious traumatisation and secondary traumatic stress (STS). Also included is a list of resources such as helpful specialist organisations, and a list of further reading to increase awareness and understanding of complex trauma.

The handbook is designed in such a way that you can dip in and out of it as you need to. You do not have to read all the chapters, or in any particular order. It is a flexible resource to be used in the way it most suits you. It is designed to help you to create a safe, secure base in which you can introduce skills and exercises that facilitate the management of trauma symptoms and help survivors to make sense of their traumatic experiences. Each chapter can be read as a stand-alone and includes a range of top tips, knowledge, core symptoms, warnings and exercises.

USE OF LANGUAGE

To legitimise the experience of complex trauma, the terms abuse, violence and assault will be used to include not just the use of physical force and assault but also the myriad forms of psychological, emotional, financial or sexual coercion designed to entrap individuals and keep them in thrall to the abuser. Practitioners may find the distinction between 'victimisation' and 'traumatisation' helpful when working with survivors of complex trauma as it enables survivors to acknowledge that while they were victims during the abuse, the pervasive effects have led to traumatisation rather than victimisation. This circumvents the pejorative effects of being labelled or identified as victims and its associated connotations. Practitioners also need to acknowledge that survivors are rarely passive victims and have invariably developed strategies to manage the abuse. To emphasise these active responses, and to dispel the negative connotation associated with the term 'victim', the term 'survivor' will be used. While the author acknowledges the differences and similarities between counsellor and therapist, these terms will be used synonymously, alongside the terms clinician and practitioner.

ICONS

The following icons are used to signpost the books main features:

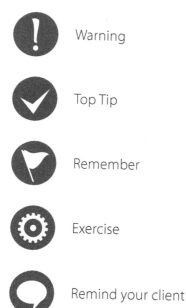

Warning

Top Tip

Remember

Exercise

Remind your client

Part 1

UNDERSTANDING COMPLEX TRAUMA

1

UNDERSTANDING TRAUMA
AND COMPLEX TRAUMA

Trauma is commonly defined as exposure to actual or threatened death, serious injury or sexual violation (DSM-V, APA, 2013) in which intense fear, horror or helplessness predominates. This can occur either through one single event or multiple and repeated traumatic events. Complex trauma is usually associated with prolonged, repeated traumatic experiences which involve multiple violations such as sexual assaults, physical violence, emotional abuse and neglect, often committed by someone known to the victim. In contrast to a single traumatic event, the repeated betrayal of trust, in which 'abuse masquerades as protection or affection' (Sanderson, 2010a, p.72) gives rise to a range of symptoms such as dissociation, alterations in sense of self, and a fear of intimacy in relationships.

This chapter explores the nature of trauma and complex trauma and how these impact upon individuals. The main focus will be on complex trauma and the range of symptomatology associated with repeated trauma within dependent relationships in which there is no escape. It will also present the current Diagnostic and Statistical Manual (DSM-V, APA, 2013) criteria and symptoms for Post-Traumatic Stress Disorder (PTSD) and symptoms associated with complex trauma.

WHAT IS MEANT BY TRAUMA?
There is often considerable variation in what is meant by trauma amongst clinicians, researchers, practitioners and survivors of trauma. In the recent revision in the American Psychiatric Association's Diagnostic Statistical Manual V (APA, 2013) criteria for trauma leading to PTSD now include not only direct exposure to actual or threatened death, serious injury or sexual violation, but also the witnessing of such traumatic events, learning

about such events happening to a close family member or friend, and experiencing repeated or extreme exposure to aversive details of traumatic events by emergency workers or police officers (APA, 2013). This last category equally applies to practitioners who specialise in working with survivors of trauma (see Chapter 24).

While this revision includes not just trauma through combat or natural disasters, but also sexual violation, it does not fully explain the impact of pervasive and repeated physical, sexual or psychological violations, or the habitual unpredictability and lack of control within attachment relationships such as child physical abuse (CPA), child sexual abuse (CSA), domestic abuse (DA), or institutional abuse. It also does not account for the complexity of abuse by those who have power and authority over the individual such as religious or faith leaders (Sanderson, 2011), cult leaders, or abuse by professionals such as doctors, psychotherapists or counsellors (Sanderson, 2010a). As a result the current criteria do not unravel how persistent threats to psychological integrity from prolonged abuse within an attachment relationship can undermine self-structures and related mental capacities.

Several clinicians and researchers (Herman, 1992b; Rothschild, 2000; Sanderson, 2010a; Terr, 1991) have highlighted the significant differences between a single event trauma, what Terr (1991) refers to as Type I Trauma, and multiple or Type II Trauma, especially in terms of impact and long-term effects. According to Terr (1991) Type II Trauma is associated with much greater psychobiological disruption, including complex post-traumatic stress reactions, dissociation, alterations in perception, dissociative amnesia for past and present experiences, memory impairment, loss of continuity and loss of meaning.

Rothschild (2000) further distinguishes between Type II Trauma and degrees of resilience. According to Rothschild (2000), Type IIA Trauma consists of multiple traumas experienced by individuals who have benefited from relatively stable backgrounds, and thus have sufficient resources to separate individual traumatic events from one another. In contrast, Type IIB Trauma consists of multiple traumas which are so overwhelming that the individual cannot separate one from another. Type IIB Traumas are further divided into Type IIB (R) in which the person has experienced sufficient stability to develop resources but the complexity of traumatic experiences are so overwhelming that resilience is impaired. In contrast, in Type IIB (nR) Trauma the individual has never developed resources for resilience. The latter is characteristic of survivors of complex trauma who have a history of childhood trauma such as CPA or CSA, and adult re-victimisation.

TRAUMA WITHIN ATTACHMENT RELATIONSHIPS

Repeated acts of violence, abuse or humiliation within attachment relationships can have more pervasive immediate and long-term effects due to the aversive dynamics such as the betrayal of trust, violation of dependency and protection needs and the severing of human connection, which threatens the sense of self and self-identity. Such failures in attachment and lack of protection when most needed can result in disruptions to, or fragmentation of personality, resulting in a chronic sense of emptiness, future relationship difficulties, and traumatic loneliness.

Trauma within attachment relationships in which the person is dependent on the abuser to satisfy basic human needs such as safety and protection, gives rise to a range of psychobiological defences that can result in dissociation and alterations in perception. To reconcile the paradox of abuse within a caring relationship or 'Knowing what you are not supposed to know and feeling what you are not supposed to feel' (Bowlby, 1988, p.99) survivors have to deny the traumatic nature of the abuse in order to hold onto a positive image of the abuser on whom they depend to have basic human needs met. In addition, when the abuser wields power and authority over the individual, acknowledging the abuse can have terrifying consequences: it can feel safer to deny the traumatic nature of the experience. This can lead to traumatic bonding (see Chapter 4, pp.61–2), confusion and distortion of reality.

In addition, the constant threat of physical or psychological annihilation, unpredictability and lack of control forces the individual to disown basic human needs and to deny any experience of vulnerability. Dehumanising the individual and distorting their reality prevents the individual from legitimising or naming the experience as abuse or trauma. This is further compounded when violations are initially not perceived as painful, terrifying or traumatic due dissociation, the distortion of reality by the abuser, or normalisation. Many abusers coerce victims through establishing a 'special' relationship in which sexual contact or physical punishment is presented as normal, making it hard to define as abuse or trauma. Awareness of the abusive nature of such coercion may not penetrate conscious awareness until much later when the person is in a place of safety and is able to reflect on their experience, or through cognitive reappraisal.

In the absence of being able to validate the trauma it becomes difficult to generate meaning, or make sense of experiences. As a result all relationships are seen as dangerous, a source of anxiety or terror and anticipated re-traumatisation, making it hard to trust and connect to others, including professionals.

COMPLEX TRAUMA

Despite significant differences between single event and multiple prolonged trauma, and proposals for a separate category of complex traumatic stress disorder (Herman, 2006), the APA have not included this in DSM-V as a separate, stand-alone diagnostic category. The revised International Classification of Diseases 10 (ICD 10, WHO, 2007) has taken into account both prolonged trauma and the delay or protracted responses to it in their categorisation of PTSD '…as a delayed or protracted response to a stressful event or situation (of either brief or long duration) of an exceptionally threatening or catastrophic nature, which is likely to cause pervasive distress in almost anyone…[that] may follow a chronic course over many years, with eventual transition to an enduring personality change' (www.who.int/classifications/icd/icdonlineversions/en).

Despite not being included in DSM-V (APA, 2013) there is considerable clinical evidence that, 'Survivors of prolonged abuse develop characteristic personality changes, including deformations of relatedness and identity…' (Herman, 1992b, p.379) and that conceptualising these dynamics within complex trauma aids clinicians in understanding the impact of pervasive and adverse traumatic events such as repeated sexual or physical abuse both in childhood and adulthood, committed in the absence of adequate emotional or social support. As such complex trauma more adequately highlights the symptoms seen in cases of repetitive and inescapable abuse in intimate relationships such as CPA, CSA, DA, elder abuse, institutional abuse, sexual slavery, or those held in 'captivity', or in thrall to their abuser who are not accounted for in current formulations of post-traumatic stress responses (Sanderson, 2010a).

POST-TRAUMATIC STRESS DISORDER (PTSD)

About one third of survivors of trauma and complex trauma develop symptoms of PTSD and it is more commonly diagnosed in females

(Chu, 2011), probably due to females seeking help for their symptoms, while males tend to mask or regulate their symptoms through self-medication and the use of alcohol or drugs. The main criteria for the diagnosis of PTSD are divided into the following four categories: intrusive symptoms, avoidance symptoms, alterations in cognitions and mood and alterations in arousal.

Box 1.1 Symptoms included in Criteria for PTSD (adapted from DSM-V, APA, 2013)

1. Intrusion symptoms – intrusive distressing memories; recurrent distressing dreams; dissociative reactions such as flashbacks through to complete loss of awareness of present surroundings; intense or prolonged psychological distress at exposure to internal or external cues that symbolise or resemble the traumatic event(s); marked physiological reactions to reminders of the traumatic event(s)

2. Avoidance symptoms – avoidance of distressing memories, thoughts, or feelings associated with the traumatic event(s); avoidance of external reminders (i.e. people, places, conversations, activities, objects, situations) that arouse distressing memories, thoughts of, or feelings associated with, the traumatic event(s)

3. Alterations in cognitions and mood – dissociative amnesia for important aspects of the traumatic event(s); persistent and exaggerated negative beliefs or expectations about oneself, others, or the world; distorted blame of self or others about the cause or consequences of the traumatic event(s); persistent negative emotional state (e.g. fear, horror, anger, guilt, or shame); diminished interest in significant activities; feelings of detachment or estrangement from others; persistent inability to experience positive emotions (e.g. unable to have loving feelings, psychic numbing)

4. Alterations in arousal and reactivity – irritable or aggressive behaviour; reckless or self-destructive behaviour; hyper-vigilance; exaggerated startle-response; problems with concentration; sleep disturbance

---

While the current DSM-V (APA, 2013) criteria for PTSD attempt to account for a wide range of trauma reactions they do not offer a comprehensive account for all the symptoms associated with complex trauma. In essence the criteria focus on the primary reactions to trauma such as neurobiological and physiological responses, for example hyper-arousal; intrusive symptoms such as flashbacks; avoidance symptoms; and alterations in cognitions (see Box 1.1). However, the new criteria do not fully account for all the secondary responses that develop in an attempt to cope with the primary traumatic effects such as self-harm, eating disorders, obsessive-compulsive disorders and addictions, which distract from the painful traumatic experiences. The criteria also fail to fully explain changes in personality, profound relationship difficulties or traumatic loneliness.

COMPLEX TRAUMA SYMPTOMS

In the case of complex trauma the symptoms become chronic as they begin to affect the very core of the self. Complex trauma reactions are commonly seen in people who have experienced prolonged sexual or physical abuse, or torture, especially if this is accompanied by the use of deception, falsification of reality and annihilation of the subjective self. Like PTSD, complex trauma elicits overwhelming, out-of-control physiological reactions such as hyper-arousal, flashbacks and intrusive memories. It also impacts on how survivors think about themselves and others, how they feel about their bodies, and how they relate to others. In addition, complex trauma can result in the distortion of reality, stigmatisation and a deep sense of shame. To manage such strong reactions can lead to an avoidance of all feelings, even pleasurable ones, and a withdrawal from others leading to social isolation. In order to avoid shame, you may find your client retreating from the world and expressing feelings that they are living their lives in a bubble.

Although complex trauma has not been adopted as a separate category by the APA they have added a new subtype of PTSD which is referred to as post traumatic stress disorder – with prominent dissociative (depersonalisation/derealisation) symptoms, in which the individual meets the diagnostic criteria for PTSD and has additional persistent or recurrent symptoms of either or both: depersonalisation which is characterised by feeling detached from, and as if one is an outside observer of one's mental process or body (i.e., feeling as though one is in a dream, a sense of unreality of self or body, or time moving slowly). Or derealisation which is characterised by experiences of unreality of one's surroundings (e.g. world around the person is experienced as unreal, dreamlike, distant or distorted) and which is not due to the direct physiolgical effects of a substance (e.g. drugs or alcohol intoxication), or a medical condition. While this offers some aspects of complex trauma it does not account for all the symptoms associated with prolonged and repeated trauma (see Box 1.2).

Box 1.2 Symptom clusters associated with complex trauma

1. Impairment in regulating affective impulses, rapid and unexpected changes in emotion and impulses, in particular anger directed at both self and others

2. Chronic self-destructive behaviours such as self-mutilation, eating disorders or drug abuse

3. Alterations in attention and consciousness leading to dissociative episodes, dissociative amnesia and impaired memory, difficulties with attention and concentration, sense of 'spaciness'

4. Alterations in self-perception manifested by a chronic sense of guilt, shame or inflated sense of responsibility, negative feelings and thoughts of self, unlikeable, unlovable, stupid, inept, dirty, worthless, lazy…

5. Alterations in relationships with others, primarily evident by the inability to trust and enjoy emotional intimacy, fear of intimacy, rejection, abandonment or criticism, relational conflicts, or over trusting

6. Complaints of diffuse somatic pain and dysfunction for which there is no medical explanation, such as abdominal pain, headaches, joints, muscle, elimination problems

7. Alterations in systems of meaning, such as loss of existing belief systems or the value and meaning of one's life, loss of faith in good things happening, loss of belief that others or the world are benign, sense of hopelessness, future bound to be as bad as past, sense of foreshortened future, premature death, despair or unrealistic optimism

---

COMPLEX TRAUMA AND ASSOCIATED DISORDERS

PTSD and complex trauma can produce a range of other psychological effects and disorders, especially anxiety disorders such as agoraphobia and social phobia, depression, obsessive compulsive disorder (OCD), borderline personality disorder, and chronic fatigue syndrome. They can also give rise to a number of physical complaints such as headaches, irritable bowel syndrome and unexplainable aches and pains, which are the body's way of expressing emotional distress or the effect of chronic stress (see Table 1.1).

In the case of associated disorders or dual-diagnosis it may be more beneficial to treat the secondary, or non-trauma related symptoms first to ensure sufficient stabilisation before addressing the traumatic experiences (Chu, 2011). This is especially the case in self-harming behaviours and addictions. Conversely, if associated symptoms such as depression are unresponsive to medication it may indicate that PTSD symptoms need to be prioritised and given greater therapeutic focus.

It is critical to identify primary traumatic reactions as well as those associated with complex trauma and secondary symptoms. To do this it may help to invite the client to engage in this exercise.

Table 1.1 Associated psychiatric disorders and physical illnesses	
Associated psychiatric disorders	**Associated physical illness**
Personality disorders – borderline personality disorder, antisocial personality disorder PTSD Dissociative disorders Depression Anxiety disorders Phobias – agoraphobia, social phobia OCD Eating disorders Substance dependency Self-harming behaviours Schizophrenia	Irritable bowel syndrome Chronic fatigue syndrome Chronic pelvic pain Increased risk of obesity Type II Diabetes Hypertension Recurring throat problems Ageing and degeneration of brain structures, including hippocampus

 Exercise
Identifying PTSD symptoms and coping strategies

1. With your client try to identify which, if any, PTSD symptoms they have experienced in the past or present and rank the order in which they are most troublesome.

2. Invite your client to make a list of coping strategies used in the past or present. Check which ones are most effective and adaptive and agree to reduce those that are no longer effective or adaptive.

3. Invite your client to add more strategies over time.

Alongside this, it is important to identify adaptive and maladaptive coping strategies that the client uses to regulate out of control emotions and trauma reactions such as self-injury or self-medication through food, alcohol or substance misuse, sex addiction or gambling. While these behaviours are adopted to either numb or release emotional or psychological pain, they are commonly accompanied by chronic feelings of ineffectiveness, shame, despair or hopelessness and feeling permanently damaged. This can compound distorted perceptions and negative thoughts such as self-blame. Shame and the loss of trust in others invariably leads to defensive tactics such as avoidance or hostility, and a lack of trust in a safe or benign world.

Remind your client

Even if their trauma experience was subtle and non-violent and not consciously experienced as trauma it can still be traumatising in distorting their reality and overall sense of confusion.

To manage the effects of PTSD and complex trauma it is crucial to have a thorough knowledge of trauma reactions and to be able to convey this to survivors in such a way that they can better understand their physiological reactions and symptoms. Enabling survivors to make sense of their trauma reactions can reassure them that they are not 'going crazy' and allow them to regain more control over their bodily reactions. The following chapter aims to enhance understanding of trauma and trauma reactions, which can be used to make survivors more aware of the link between trauma and their symptoms.

Remember

Not all survivors of complex trauma develop PTSD symptoms.

2

UNDERSTANDING
TRAUMA SYMPTOMS

To fully understand the impact of trauma and complex trauma, practitioners will need to familiarise themselves with the primary symptoms of trauma. While each survivor's reactions to trauma are unique and will vary from person to person and depend on the type of trauma, age, the frequency and duration of the abuse, and the relationship to the abuser(s), there are a number of commonalities. It is crucial that survivors are helped to recognise that the physical and psychological reactions to trauma are normal responses which serve to protect us, and are elicited outside of conscious awareness or control. These reactions are like an emotional immune system, which instead of fighting invading bacteria or viruses, fights to protect us from harm.

To help survivors understand their reactions to trauma, practitioners need to be able to convey the following information in a way that is easily understood by the client and that makes sense to them. This can be supported with directed reading or self-help books such as *The Warrior Within* (Sanderson, 2010c).

Persistent re-experiencing of trauma can be triggered by both internal and external cues. This means that even if the survivor is currently not in actual external danger, inner feelings and sensations can trigger a range of PTSD reactions. Given that they may already be in an elevated state of anxiety, it is easy to set off an already highly sensitive alarm system on the basis of internal physiological arousal. This is potentially dangerous as it prevents the survivor from recognising actual external danger and makes it hard to assess objectively the degree of safety.

THE ALARM SYSTEM

To help survivors understand the neurological and physiological responses to trauma it is helpful to explore their knowledge of how the body reacts to danger. When in the presence of danger primitive biological mechanisms such as the alarm system are activated to aid survival. As a result the brain releases a cascade of neuro-chemicals which start a complex chain of bodily reactions, all of which are designed to protect us from the harmful effects of trauma. Although the alarm system does not stop the emotional pain, stress or trauma from happening, it does cushion the trauma and helps us to deal with it.

The alarm system acts as an emotional immune system, which like the physical immune system, is activated outside of conscious awareness and is therefore not under our control. It is vital that survivors understand that whatever their reactions during the trauma, these were outside of conscious control and therefore they are not to blame or at fault for how they responded. Recognising this can dramatically reduce any crippling feelings of shame, self-blame, or guilt.

 Remind your client
Reactions to trauma are outside of conscious control and they are not to blame for how they responded during the abuse.

When the body's alarm system is tripped and goes on red alert it sends signals to the brain to prepare for fight, flight or freeze. This sets off two crucial biological defence systems: the sympathetic nervous system and the parasympathetic nervous system. The sympathetic nervous system mobilises high level energy necessary for fight or flight, while the parasympathetic nervous system slows down the heart and metabolic rate which results in the freeze response.

The two structures in the brain that regulate the alarm system are both located in the limbic system, the amygdala and the hippocampus. The role of the amygdala is to detect threatening information through external senses such as touch, taste, sound, smell or vision. The amygdala is responsible for determining whether incoming stimuli are desirable, benign or dangerous. To maximise survival, this evaluation is instantaneous but crude and primitive in that it does not use deeper analysis, reason or common sense. This is why it is often referred to as the 'fast and dirty route'.

If the stimulus is life threatening, stress hormones such as adrenaline and cortisol are released, which send messages through the nervous system to the muscles and internal organs to either attack, run or play dead. The amygdala is highly sensitive to any danger and is easily activated to increase readiness to attack or defend (fight), run (flight) or submit (freeze).

In contrast to the 'fast and dirty' route of the amygdala, the hippocampus is a much slower route in that it evaluates the external threat through deeper analysis using conscious thought, memory, prior knowledge, reason and logic. The hippocampus is also critical in laying down new memories and experiences. If the danger is truly life threatening, the hippocampus will send messages to continue with appropriate responses. If however the deeper analysis concludes that the stimuli are not dangerous it will send messages to deactivate the responses. In most cases of threat these two structures work in harmony to balance appropriate responses to the situation.

When the trauma is prolonged and repeated such as in complex trauma, the feedback loop that controls these two systems malfunctions and floods the body with high levels of stress hormones. While these stress hormones are critical for survival, they are highly toxic and only designed to circulate for short periods of time so that the individual can get to a place of safety or remain safe until the threat is over. In the case of certain traumas such as CPA or CSA where the child cannot fight or run to safety, the only option is to freeze. This means that the stress hormones cannot be discharged and remain in the system, which can have a number of negative consequences, not least forcing the alarm system to remain on red alert, or 'online' (Sanderson, 2010c).

Evidence shows that high levels of cortisol that are not discharged can lead to the destruction of brain cells which can affect the function and size of the amygdala and hippocampus (Gerhardt, 2004; Teicher, 2000). Such malfunction leads to increased arousal, fear and anger responses, as well as memory impairments.

When the brain and body are flooded with chronic levels of stress hormones the hippocampus goes 'offline' and is unable to accurately evaluate the degree of threat or danger. It is also not able to assess whether the danger is internal or external, or whether the traumatic incident is over or on-going, and cannot send the appropriate messages to the amygdala to deactivate the alarm system. This leads to the alarm system remaining on constant red alert and the continued release of stress hormones.

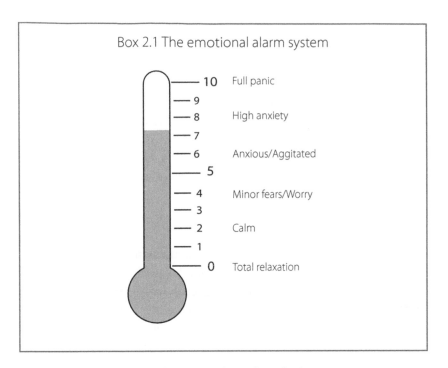

Box 2.1 The emotional alarm system

As a consequence the body responds as though the trauma is on-going, even after the threat is over. Over time the alarm system is reset on a default setting of 'on', with survivors feeling as though they are being repeatedly traumatised. This leads to a heightened or continuous state of danger, known as hyper-arousal. This hyper-arousal forces stress hormones to continue to flood the body and brain, and the tyranny of post-traumatic stress responses.

Since the hippocampus is not able to regulate the alarm setting, or halt the release of chronic levels of stress hormones, its ability to store new memories is reduced. This means that the trauma is not stored within context or time, making it seem as though it is continuous and never ending. This in turn prevents the processing of the trauma keeping it 'online' with the same vividness and intensity as when the actual assault happened.

Not being able to process the traumatic experience makes it harder for survivors to store it in memory or to recall it leading to amnesia, or incomplete or fragmented memories. A crucial goal in recovering from complex trauma is to bring the hippocampus back 'online' so that its function can be restored to regulate the alarm system to evaluate danger, and differentiate between internal and external threat.

DAMAGE TO PHYSICAL WELL-BEING

Prolonged release of high levels of stress hormones impacts on physical well-being leading to a range of physical problems such as hypertension, physical exhaustion, chronic fatigue syndrome (CFS), sleep impairment, and digestive, respiratory and endocrine problems. In addition, chronic fear reactions and high levels of adrenaline evoke waves of overwhelming anger which survivors cannot release for fear of consequences, thereby creating even further stress. Hyper-arousal also affects concentration and the ability to reflect on or process experiences, preventing survivors from making sense of their experiences.

ROLE OF THE FREEZE RESPONSE

While the alarm system can activate three alternative reactions – fight, flight or freeze – in most cases of complex trauma, especially when it occurs in childhood, there is only one option: to freeze. The freeze response is designed to conserve energy so that the individual can escape when the danger is over. Young children are not able to outrun or fight an adult effectively, and are thus left with no option but to freeze. While the freeze response protects the individual from the greater threat of the consequences of fighting back or running away, it is often experienced as passive submission. This can make survivors feel as though they were weak in not fighting back or running away, which can lead to shame, self-blame and guilt.

It is important to convey to survivors that realistically children are not able to escape, especially if the abuser is a significant figure in the child's life such as a parent, relative or priest. In that moment they are both powerless and helpless. However, the sense of submission can often haunt them and leave them feeling ashamed that they did not do more to prevent the abuse. This is also true for adults who are in thrall to an abuser who has power and authority over them.

The freeze response also protects individuals from the full impact of the pain of the abuse. As the parasympathetic nervous system kicks in, a sense of calmness descends on the brain, slowing everything down, and the body begins to feel numb in order to cushion the anticipated pain and the emotional terror of the trauma. Once the danger is over, these reactions fade and the stress hormones are discharged through movement.

In complex trauma in which there is no escape, these hormones are not discharged and continue to circulate leading to increased numbness, paralysis, dissociation, psychological deadness, or collapse. Thus the terror and distress do not go away but tend to grow stronger over time, causing even more intense distress which the mind tries to block through avoidance, psychic numbing and dissociation (see Chapter 3).

 Remind your client
Freezing is NOT giving up or a passive act of submission. It protects them from further harm and is not a conscious choice but part of the body's alarm system when in danger with no means of escape.

POST-TRAUMATIC STRESS SYMPTOMS

As complex trauma impacts differently on each individual it might be helpful to examine how it has affected your client in particular. It is helpful to identify which post-traumatic symptoms, if any, affect each individual client and which ones impair functioning the most so that these can be targeted specifically. Encourage your client to look at the range of post-traumatic stress symptoms (see Box 1.1, p.21) and encourage them to list which symptoms apply to them, both in the past and present. Look at this list with your client. While examining this list ask how the survivor has coped with the traumatic experiences. It is important to check the main reactions in terms of intrusive symptoms such as flashbacks, intrusive memories and nightmares; or avoidance such as dissociation, withdrawal and isolation as well as degrees of hyper-arousal, hyper-vigilance or hypo-arousal.

It is vital to remind the client that these are all normal reactions to trauma which helped them to survive. These symptoms may seem crazy-making and frightening but they do have an adaptive function and make sense. For instance hyper-vigilance ensures that we are alert in a hostile world, while dissociation anaesthetises the psychological pain making it easier to survive emotionally. While these reactions may have helped in the past, this has exerted a huge cost in not being able to regulate emotions, leading to a sense of feeling out of control, high levels of anxiety, suicidal thoughts or destructive behaviour such as self-injury. To soothe these symptoms the survivor may use drugs, alcohol or food as a form of self-medication. To gain some control over post-traumatic stress reactions it is helpful to have a deeper understanding of the range of symptoms.

Hyper-arousal

A classic post-traumatic stress reaction is hyper-arousal in which the individual is in a constant state of high alert due to the increased levels of stress hormones such as adrenaline and cortisol flooding the body. This results in feelings of restlessness, anxiety, irritability, or out of control emotions. High levels of adrenaline lead to physiological responses such as elevated heart rate, palpitations, and sweating. They also increase feelings of uncontrollable anger or rage and wild mood swings. As the nervous system becomes overloaded with stress hormones survivors may sway between high levels of agitation and total exhaustion.

Practitioners need to convey to clients that their alarm system is on a default setting of high alert which means that all their energy and resources are diverted to managing stress reactions and survival. As a result it is harder to think clearly, evaluate external or internal cues accurately, or make sense of the experience. In essence clients are unable to use their 'brake' to regulate their reactions making it difficult to gain control over their body, thoughts or feelings (see Chapter 11).

In hyper-arousal, survivors' physiological reactions take on a life of their own and they feel less able to control them. This can happen with negative as well as pleasurable experiences. For example, excitement, physical exercise or sex have similar internal sensations such as increased heart rate and breathing, sweating and muscle tension, which mirror those seen in fear responses and therefore can trip the alarm system. This means even pleasurable feelings or activities are experienced as dangerous thereby reducing the ability to enjoy life.

Hyper-arousal also disrupts sleep, rest and eating patterns. At times survivors may be so stressed that they simply cannot eat or sleep, let alone rest. This can cause further problems as the body is not able to recuperate through rest, which can result in exhaustion and chronic fatigue. Hyper-arousal can become such a normal state that survivors may have no conscious awareness of its effect, its origins, or its link to abuse.

Reminding the client that recognising that hyper-arousal is not a sign of 'going crazy' is the first step in taking control. It is vital for them to discharge the high levels of stress hormones so that their body can rest and reset the alarm system. Chapter 10 explores ways in which survivors can release stress hormones in a healthy way; through movement, exercise, and skills to allow them to take more control over their post-traumatic reactions.

Hyper-vigilance

A predominant symptom of hyper-arousal is hyper-vigilance, which makes it hard for survivors to relax or let their guard down. As they invariably anticipate threat they are on high alert and constantly monitor the environment for any signs of danger. This is seen in an increased startle-response, where survivors may jump at any loud noise or stimuli, and are in a constant state of watchfulness. In contrast, some survivors are so immersed in, and preoccupied by, internal sensations that they 'tune out' from their environment, and become hypo-vigilant. This puts them at risk of threat as they are not aware of actual dangers in their surroundings (see Chapter 11). It is also not uncommon to alternate between hyper-arousal and hypo-arousal, which accounts for some of the extreme mood swings seen in some survivors of complex trauma.

Avoidance

One way that survivors manage trauma is through avoidance. This can include avoidance of trauma cues: people, places or activities associated with the trauma including intimacy and sexual relationships. All of these can lead to social isolation and a deep sense of aloneness. Alternatively, they may avoid feelings and thoughts through numbing or dissociation as a form of anaesthesia. Survivors might avoid feelings and thoughts through sleep, watching endless television, relentless work schedules, obsessive thoughts or compulsive behaviours to keep themselves physically and mentally busy at all times.

This is a method of escape, to distract or block any distressing feelings. Survivors might also avoid feeling through the soothing or numbing effects of food, alcohol, drugs, self-injury or obsessive-compulsive behaviour. While these provide them with short term relief, avoidance actually intensifies negative feelings and thoughts. Every time these are avoided they become 'stamped in' as they remain unprocessed and un-integrated.

Some of major post-traumatic stress reactions occur largely due to avoidance or a lack of reflective functioning which impedes emotional processing and prevents feelings from becoming fully integrated. In addition, when people avoid feelings or thoughts, they are more likely to intensify and be twice as likely to recur, generating even more distress (Sanderson, 2010c). Most significantly, un-integrated experiences are more likely to give rise to flashbacks – one of the hallmark signs of PTSD.

Flashbacks

Flashbacks are very intense and vivid recollections of traumatic experiences that have not been fully processed and integrated into the memory system. As they are so intense they can activate the same cascade of bio-chemicals and stress hormones as the original trauma. This sets off similar bodily reactions such as pounding heart, changes in breathing, sweating and muscle tension designed to fight or flee. As survivors have the flashback, their bodies may begin to take on the same postures and survival mechanism they used during the original trauma such as cowering, freezing, submission or playing dead. For methods to help your client manage flashbacks more effectively turn to Chapter 12.

Remind your client
Flashbacks are a normal reaction to traumatic experiences and they do not mean that they are going 'crazy'.

It is critical that your client acknowledges that they are NOT being abused again, but that the flashback is a memory of a something that happened to them in the past. In effect it is a flashback to a previous experience, which due to its intensity fools the mind and body into feeling and believing that the past event is happening now in real time.

Flashbacks can be triggered in a number of ways, and represent a single event, or encapsulate a series of traumatic incidents. Common triggers are being in the presence of actual threat in the environment, or activation of internal bodily sensations which are similar to when they were in danger in the past. Sensory stimuli such as images, sight, sound, smell, taste, touch or the position of the body associated with the trauma can also trigger flashbacks. Certain actions, intentions or emotions reminiscent of the trauma or certain words, places, objects, or someone who resembles their abuser can also act as triggers. If the survivor is currently experiencing trauma or struggling with loss this can also ignite flashbacks.

Nightmares and vivid dreams

Nightmares are the night-time equivalent of flashbacks and therefore represent unprocessed aspects of the traumatic experience. Nightmares also symbolise emotional aspects of the trauma such as feelings of shame, humiliation and anger. Like flashbacks, dreams and nightmares help to sort through experiences in order to file them away in our memory banks, albeit while asleep rather than awake. Some survivors find that their nightmares are more terrifying than flashbacks. This is because while we are asleep our resources and coping strategies are 'off line' making it harder to manage them.

If nightmares and dreams remain unprocessed they will keep recurring, generating fears around going to bed and difficulties sleeping. Interrupted sleep will leave survivors feeling constantly tired and exhausted. When nightmares occur several times a night energy levels and resilience will be eroded making it extremely hard to function during the day. If left unresolved, the lack of rest and sleep can make survivors vulnerable to chronic fatigue syndrome.

 Top tip
To help survivors manage their nightmares and dreams, get them to keep a dream diary so that they can process them and improve their sleep patterns.

If your client suffers from recurring nightmares turn to Chapter 12 to find tools to help them manage nightmares and how they can process traumatic memories more effectively.

Panic attacks
Panic attacks are characterised by a sudden surge of intense anxiety and are often due to prolonged periods of stress. They can be triggered by something specific that is frightening, or more often they will occur spontaneously for no apparent reason. As they can happen any time, they can prevent survivors from going out or tolerating situations in which the panic attack first occurred. The fear of having a panic attack can lead to fear of leaving the house, social withdrawal and isolation.

It is helpful for survivors to recognise the signs of panic attacks such as shortness and shallowness of breath, pounding and irregular heartbeat, a sense of feeling 'unreal', pains or tightness in the chest similar to a heart attack, unsteadiness, trembling and dizziness, and the feeling that the world is spinning around. Survivors may also experience excessive sweating, feeling faint and light-headedness, a fear of losing control, going crazy or even dying. This is often accompanied by tingling in the hands and feet, choking or feeling as though being smothered, flushed skin, an urgent intense need to run away, nausea and a powerful urge to scream. The intensity of the symptoms can make survivors feel as though they are having a heart attack. To help your client manage their panic attacks, see Chapter 12.

INTRUSIVE MEMORIES

In order to understand intrusive memories it helps to understand the role of memory in survival. Memory is a necessary aid to survival as it stores both positive and negative experiences. Positive or pleasurable experiences are stored so that they are repeated, while negative or unpleasant experiences are stored so that they can be avoided. Memory is very complex and dynamic. It is not static like a video recording, but constantly adds and subtracts when integrating new experiences into past experiences.

In essence, we process experiences by reviewing them, elaborating on them and linking them to other experiences. This then allows them to be stored as memories in order to direct future behaviour. In addition, as we process experiences we will be able to make them less frightening by reducing their emotional intensity. To use a computer metaphor, it's a bit like saving your document in a folder to be accessed when you need to rather than not saving the document at all so it stays 'on line' waiting for your attention every time you go to your computer.

Remind your client

Unprocessed experiences are harder to store in memory because they are still 'alive', demanding constant attention. This means they will remain as frightening as when they first experienced them.

Figure 2.1 illustrates how this occurs and can be used as a visual aid with clients to explain the nature of intrusive memories. Traumatic experiences are usually triggered by sensory cues such as sound, smell, touch, taste or vision, as well as perception and certain words. These demand attention through the return of intrusive memories.

Intrusive memories are so distressing that survivors will try to avoid them, not realising that this makes them even more vivid and frightening, and twice as likely to recur. The more they try not to think about them, the more they will spontaneously recur and demand attention. Rather than reflect or process memories survivors tend to try to block them out through dissociation, the use of alcohol, drugs, food or self-injury. Alternatively, they might try to distract themselves by keeping busy/ working endlessly/preoccupying themselves so that they do not have to feel, think or talk about them.

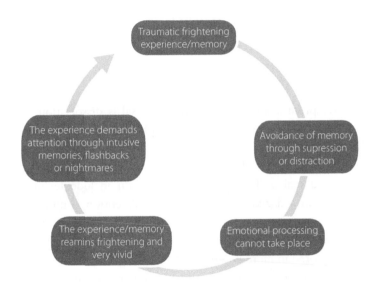

Figure 2.1 How traumatic experiences become intrusive memories

HYPO-AROUSAL

In hypo-arousal the survivor avoids sensations, emotions or situations that evoke intense negative or positive feelings. This commonly manifests as phobic avoidance of emotions (see Chapter 3, p.40). Hypo-arousal is an automatic, unconscious physiological response mediated by the parasympathetic nervous system in which heart rate and breathing slow down, muscle tone goes limp, and the mind and body seem to collapse. This state of hibernation, or feigned death, induces numbness to avoid the experience of physical and emotional pain. It is characterised by shutting down for periods of time in an almost trance like state in which the survivor may feel drowsy to the point of sleep. This can lead to becoming unresponsive to the environment, tuning out all external stimuli and not being able to hear or respond to others.

Such numbness and detachment from self and others makes it very difficult for survivors to think or reflect on their experiences, past or present, making it difficult to process these or to feel any empathy for self or others. This in turn makes it extremely hard to reach out for help from others, preventing them from accessing much needed support. Hypo-arousal can lead to hypo-vigilance in which the individual becomes oblivious to their environment and is not able to accurately detect safety or danger. As this can put the survivor at risk of further traumatisation, it is critical to manage the symptoms of hypo-arousal (see pp.69–71), especially dissociation.

Dissociation

A classic symptom associated with hypo-arousal is dissociation, which is often described as a 'mental flight when physical flight is not possible' (Kluft, 1992) and is a highly adaptive response to inescapable trauma. It can provide a 'mental shield' allowing survivors to detach from feelings, bodily sensations and reality. The signs of dissociation include feeling spaced out, or being in a dazed or dreamlike state. Attention is more narrowly focused as they tune, or screen out the world around them. As dissociation underpins much of complex trauma and gives rise to a range of symptoms, it will be explored in more depth in the following chapter.

Once clients have a better understanding of the nature of trauma and post-traumatic stress reactions they can begin to normalise their symptoms rather than continue to feel as though they are 'going crazy' or are irreversibly damaged. This will allow them to start the process of taking control over bodily reactions by learning more effective skills to manage trauma symptoms. These skills, alongside a range of useful exercises, will be explored in Part 3.

 Remember
Remind clients that post-traumatic symptoms are normal reactions to trauma.

3

UNDERSTANDING THE ROLE OF DISSOCIATION AND DISSOCIATIVE DISORDERS

Dissociation is an adaptive survival mechanism in the presence of overwhelming externally threatening experiences from which the victim cannot escape physically but may escape psychologically, by splitting off from the experience and associated sensations, feelings, thoughts and memories (Sanderson, 2006). It is what Lifton (1979) has described as a 'paralysis of the mind' when there is no escape. Invariably the individual also screens out the external world so that it appears unreal or surreal and in which time has slowed down, or speeded up, or in which familiar places, people or objects seem alien or appear not to exist, known as derealisation.

This is often accompanied by unusual bodily sensations such as a sense of floating away, looking at the self from a distance or a feeling that the body has separated from other parts. As a result the individual feels as though experiences are not happening to them, but to someone else. In being out of contact with the body and not being able to process the experiences, there will be huge lapses in time and memory. As the mind unconsciously blanks out part or all of the experience and associated memories, the individual loses the sense of continuity, of who they are and their reality. This is known as depersonalisation.

While dissociation is a normal response to trauma, it can impact on everyday functioning and over time can result in changes in the individual's sense of self, reality and time, and memory. Survivors can become so out of contact with their body that they only inhabit their head and lose contact with all inner sensations. This makes it increasingly difficult to monitor threat or danger or to access internal signals that something is not right. Frequent detachment from bodily experiences also gives rise to a loss of reality and uncertainty about whether the experience actually happened. Such unreality about body and self can result in the survivor feeling like a shadow of a person, rather than a fully integrated human being. In severe cases of dissociation, some survivors can become so fragmented in their sense of self that they develop separate personalities as seen in dissociative identity disorder (DID; see below).

Although emotional anaesthesia initially aids survival, over time it can develop into phobic avoidance of feelings, which can make survivors unresponsive to feelings, including pleasurable ones, leading to a sense of emotional and psychological deadness or frozenness. Moreover, dissociation requires huge mental energy, which is both physically and mentally exhausting and draining. The absence of any emotional experiencing can make survivors appear cold and unfeeling. This prevents others from connecting with them, thereby reducing opportunities for intimacy or caring and loving relationships. This can increase the sense of aloneness and traumatic loneliness. Given the dangers of dissociation it is critical that survivors understand the nature of dissociation and recognise the dangers of avoiding sensations, feelings and thoughts. This chapter aims to enable practitioners to have a better understanding of dissociation so that they can identify the hallmark cues to dissociation and assess the range of dissociative disorders, including DID. With such knowledge they will be better equipped to work with dissociative clients, and more able to help survivors to understand and manage the range of symptoms.

SPECTRUM OF DISSOCIATION

Everyone dissociates to some degree whether through daydreaming, being on auto pilot, or detaching from different aspects of experiences. This can be seen when immersed, or 'getting lost' in, reading a good book, gardening, watching a film or when listening to music. These are all normal and healthy forms of detaching from reality. It is also present when engaged in creative activities and when meditating.

Screening out the environment can be highly adaptive in enhancing focus and concentration and is often what enables emergency workers and surgeons to optimise functioning when there is threat, danger or chaos around them. Many mental health practitioners may also use a degree of dissociation in order to contain their own or their client's anxieties or feelings, especially when highly distressed or traumatised. It might help to identify and list your own experience of dissociation in your everyday and clinical life.

Dissociation is commonly found in children and is most pronounced in their ability to become absorbed in play, fantasy and imagination. In some children the capacity for fantasy and imaginative dissociation allows them to create imaginary companions and entirely separate identities (Trujillo Lewis, Yeager and Gidlow, 1996). While this is a normal part of development allowing children to experiment with different identities, some children are more adept at this than others due to genetics and temperament (Chu, 2011). As children start to establish a coherent sense of self and self-identity, they tend to engage more with their external world and their agency in it.

Some children however continue to live in a fantasy world, especially when there is a need to escape their environment, or as a result of traumatisation. They are more likely to escape into dissociative imagination and fantasy, with some retaining imaginary companions into adulthood. In the case of severe traumatisation, they may develop entirely separate identities to manage unprocessed experiences which can result in DID, formerly known as multiple personality disorder (see pp.49–50).

CONTINUUM OF DISSOCIATION

Most people experience a range of states of alertness and detachment in any one typical day and these will vary depending on energy levels, daily activities and tasks that need to be achieved. Thus there will be moments of high physical activity and focused mental concentration, which demand alert consciousness and awareness of both internal external states. A typical day will also consist of times for relaxation, daydreaming, reading a book or watching a film; or mild detachment in which attention and awareness are narrowed. This can also happen when engaged in a habitual activity such as driving a car or riding a bicycle in which there is little awareness of the activity performed and a sense of being on auto-pilot. This is known as automaticity in which repetitive and practised activities are performed outside of conscious awareness.

In addition, it is normal to move through multiple experiential states or roles such as parent, spouse, teacher, friend, sibling or work colleague with a continuous sense of core identity. All of these are normal aspects of experiencing. In clinical dissociation the degree of detachment may be so extreme that the person becomes so immersed in their internal world that they lose contact with reality, their body and sense of self for periods of time resulting in dissociative amnesia in which all sense of time is lost, with no memory of experiences, events or activities. In severe detachment this is accompanied by a loss of continuity in identity in which separate identities or personalities seem to inhabit the individual.

As can be seen clinical dissociation differs markedly from everyday dissociation in how this is experienced by survivors. As many survivors are unable to recognise dissociative symptoms they are rarely able to find words to describe them. Those that are able to commonly report a sense of falling apart or shattering, feeling fragmented or fractured, or feeling 'beside myself', or of hovering between two parallel states such as sanity and insanity. This is often accompanied by a sense of lack of control over thoughts, feelings, actions and memories which exacerbates the sense of 'going crazy'. Some survivors report an overwhelming sense of 'not me' and separate parts or identities with different voices and experiencing.

Survivors experiencing dissociative amnesia describe memories as 'foggy', 'full of black holes', or 'Swiss cheese holes'. They also report a sense of being 'wrapped in cotton wool', being frozen or dead inside, being like cardboard, robotic, or one dimensional and doubting their very existence. All of these are signs of failure of integration of experiences and associative capacities in which they are unable to access thoughts, feelings, judgements, behaviours or experiences. This prevents them from organising aspects of self and experience into a unified whole which prevents the continuity of self and development of an integrated coherent life narrative. It is for this reason that part of the therapeutic work needs to focus on enhancing awareness of dissociation, linking these symptoms to trauma and enabling clients to verbalise and reflect on dissociative experiences in order to begin to make sense of them, so as to integrate them.

CLINICAL DISSOCIATION

In the presence of overwhelming trauma from which there is no escape the ability to dissociate becomes a powerful survival strategy. There are three types of dissociation that can be seen in the presence of trauma, all of which aid survival. Primary dissociation occurs in the face of overwhelming trauma or threat preventing the individual from integrating what is happening to the extent that experience remains fragmented. Secondary, or peritraumatic dissociation is activated during trauma where there is no escape and represents what Kluft (1992) has called 'psychological flight when physical flight is not possible'. It is a form of 'psychic anaesthetising' and can be accompanied by out-of-body experiences and a sense of 'leaving the body'. Tertiary dissociation is associated with severe childhood abuse and complex trauma in which distinct ego-states emerge to contain the traumatic experience, which can result in DID.

Dissociation in the presence of trauma is mediated through the release of endorphins, the body's natural opiates. The anaesthetising effect of endorphins is similar to morphine in taking away pain and calming the individual. When the body is flooded with these endogenous opioids a floaty, dreamlike state is induced. In extreme trauma, out-of-body experiences may occur in which survivors experience a separation from self and body, and report seeing themselves outside of their body. If this is frequently repeated such as in complex trauma it can lead to a sense of more permanent separation of self (or selves) from the body, characteristic of DID.

Young children are particularly vulnerable to dissociation as they lack the ability to integrate traumatic experiences due to insufficient maturity and lack of emotional and social support necessary to help them manage such overwhelming states. As a result the traumatic experience becomes locked into the right brain preventing access to left brain processing and analysis (Allez, 2010; Chu, 2011).

For many survivors dissociation becomes an adaptive response to overwhelming external and inner states as it calms and soothes unbearable states. The powerful effect of dissociation means that survivors can become phobic of inner experiencing and avoid all sensations, feelings and thoughts. However this can become maladaptive over time in that inner experiences are not integrated and appear to exist separately from the person, take on a life of their own, and present as separate identities or personalities. Consequently survivors begin to experience a 'not me' quality in experiencing thoughts, feelings, behaviour and memories which appear outside of conscious control. As these split-off experiences become fixed they can evolve into separate identities, with their own voice, name, age, individual view of self, feelings, thoughts and behaviour as seen in DID.

While initially adaptive, dissociation can become maladaptive in becoming a learnt response to all feelings and sensation, even positive ones. This can lead to impaired emotional processing in which emotions are either numbed or frozen, or spiral out of control. In addition it affects thinking and impairs cognitive processing leading to a range of perceptual and cognitive distortions, dichotomous thinking and a trauma worldview (see Table 3.1).

Table 3.1 Positive and negative aspects of dissociation	
Positive aspects of dissociation	**Negative aspects of dissociation**
1. Biologically mediated, not voluntary control	1. Can become a pattern, addictive, default setting, obsessive
2. Anaesthetises physical and psychic pain	2. Leads to isolation, traumatic loneliness, lack of friendships, and intimacy
3. Survival strategy	3. Relationships suffer as not emotionally present
4. Compartmentalisation	
5. Can sharpen focus in short term	4. Can lead to imaginary/unrealistic and dichotomous thinking, and unrealistic expectations
6. Allows person to get on with daily life without being overwhelmed by traumatic experiences	5. Reduces attention span and impedes learning
	6. It can limit change and growth
7. Allows for a degree of functioning in everyday life	7. Can endanger personal safety, and that of children, pets, or dependents

Warning

To ensure your client's safety while dissociating, you must remind them not to drive or operate machinery, and ensure that young children, pets or dependents are safe.

STRUCTURAL DISSOCIATION

The most common form of dissociation seen in survivors with complex trauma is a vertical split in consciousness as a way of shielding oneself from overwhelming fear of annihilation and cognitive knowledge of traumatic events (Davies and Frawley, 1994). Such dissociation has been variously described as ' ...a separation of mental and experiential contents that would normally be connected' (Howell, 2005, p.307), ' ...a failure of integration of ideas, information, affects and experience' (Putnam, 1997, p.19), and in the BASK Model of dissociation as a ' ...fragmentation between behaviour, affect, somatic sensation and knowledge' (Braun, 1988, p.5). Such splits promote the parallel owning and disowning of conflictual or paradoxical experiences which is all too common in complex trauma within attachment relationships. It is this lack integration which prevents the integration of self-states in young children, or fragmentation of integrated systems of experiencing, and de-coupling of self-states in adults (Bromberg, 1998).

An invaluable and clinically useful way of understanding and working with dissociation in complex trauma is the concept of structural dissociation. Structural dissociation aptly accounts for the split between what appears to be highly functioning aspects of the self, and those aspects of self that are locked into traumatic re-experiencing. Thus the 'apparently normal personality' (ANP) detaches and avoids any contact with trauma related alternates while the 'emotional personality' (EP) remains embedded in the trauma (Myers, 1940; Steele, van der Hart and Nijenhuis, 2001). In what is called primary structural dissociation, the ANP is highly functional in managing daily life, work and social interaction albeit emotionally and physically numb, while the EP is locked into reliving the trauma through post-traumatic symptoms such as hyper-arousal, flashbacks, amnesia, and disorientation.

In prolonged and severe complex trauma, secondary structural dissociation can occur in which the EP fragments into two or more separate EPs with a single ANP, which underpins most of the dissociative disorders and some personality disorders such as borderline personality disorder (BPD) (Steele *et al.*, 2001). Tertiary structural dissociation occurs when the ANP becomes overburdened by the intrusion of trauma and trauma symptoms and begins to fragment alongside fragmented EPs, leading to features of DID.

HIGH FUNCTIONING DISSOCIATION

Some survivors with primary or secondary structural dissociation present as extremely high functioning with successful careers, and yet encounter a range of difficulties in their close personal relationships. This is often confusing as it is in sharp contrast to their success in their working lives. High functioning clients often enter therapy trying to understand why their intimate relationships are fraught with difficulties. Such clients either fear intimacy and are generally avoidant in their relationships or display high level or dependency and fear of abandonment. This represents a split in attachment style wherein the ANP is avoidant and dismissive of attachment needs, while the EP is insecurely dependent upon and preoccupied with attachment needs. As high functioning clients are in thrall to the ANP and not consciously aware of any traumatic experiences or that they are dissociative, they are often bewildered by their lack of success in their personal relationships in which the EP threatens to emerge.

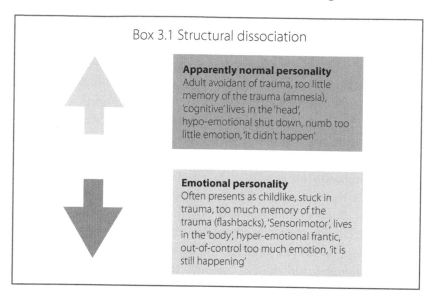

Box 3.1 Structural dissociation

Apparently normal personality
Adult avoidant of trauma, too little memory of the trauma (amnesia), 'cognitive' lives in the 'head', hypo-emotional shut down, numb too little emotion, 'it didn't happen'

Emotional personality
Often presents as childlike, stuck in trauma, too much memory of the trauma (flashbacks), 'Sensorimotor', lives in the 'body', hyper-emotional frantic, out-of-control too much emotion, 'it is still happening'

In separating the ANP and EP survivors get on with daily life without being overwhelmed by trauma or internal and external stress. While they are out of contact with unresolved trauma they are never able to integrate traumatic experiences. Over time high functioning clients can develop what van der Hart, Nijenhuis and Steele (2006) call 'a phobia of inner experience'. Although they often present as emotionally literate this is commonly a cover up for an internal emotional desert, vacuum or emptiness. When they do talk about emotions these are rarely 'felt' and commonly represent 'thought' emotions in which the right emotion is cognitively identified rather than experienced.

Such clients are rarely aware that they avoid inner experiencing this often and how this impacts on a range of mental activities such as perception, sensing and remembering as well as predicting and planning, or the accompanying cognitive errors in interpretation and judgement. To fully unlock complex trauma it is crucial that survivors become aware of inner experiencing and learn to tolerate and regulate it in order to facilitate change. They need to be in contact with the full range of feelings such as sadness, rage, anger, shame, or disgust. Clients might also feel overwhelmed by being in contact with physical sensations such as rapid heartbeat, difficulty breathing or sweating as it is reminiscent of the trauma.

To maintain phobic avoidance inner experiencing survivors will adopt a wide range of avoidance strategies that support high functioning and have ensured success in some areas of their lives. The most commonly seen avoidance strategies associated with high functioning clients are compartmentalising the trauma by sealing it off, retreating into cognitive appraisal and understanding of the world and experiences by 'living in their head' rather than inhabiting their bodies; keeping busy or working endlessly so that feelings do not come to the surface or intrude; and self-criticism and perfectionism to avoid the experience of shame. In addition they may withdraw from others and shun intimacy so that feelings are kept at bay, or engage in obsessive-compulsive behaviours to feel more in control. Less well functioning clients may resort to the use alcohol or drugs to block out inner experiencing, or use self-injury, food or addictions to regulate overwhelming inner experiences.

Some high functioning clients create a parallel world to enable the ANP to function. This usually consists of a fantasy world which is bounteous, beautiful, benign and full of harmony to escape the real world of despair, trauma and abuse. While escape into this internal fantasy world can be adaptive at times to visualise post-traumatic growth, over time it can become addictive and obsessive. Persistent and prolonged withdrawal into the fantasy inner world means that survivors become increasingly more detached and dissociated from the real world. This impacts negatively on relationships and communication, which exacerbates a sense of aloneness and can affect the ability to work effectively by reducing focus and attention, and can hamper collegiate relationships.

Some of these difficulties can also become manifest in the therapeutic relationship in which the client loses focus, leading to selective abstraction. When clients dissociate or enter their fantasy world they tune out and don't hear all that is said, which can lead to gross misinterpretation and miscommunication. This can create significant barriers in therapeutic relationships such as mis-attunement, leading to defensive reactions, criticism, projection, and negative transference and counter-transference reactions (see Chapter 6).

Box 3.2 Dissociative disorders (adapted from DSM-V, APA, 2013)

- Depersonalisation-de-realisation disorder: Depersonalisation is characterised by episodes of unreality, or detachment from thoughts, feelings, sensations, body, or actions, as well as alterations in perception, distortion of time, physical and or emotional numbing, and self. Derealisation is characterised by sense of unreality or detachment from surroundings in which individuals or objects are visually distorted, or experienced as unreal, dreamlike, foggy or lifeless

- Dissociative amnesia: Characterised by the inability to recall important autobiographical information, usually of a traumatic or stressful nature. There are two sub-types: selective amnesia for a specific event or events and generalised amnesia for identity and life history. Some individuals may experience dissociative fugue, a state which involves bewildered wandering or travel

- Dissociative identity disorder (DID): Disruption of identity characterised by two or more distinct personality states or an experience of possession involving a discontinuity in sense of self and sense of agency, accompanied by related alterations in affect, behaviour, consciousness, memory, perception, cognition and/or sensorimotor functioning and recurrent gaps in the recall of everyday events, important personal information, and/or traumatic events

- Dissociative disorder not elsewhere classified (DDNEC): This includes dissociative symptoms that do not meet the criteria for any specific dissociative disorder such as identity disturbance in individuals who have experienced prolonged and intense coercive persuasion through brainwashing or indoctrination while captive, tortured, or during long-term political imprisonment, or recruitment by cults or terror organisations. These are characterised by moderate disturbance and alterations of identity, episodes of possession and self-agency and a range of dissociative symptoms, such as depersonalisation, de-realisation, amnesia, flashbacks, disruptions of consciousness, stupour, catatonia, auditory or visual hallucinations, delusions, disturbed behaviour and dissociative trance, in which there is narrowing or complete loss of awareness of immediate surroundings sometimes accompanied by stereotyped involuntary movement or behaviour

THE RANGE OF DISSOCIATIVE DISORDERS

Persistent and chronic dissociation can result in a wide range of symptoms and dissociative disorders that are commonly seen in survivors of complex trauma. The classification for DSM-V (APA, 2013, see Box 3.2) consists of four categories: depersonalisation-derealisation disorder, dissociative amnesia, DID and dissociative disorder not elsewhere classified

(DDNEC). These classifications emphasise that the criteria involving possession or trance like states cannot be applied in the case of normal and broadly accepted parts of cultural or religious practices. In addition, there is acknowledgement and recognition that some of the symptoms in DDNEC may be due to prolonged and intense coercive persuasion through brainwashing or indoctrination while captive, tortured, or during long-term political imprisonment or recruitment by cults or terror organisations. Arguably this would also include repeated and prolonged abuse as seen in complex trauma due to CPA, CSA, DA, institutional abuse, and abuse experienced within religious, cult, or faith communities.

DID (DISSOCIATIVE IDENTITY DISORDER)

The most severe of the dissociative disorders is DID as it can seriously compromise everyday functioning. Although DID is relatively rare, with an estimated prevalence rate of 1–3 per cent of the population (ISSTD Guidelines, 2011), it is not unknown for survivors of complex trauma to display features of DID. Many survivors are not aware that they have separate identities and these may not manifest until much later in the therapeutic process when 'alters' (personalities) appear. The nature of DID necessitates specialist treatment and practitioners who are not trained to work with DID will need to refer DID clients to more appropriate or specialist agencies. It is crucial that practitioners undertake a comprehensive assessment of the client's level of functioning and are objective and realistic in their ability to provide the most effective treatment.

Despite the inclusion of DID in DSM-V (APA, 2013) it is surrounded by considerable controversy with many clinicians disputing its existence as a clinical disorder. This is in part due to the nature of evidential data, much of which is anecdotal, and its co-morbidity with other disorders such as PBD and bipolar disorder. Lilienfield et al. (1991) found that between 35 per cent and 71 per cent of DID patients also met the diagnostic criteria for BPD, bipolar disorder and other conditions characterised by instability.

There is also significant disagreement between researchers, clinicians and clients in terms of understanding the manifestation of separate identities. Boon, Steele and van der Hart (2011) argue that while survivors experience alters as separate identities co-existing within the same body, these '…dissociative parts of the personality are not actually separate identities or personalities in one body, but rather parts of a single individual that are not yet functioning in a smooth, coordinated and flexible way'. This implies that although patients believe that their mind houses multiple entities, this is merely a metaphor for different parts or aspects of themselves to explain unstable moods, self-destructive behaviour, impulsivity and erratic relationships. In essence, it is an attempt to make sense of bewildering behaviours and feelings which appear to be outside of voluntary control.

Some researchers such as Spanos (1996) have also been critical of the use of hypnosis as the preferred form of treatment as this may fuel difficulties in distinguishing fantasy from reality. In addition, integration wherein alters are encouraged to communicate with each other may be counter-productive in supporting false beliefs that thoughts and feelings reside separately and thereby preserve dissociation. This can perpetuate dissociation as a phobic avoidance of the full range of inner experiencing. A more effective therapeutic strategy is to reduce dissociative states and identities by understanding that these are painful experiences that have been split off from the ANP and not a separate identity. Clients need to be able to recognise, acknowledge and take ownership of the full range of their feelings, thoughts and behaviours rather than splitting them off.

Warning
Clients with DID need specialist treatment and unless you are trained to work with this client group you will need to refer clients to more specialist agencies.

ASSOCIATED DISORDERS

Severe and chronic dissociation can also lead to a range of associated disorders, in particular somatoform disorders and personality disorders. In somatoform disorders, dissociated traumatic experiences which are outside of conscious awareness can become somatised and manifest as a range of physical illnesses, or bodily aches and pains, for which there is no medical or biological cause. Thus psychological pain and unbearable internal states manifest as bodily symptoms which can range from recurring or constant minor aches or pains – such as breast pain, pelvic pain, constant sore throat – through to hypochondriasis, in which physical pain replaces psychic pain. These invariably consist of somatic re-experiencing, often referred to as body memories, in which physical sensations, focused pain or involuntary spasms associated with the trauma and embedded in the implicit memory system re-emerge as bodily sensations.

Avoidance of inner experiencing and dissociation is also highly correlated with some of the personality disorders, in particular BPD. The role of dissociation in BPD is to split off a range of feelings and thoughts such as vulnerability, dependency, hurt, anger, rage or hostility which can be so sealed off that they form separate self-states. These self-states commonly contain un-integrated aspects of trauma or invalidating experiences which vie for attention and often attack each other, or others, in an endless war of attrition.

The most common self-states seen in survivors of complex trauma who have been diagnosed with BPD are the abused child, the angry child, the punitive parent and the detached protector who ensures that the self-states remain split off and dissociated (Young, Klosko and Weishaar, 2003). As clients switch between these self-states, often outside conscious awareness, their behaviour is often highly volatile, impulsive and contradictory in oscillating between dependency and avoidance, submission and aggression; or passive and controlling, making it very difficult to engage in the therapeutic process (see Chapter 6).

Warning

Working with clients with BPD can be challenging and very demanding. If possible, try not to have too many clients with BPD at any one time.

WORKING WITH DISSOCIATION

As not all survivors of complex trauma are aware of the role of dissociation and how it impacts on them, it is useful for practitioners to familiarise themselves with the hallmark signs of dissociation so that they can identify the degree of dissociation. Box 3.3 summarises these in an easy checklist form. If practitioners suspect that a client may be dissociative they may wish to explore this with the client through the following two useful exercises.

Exercise

Fantasy Test

Invite your client to ask themselves, or a close and trusted friend(s) how they experience the client. Are they mentally present? Are they able to listen and remember what is said? Do they feel as though their mind drifts? Do others comment that he or she often seems far away and distant? Are they hard to access emotionally?

Exercise

Identifying dissociative symptoms checklist

This can be checked by the practitioner or you can ask your client and fill in their responses.

1. Sense of fragmentation
2. Alienation from self/not feeling real
3. Alienation from surroundings
4. Experiencing too little loss of function
5. Experiencing too much/intrusions
6. Loss of time
7. Amnesia in the present or no memory of doing something
8. Have thoughts, use words, or hear voices that are not your own, or have no control over what you say
9. Out-of-body experiences – experiencing self as outside body
10. Out of blue sensation, emotions or thoughts that don't seem to belong to you, sometimes accompanied by fear or panic
11. Hear voices in head
12. Find yourself in a place and not sure how you got there

If you suspect that the client suffers from chronic dissociation or significant clinical or diagnostic concerns then it might help to administer one of the range assessment scales to measure degree of dissociation such as Dissociative Experiences Scale (DES), the Somatoform Dissociation Questionnaire (SDQ5) and Nijenhuis *et al.*, 1996, Somatoform Dissociation Questionnaire (SDQ 20).

One of the most powerful ways of tracking the degree of dissociation and how it impacts on functioning in the present is how the client presents in therapeutic sessions. There are a range of cues to dissociation that can alert the practitioner (see Box 3.4). Counsellors need to be aware as they engage with clients for changes in verbal and non-verbal communication, somatic changes in breathing, skin tone and temperature and alternations between passive compliance and active hostility. These will all prove to be good indicators that the client is dissociating and may not be fully present or able to fully engage, and may mishear and misinterpret what is actually happening in session.

Box 3.3 Hallmark signs of dissociation

- Loss of memory, or dissociative amnesia for past and present events. Can be partial or complete. In the present no recollection of events, meeting familiar people, conversations, or topics discussed or what they have been doing
- Time loss for hours or days at a time. Find themselves somewhere with no idea how they got there, and no recollection of where they have been or what they have been doing
- Time distortions in which time passes really extremely fast, or extremely slowly, not sure where they are in terms of space or time
- Alienation or estrangement of self or body, or depersonalisation – numb, blank, outside of body, exist solely 'in the head', no control over actions, on automatic pilot
- Alienation or estrangement from surroundings, derealisation in which familiar surroundings, family and friends appear unreal and strange
- Alternations between hypo-arousal in which survivors avoid feelings and therefore experience too little, and hyper-arousal in which they experience too much as a result of the intrusion of sensation, feelings, thoughts, memories

Box 3.4 Cues to dissociation in session

1. Facial features, eyes unfocused, waxy, blank, zone out, glazed look
2. Inability to speak the unspeakable, numb with terror, prolonged silence become compliant and avoidant, helplessness
3. Robotic language – repetitive phrases, details
4. Long monologues characterised by stream of consciousness with no reflection or mentalisation
5. Changes in narrative – unfocused, disorganised, incoherent
6. Misinterpretation, miscommunication
7. Somatic cues – jerky movements, changes in temperature, freezing
8. Entering parallel worlds – fantasy 'beautiful and benign' world vs. reality 'terrifying and hostile' world
9. Submissive, compliant, 'good client'
10. Switching between submission and hostile aggression

Knowing and understanding the cues to dissociation are critical to being able to manage the rollercoaster nature of therapeutic practice when working with dissociative clients. Active dissociation in session poses enormous challenges for both client and practitioner and can create barriers in the therapeutic relationship (see Chapter 7) as well as lead to miscommunication and misinterpretations. The demands of this can result in mis-attunement leading to ruptures in the therapeutic relationship and further disconnection. It can also undermine counsellor competence, making it harder to stay connected. To minimise the impact of dissociation in therapeutic sessions and to remain connected, counsellors will need to be aware of the range of therapeutic challenges and ensure that they are able to understand dissociation as a normal response to complex trauma, and how this impacts on attachment relationships. This is further discussed in the following chapter.

4

UNDERSTANDING THE
ROLE OF ATTACHMENT

Complex trauma within attachment relationships can give rise to a range of attachment and relational difficulties. Many of these are as a result of aversive early childhood experiences and the structural dissociation that enables the survivor to split off abusive experiences so that they can remain connected to the caregiver on whom they are reliant for care and protection. This is most marked in early childhood abuse, but can also occur in the abuse of adults as is seen in DA, abuse by faith or cult leaders, and the abuse of the elderly and those with disabilities. Such traumatic experiences not only destroy bonds (Herman, 1992a), but they also impair the ability to trust and feel connected to others.

This chapter will explore the impact of complex trauma on attachment and relational worth and how this affects future relationships throughout the lifespan, including the therapeutic relationship. It will look at how complex trauma can lead to traumatic bonding and increased dependency needs and how this shapes attachment patterns and attachment style. Finally it will examine how the betrayal of trust can lead to a range of relationship difficulties such as the avoidance of attachment and intimacy, which in turn leads to isolation and traumatic loneliness.

THE FUNCTION OF ATTACHMENT

Attachment is an innate psychobiological imperative that aids physical and psychological survival. To maximise survival it is essential that young infants form attachment bonds to others who will protect them from danger and harm. These bonds shape the baby's brain (Gerhardt, 2004) to ensure healthy psychological development, and provide a secure base in which physical and emotional needs are satisfied. In meeting these needs the child learns that others can be trusted to respond appropriately to a range of needs, and that internal states can be regulated (Bowlby, 1965; Cairns, 2002).

The primary purpose of early attachment bonds is to support the experience-dependent maturation of the developing brain (Schore, 2011) before autonomy and affect regulation develop (Howe, 2005; Tronick, 1998). Thus the primary caregiver acts as an external affect regulating system to facilitate the child's own regulation of arousal and emotional inner psychological mental states (Gerhardt, 2004; Howe, 2005; Schore, 2001). Learning to regulate affect promotes learning to understand feelings, somatic experiences and mental states and how these influence behaviour and social-emotional interaction. It is in consistent, appropriately responsive caregiving that the infant learns that distressing internal states can be soothed and regulated, which allows them to be integrated. From this the infant learns that others are safe and can be relied upon to respond to them when needed, which regulates stress responses and aids socialisation. The bonding process also releases critical hormones such as oxytocin and vasopressin which mediate the sense of comfort, pleasure and delight experienced when in a close relationship (Zak, 2008).

Early experiences of caregiving give rise to templates, or inner working models (IWM) (Bowlby, 1973) of what can and cannot be expected in relationships and how others respond to needs. These predictive expectancies are best developed in the presence of consistent and predictable caregiving. When caregiving is unpredictable, absent or abusive the infant is less able to predict accurately leading to fear or lack of trust in others and increased stress responses (Gerhardt, 2004). This can lead to impaired regulation of stress responses which can in turn lead to an over dependence on others to regulate these, or to excessive self-sufficiency and auto-regulation.

As attachment bonds facilitate the regulation of emotions, the infant learns that unbearable states can be managed. Over time the child will be able to move from external or relational soothing to self-soothing. In managing emotional states the child is more able to reflect on and integrate emotional states and experiences, which increases their ability to learn from them. This promotes the integration of self-states which enhances empathy for self and others and the necessary skills that aid emotional and social functioning. In trusting self and others, a healthy balance between dependence and independence is achieved, which promotes healthy connection to others.

In being connected to others the child learns to understand other people's mental states and develops empathy for others which aids social interaction and promotes healthy relationships. Through secure attachment the child can develop mindful reflection to find a healthy balance between autonomy, dependence and interdependence. With this they are able to set clear boundaries so that they can relate to others with mutual respect, empathy and equality. This makes it easier to resolve conflicts, talk about inner feelings without fear of rejection or humiliation, and manage the cycle of connection, disconnection, and reconnection that underpins healthy relationships (Boon *et al.*, 2011).

In complex trauma children are not able to achieve self-integration or develop the IWMs necessary to feel safe around others which leads to disruption in the attachment system. This gives rise to insecure attachments, in which they become either excessively dependent on others or fiercely independent. These early attachment styles shape relational worth and influence later relationships throughout the lifespan (Sanderson, 2010a). This can lead to insecure attachment in close relationships in which survivors become overly preoccupied with attachment figures or avoid close relationships and attachment (see Table 4.1 below). As a result relationships become dangerous and terrifying rather than a source of pleasure or comfort making them complicated and exhausting rather than soothing.

 Remember

Survivors of complex trauma experience relationships as dangerous and terrifying rather than as a source of pleasure.

ATTACHMENT STYLES

As attachment is critical to the development of healthy neurobiological and social-emotional functioning, there has been considerable research on attachment styles in both children (Ainsworth, Mary, Blehar, Waters and Wall, 1978; Main and Solomon, 1986) and adults (Bartholomew and Horowitz, 1991; Hazan and Shaver, 1987) with a range of assessment measures. Box 4.1 contains some questions that are useful in identifying early attachment experiences and how these might persist into adulthood which practitioners may use in assessing client's attachment style, and indeed their own.

Box 4.1 Attachment questions

- Give five adjectives to describe your early relationship with caregivers
- Recall specific memories to support each word
- How did you seek comfort when ill, frightened or upset?
- How did your attachment figures respond?
- Did you experience any separations, losses or bereavements in early life? If so, say more
- Were you ever threatened, even jokingly, with being abandoned or sent away?
- Did you experience any emotional, physical or sexual abuse as a child?
- Why do you think he/she behaved in that way?
- Has that relationship changed over time? If so, how?

As clients with fragmented memories, or who suffer from dissociative amnesia, may find it difficult to answer questions related to childhood experiences, they may benefit from George and West's (2001) Adult Attachment Projective (AAP) Test. This projective test consists of eight drawings representing themes of attachment and loss allowing access to more implicit memories of attachment experiences rather than relying on conscious memories. Alternatively, practitioners can use non-verbal ways of identifying attachment relationships such as drawing circles representing self and significant others in relation to each other (see Box 4.4 at the end of this chapter, page 68 for useful exercises to identify attachment patterns and styles).

There are five primary adult attachment styles: 1) secure; 2) anxious-preoccupied; 3) dismissive-avoidant; 4) fearful-avoidant; and 5) disorganised/disoriented/dissociated (Bartholomew and Horowitz, 1991; Main and Solomon, 1986). The secure attachment style in adults corresponds to the secure attachment style seen in children. The anxious-preoccupied attachment style in adults corresponds to the anxious-ambivalent attachment style in children. However, the dismissive-avoidant and attachment style and the fearful-avoidant attachment style, which are distinct in adults, correspond to a single avoidant attachment style in children (Ainsworth *et al.*, 1978; Bartholomew and Horowitz, 1991).

The disorganised attachment style identified by Main and Solomon (1986) in children is the same as that seen in adults and is the one most frequently associated with trauma and complex trauma.

Secure attachment

This style of attachment is associated with a history of warm, responsive and consistent relationships both in childhood and adulthood, and a positive view of self, others and relationships. Such individuals also commonly report greater satisfaction and adjustment in their relationships as they balance intimacy with independence. Securely attached people find it easy to be emotionally close to others and are generally comfortable depending on others and having others depend on them. They do not tend to worry about being alone or having others not accept them.

Insecure attachment

In contrast to adults with a secure attachment style, those with an insecure attachment style generally report unpredictable, emotionally unavailable, lack of support or aversive attachment relationships in childhood and adulthood. Due to inconsistency, or lack of responsiveness to needs, there has been insufficient support in regulating inner experiencing and mental states resulting in disruptions in emotional regulation and integration. This impairs the ability to fully trust others and elicits the expectancy that partners will be unavailable, unpredictable or absent. Such expectancies give rise to either an insecure preoccupied attachment style which is linked to excessive dependency, or a dismissive-avoidant or fearful-avoidant attachment style which is characterised by fierce independence and avoidance of relationships.

In the case of severe aversive early child experiences such as rejection, neglect or physical, emotional or sexual violence, the child and later adult is more likely to develop a disorganised/disoriented/dissociated attachment style (Main and Solomon, 1986). This attachment style has become synonymous with traumatic childhoods (Carlson, Cicchetti *et al.*, 1989) and is characterised by dissociation, trance-like states, freezing, hyper-vigilance, hyper-activity, hyper-arousal, low or high tolerance window for stress, stereotypical automaton motor movements, attention deficit, speech disorders, cognitive deficits, lack of empathy, and failure to thrive (Hesse, Main, Abrams and Rifkin, 2003).

Table 4.1 Insecure attachment style (adapted from Bartholomew and Horowitz, 1991 and Main and Solomon, 1986)			
Anxious-preoccupied attachment	Dismissive-avoidant attachment	Fearful-avoidant attachment	Disorganised/disoriented/dissociated
• Need to be emotionally close, intimate • Obsessive needs for reassurance and approval • Overly dependent on others – clingy • Negative view of self, self-worth • Obsessive rumination about relationships • Jealousy • Obsessive compulsive disorders • Dependent or histrionic personality disorder	• Deny need for close relationship • Independent and self-sufficient • Avoidant • Display invulnerability • Deny needing relationships • Distant • Frozen • Shame • Social isolation • Depression • Paranoia • Schizoid, schizotypal, paranoid or obsessional personality disorder	• Ambivalent about relationships – approach-avoid • Lack trust • Anxious about getting hurt • Negative view of self, and others • Suppress and hide their feelings • Unpredictable and inconsistent • Moody • Impulsive • Bipolar disorder • Borderline personality disorder	• Lack of coherent organised attachment • Hyper-vigilant • Dissociation • Trance like states – freeze response • Hyperactivity • Low window of tolerance for stress • Attention and cognitive deficits • Lack of empathy • Self-harm, substance abuse • Suicidal ideation • Borderline personality disorder

This attachment style best fits what is seen in complex trauma, not just in childhood but also in adulthood wherein the individual is put into an irreconcilable paradox of approach and avoidance as the significant other is both a safe haven and a source of terror. This leads to what Main (1995) has called 'fear without solution'. As a result relationships are experienced as paradoxical and at times so terrifying that dissociation is the only form of escape. As the mirror provided by the caregiver is absent or shattered into a thousand fragments, the child or adult cannot form a coherent sense of self or organised attachment strategy (George and West, 2001). This results in extremely chaotic attachments in which survivors oscillate between seeking comfort and defending against caregiving (for a summary of these attachment styles see Table 4.1).

In the long term, entrenched insecure attachments styles can lead to a range of attachment disorders in children such as reactive attachment disorder (DSM-V, APA, 2013) in which all attachment is avoided or disinhibited social engagement disorder (DSM-V, APA, 2013) which is characterised by indiscriminate attachments, in which the child trusts indiscriminately and will accept anyone, even strangers, as caregivers, putting them in greater danger of further abuse. They can also shape the adult personality wherein those with an avoidant attachment are vulnerable to developing obsessional, paranoid, schizoid or schizotypal personality disorders; those with preoccupied attachment are at risk of developing histrionic or dependent personality disorder; while a disorganised attachment is highly correlated with BPD (Fonagy *et al.*, 1996).

COMPLEX TRAUMA AND ATTACHMENT

Most survivors of complex trauma suffer a dual liability in not being able to seek comfort from their attachment figure, as they are also the abuser, which reinforces the sense of terror and aloneness as the very person who can alleviate the terror is also the source of that fear (Sanderson, 2010a). While each survivor will react differently to their traumatic experiences they commonly do develop one of the above insecure attachment styles (Hesse, 1999; Liotti, 1999; Main and Morgan, 1996). In addition, the denial, minimisation, distortion of reality, secrecy and lack of adequate support following traumatisation means that traumatic experiences are split off from conscious awareness so that the ANP can continue to function and behave as though nothing is wrong. This can lead to traumatic bonding with the abuser.

TRAUMATIC BONDING

Traumatic bonding has been described by Dutton and Painter (1981) as the ' …strong emotional ties that develop between two persons where one person intermittently harasses, beats, threatens, abuse or intimidates the other' (p.140) which is characteristic of complex trauma in both childhood and adulthood. It is most likely to occur in the presence of inescapable life threatening trauma which evokes fearful dependency and denial of rage in the victim. As the core feature of traumatic bonding is that the abuser is both the source of preserving life and destroying life, the victim cannot afford to access rage or anger as this will elicit further threat and danger, and so must be denied.

For traumatic bonding to occur certain dynamics need to be present. First there has to be an imbalance of power in which one person has control and authority over another. Second, the abuse is sporadic or intermittent, whereby highly positive, caring and affectionate behaviour alternates with intensely negative and aversive behaviour such as physical, emotional or sexual violence. To manage and survive these two highly contradictory acts the survivor has to deny, dissociate or compartmentalise the abuse components in the relationship in order to focus on the positive, caring and loving aspects. In order to survive the abuse, the survivor has to distort reality and override the true nature of the abusive relationship and normalise the abuser's behaviour. This allows them to mask the abuse and develop an increasingly higher tolerance for abuse, which can become so entrenched that the survivor is unable to admit the abuse to self or others.

The alternation between abusive and loving behaviour becomes the 'superglue that bonds' (Allen, 2001, p.70) the relationship. This bond can sometimes be so strong that anything that may threaten that bond, including therapeutic exploration, will be resisted. To manage the cognitive dissonance, the survivor is compelled to seal off any negative beliefs about the abuser and to humanise rather than demonise them. As a result many survivors adopt the abuser's belief system and come to identify with the aggressor. These changes in perception and powerful cognitive distortion are a central feature of many of the distorted core beliefs that survivors have about self, others, and relationships.

 Remember

Dissociation facilitates traumatic bonding and increases window of tolerance of abusive behaviour.

Along with dissociation and disconnection from aspects of the self, other detrimental relationship dynamics may emerge such as impaired relational worth and the false belief that all relationships are fraught with fear, anxiety, confusion, and conflict rather than a source of pleasure. This can lead to fear of dependency, intimacy and closeness, as well as an intense fear of rejection or abandonment. To combat these fears some survivors become dependent, compliant and submissive in their relationships while others become aggressive or controlling. Many of these attachment dynamics emerge in the therapeutic process and will need to be addressed.

FEAR OF ATTACHMENT AND DEPENDENCY

Fear of dependency can be expressed as either excessive dependence or excessive independence (Steele *et al.*, 2001). When healthy dependency needs are not met some survivors actively seek to have these met through pursuing relationships at all costs in the hope that this will soothe, comfort and reassure them that they have some worth. In this the quality of the relationship is rarely assessed as any relationship is better than none to assuage the fear of being alone. In this, some survivors become compliant and submissive to ensure that the relationship is preserved, while others resort to the use of power and control to keep the relationship intact. Some individuals switch between submission and control in order to bind their partners to them, which is commonly seen in domestic abusers (Sanderson, 2008; Sanderson, 2010a).

Unmet dependency needs can also be expressed through what is known as counterdependence (Steele *et al.*, 2001) whereby the individual becomes fiercely independent and self-sufficient. In this the shame of having needs, and not having them met, leads the individual to deny their needs. As a result they develop an almost phobic avoidance of attachment and attachment loss (Steele and van der Hart, 2009).

Steele and van der Hart (2009) have identified two significant fear responses related to attachment. The first, which they call 'phobia of attachment' is defined as 'an intense aversion of becoming too emotionally or physically close to another person' (Steele and van der Hart, 2009, p.85), while the second they call 'phobia of attachment loss' which is defined as 'an intense fear and panic about losing important relationships' (Boon *et al.*, 2011, p.348). It can be seen from Table 4.2 that while both have a common source such as a desperate need for connection, shame for having attachment needs or chronic fear of dependency needs, how these manifest is quite different with the phobia of attachment activating avoidant behaviours and the phobia of attachment loss activating clingy behaviours.

Table 4.2 Signs of phobia of attachment and attachment loss (adapted from Boon *et al.*, 2011)	
Signs of phobia of attachment	**Signs of phobia of attachment loss**
• Self or auto-regulation rather than relational regulation • Fiercely self-sufficient • Ashamed of dependency needs • Relationships experienced as conflictual and exhausting • Relationships act as a stressor rather than source of comfort or pleasure • Fear of intense feelings, needs and yearnings which characterise close relationships • Avoid trauma triggers by avoiding relationships	• Relational regulation due to lack of self-regulation • Seek out people to avoid being alone • Panic when alone • Fear being alone forever • Expectancy of being abandoned or rejected • Intense fear and rage • Overwhelming arousal and dys-regulation • Deeply ashamed of dependency needs • Stuck in trauma time with no access to care or support • Clinging and seeking behaviours • Submissive and people pleasers • Unaware of and unable to express own needs • Lack of emotional intimacy prevents needs being met

When survivors switch between these two phobic reactions it can generate the very thing they fear, which is chaotic and conflictual relationships. This represents the inner conflict and confusion around close relationships, and the lack of integration between two dissociated states. Ultimately this sends extremely mixed messages to others which is at best confusing and at worst so frustrating that people are reluctant to connect, which reinforces the survivor's fears. As a result many survivors end up feeling isolated and alone, which can lead to traumatic loneliness.

Such dynamics may also manifest in the therapeutic relationship which can be challenging and demanding for both client and practitioner. It is crucial that clients are helped to normalise their dependence needs, and not made to feel ashamed of these. Counsellors need to provide a secure base in which they offer containment and relational regulation, which can be incorporated by the client so that they can learn the skills to self-regulate. It is in such a setting that the survivor can begin to integrate dissociated dependency needs and vulnerability, and begin to develop a secure attachment style (Siegel, 2002; see Box 4.2).

Box 4.2 Learned secure attachment style

- Respectful and accepting of self and others
- Balance between dependence and independence
- Able to set healthy boundaries
- Genuinely warm, engaged and human
- Emotionally available to self and others
- Authentic, honest and non-judgemental
- Empathic
- Able to connect to self and others
- Not defensively dissociated
- Able to reflect
- Able to tolerate uncertainty

TRAUMATIC LONELINESS

The legacy of complex trauma is to override the innate biological need for connection by associating this with fear and abuse rather than safety and protection. When relationships become a source of stress not comfort and pain rather than pleasure, it is not surprising that survivors withdraw and disconnect. This can lead to isolation and a deep sense of aloneness when most in need of connection. The fear of rejection and abandonment and feeling ashamed for having dependency needs can spiral into traumatic loneliness in which the survivor feels alone even when surrounded by people.

Survivors of complex trauma learn that people are not a source of comfort and that they are safer when they are alone. This is learnt during the aftermath of abuse episodes, when the survivor was alone and momentarily safe. The sense of relief and safety experienced when alone can become conditioned wherein the default setting in the presence of stressful or aversive experiences is to withdraw and be alone. Thus, rather than reach out for help and support, survivors are more likely to hide away, withdraw and become invisible. Survivors quickly learn that being visible can prompt further abuse, while being invisible can keep them safe. This dichotomy of visibility versus invisibility is a common feature in survivors of complex trauma who yearn to be seen yet need to hide to feel safe.

Remember
While being alone by choice can be healthy to allow time for contemplation and reflection, this is markedly different to being compelled to withdraw for fear of rejection or humiliation as this can lead to traumatic loneliness.

Traumatic loneliness gives rise to difficulties in perception, feelings, thoughts and expectations as well reducing opportunities to develop the social skills necessary to establish and maintain relationships. In the absence of social interaction and support survivors experience an unbearable sense of separateness which can lead to despair and intense grief. This can be so overwhelming that some survivors become actively suicidal.

Counsellors need to be aware of how pervasive traumatic loneliness can be and monitor factors that maintain withdrawal and isolation. Box 4.3 highlights some of the dynamics and behaviours that support and maintain traumatic loneliness which will need to be addressed in the initial phase of therapeutic engagement so as to facilitate change (see p.68 for helpful exercises and strategies to combat traumatic loneliness).

Remind your clients
The best antidote to the dehumanisation in complex trauma is being in the presence of genuinely safe human relationships.

Box 4.3 Factors that maintain traumatic loneliness

- Mistrust and fear of others

- Safety in solitude

- Distorted perceptions, expectations, predictions, emotions and thoughts about self and others

- Need for invisibility

- Shame of dependency needs, vulnerability, found out, revealing 'secret'

- Dissociation, split off aspects of self, ANP, EP, lack of integration self and organised attachment system

- Isolation as re-enactment of traumatic past when isolated during abuse, alone after abuse episode, default setting to retreat into isolation to gain sense of safety, hide away

- Lack of healthy boundaries – either too rigid to keep people out, or too lax so people intrude, at times switch between the two

- Hostility directed toward self and others as form of self-protection

- Relationships exhausting, frightening, complicated rather than source of pleasure or support, hard to take risks

- Lack of social skills to make friends and stay connected, undeveloped due to history of isolation

---

The range of attachment difficulties experienced by survivors of complex trauma can make it very difficult for them to seek help or enter therapy as this may re-trigger a range of fears associated with entering a relationship. Those that do seek help may fear becoming too close or dependent on the therapist, or repel any attempts to establish a therapeutic alliance, let alone relationship, by being distant and controlling. This can be very demanding and challenging and practitioners need to be aware of the pitfalls. Chapter 5 will look at the most effective forms of treatment strategies when working with survivors of complex trauma, while Chapter 7 explores how to establish and maintain the therapeutic relationship so that survivors can restore relational worth and learn secure attachment.

Box 4.4 Useful exercises for clients

1. Draw a circle representing self, and then draw circles representing significant others in relation to your circle. Reflect on the proximity and distance between the circles. Now draw the circles again as how you would like them to be in relation to your circle. Consider what skills are needed to achieve this

2. Make a list of core relational beliefs

3. Make a list of what you expect from relationships

4. Describe a healthy relationship.

5. List your experience of secure and insecure relationships including as many sensory experiences and behaviours as you can

6. List the skills you would like to have to help you reach out to others

Part 2

WORKING WITH COMPLEX TRAUMA

5
SAFE TRAUMA THERAPY

Given the range of symptoms seen in survivors of complex trauma, counsellors will need to be equipped to unlock traumatic experiences and provide the necessary skills for survivors to regain control over trauma reactions. To facilitate this, counsellors must have an understanding of the fundamental principles of trauma therapy which they can integrate with their theoretical orientation and therapeutic practice. It is essential that practitioners familiarise themselves with the components of safe trauma therapy to ensure that survivors are not re-traumatised.

To reverse the dehumanisation seen in complex trauma requires the presence of a genuine human relationship. To this effect counsellors need to provide a secure base in which to come to 'know' their clients not just 'understand' them (Bromberg, 1994). This is best achieved in an authentic human relationship rather than prescribed protocols or techniques. With this in place survivors will feel safe enough to unlock traumatic experiences, and process and integrate them. It will also enable them to restore relational worth so that they can reconnect to others without fear of further abuse. With this they will be able to enjoy full post-traumatic growth in which joy, laughter and vitality can blossom and flourish.

This chapter will look at the fundamental principles for safe trauma therapy. While there are a range of treatment modalities which address specific aspects of complex trauma, safe trauma therapy provides an approach which can be incorporated into practitioners' existing therapeutic approach. It will also highlight the importance of assessment and the use of assessment scales that measure PTSD and dissociative symptoms. This needs to be accompanied with psychoeducation so that survivors can make sense of their symptoms and normalise these within the context of complex trauma. Psychoeducation is also critical in preparing survivors for the therapeutic process, enabling them to feel more in control over their recovery and healing.

When working with survivors of complex trauma, counsellors need to be mindful of a range of factors such as power and control dynamics, session length, pacing and boundaries that can impact on the therapeutic process. These need to addressed before embarking on trauma therapy. To ensure that survivors are not re-traumatised it is crucial to adopt a phase oriented approach (Chu, 2011; Herman, 1992b; van der Hart, Nijenhuis and Steele, 2006; Rothschild, 2010; Sanderson, 2010a;) in which the initial focus is on safety, stabilisation and the acquisition of skills, before exploring the trauma narrative, and to allow for reconnection to self and post-traumatic growth.

RANGE OF TREATMENT MODALITIES

When working with survivors of complex trauma, practitioners will need to be mindful of a range of treatment modalities that they can integrate into their already existing therapeutic approach. It is hoped that trauma therapy will lend itself most easily to this in providing a framework in which safety and stabilisation are emphasised to minimise the risk of re-traumatisation. Many of the skills used to restore control over trauma reactions come from the cognitive-behavioural tradition and are combined with some of the humanistic principles.

Counsellors may also wish to familiarise themselves with the principles of traumatic incident reduction therapy when working with trauma reactions. There have been a number of so called energy therapies that have had good results in helping some of the somatosensory symptoms. Of particular note are sensorimotor therapy (Ogden, Minton and Pain, 2006), eye movement desensitisation and reprocessing (EMDR) (Shapiro, 1995), and a range of emotional freedom techniques (see Mollon, 2008 for a review). These are best combined with therapies that promote reflection, cognitive processing and integration such as Linehan's dialectical behavioural therapy (1993) and schema therapy (Young et al., 2003). Whichever model is used, counsellors need to ensure that core therapeutic goals, which are summarised in Box 5.1, are addressed.

Box 5.1 Core therapeutic goals

- Safety and stabilisation
- Creating a secure base
- Restore control over trauma reactions
- Reflection and mindfulness
- Psychoeducation and normalisation of symptoms
- Validation of existing coping skills
- Process traumatic experiences
- Restore reality and challenge distorted perceptions
- Rebuild relational worth through the therapeutic relationship
- Make sense of traumatic experiences
- Grieve losses
- Reconnect to self, others and the world
- Restore autonomy and self-efficacy
- Post-traumatic growth

In addition, practitioners need to ensure that the therapeutic process is sensitively paced to provide more than the symptom relief characteristic of time limited evidence based therapies. There is considerable clinical evidence that indicates that healing from complex trauma necessitates longer term therapeutic intervention, (Boon *et al.*, 2011; Chu, 2011; Linehan, 1993; Sanderson, 2012) and counsellors will need to consider whether they can offer such a commitment. While each survivor is unique in terms of their therapeutic needs and length of time needed to recover from trauma, practitioners who are not able to work longer term will need to refer clients to specialist agencies who can. They may also need to consider whether medication or hospitalisation are necessary in times of crisis.

 Warning
Short term symptom relief therapies are less effective than longer term therapies which focus on relational skills to facilitate post-traumatic growth.

ASSESSMENT

When working with survivors of complex trauma it is essential to be able to assess the degree of post-traumatic stress symptoms, dissociative symptoms and level of functioning. Assessment also helps the practitioner to identify primary and secondary symptoms, as well as any associated disorders (Chu, 2011). Essentially, primary symptoms consist of the trauma reactions elicited by the trauma, while secondary symptoms represent attempts by survivors to manage the primary effects such as self-harm, self-medication and withdrawal. Over time secondary symptoms can lead to associated disorders such as self-destructive behaviour, substance dependency, chronic depression and personality disorders. Counsellors need to be able to assess for both primary and secondary symptoms in order to provide appropriate therapeutic intervention, and to know when to refer on.

Generally speaking survivors of complex trauma who have been dehumanised tend to benefit more from a warm, genuinely engaged, human relationship than a distant or clinical one which is driven by standardised protocols and assessments. Survivors need to be seen as individuals with unique experiences rather than being categorised through standardised assessment. Counsellors will need to balance the at times competing demands of client needs, professional assessment and the danger of pathologising clients.

Pathologising survivors taps into their deep rooted fears that they are inadequate, flawed or crazy. It also reactivates abuse dynamics in which reality was distorted by someone more powerful than them. Counsellors must guard against reinforcing such power dynamics so that they do not re-traumatise the client. While there are a number of assessment scales, practitioners need to be mindful of how they wish to utilise these. If they feel confident or are trained to use a particular scale they may invite clients to self-administer a particular checklist or questionnaire type scale. Alternatively they may extrapolate a number of checklist items or questions and ask these more informally during the initial assessment stage. The advantage of this is that it feels less like a clinical assessment and more of an engaged therapeutic dialogue. This is often more helpful to clients who may feel distanced or pathologised by being assessed in such a clinical way. Counsellors will need to use their judgement in terms of what is most coherent with their theoretical orientation and therapeutic style, and what is most helpful for an individual client.

To aid counsellors in how to assess survivors most effectively they will need to familiarise themselves with the range of assessment scales and how they wish to use them. It is helpful to ascertain the degree of trauma by using the traumatic event scale and to check the magnitude and intensity of trauma reactions. To this effect counsellors can look at some of the post-traumatic stress and acute stress reaction scales, and those that measure dissociative experiences (see Box 5.1). Some survivors may not initially present with complex trauma or dissociative disorders and these may not emerge until later in the therapeutic process. In such cases counsellors may wish to use assessment scales only when these emerge rather than a global, generalised assessment.

Whether assessment scales are used at the beginning or when symptoms emerge, assessment will enable counsellors to assess the survivor's therapeutic needs more accurately. This will empower them to decide to what extent they can provide effective therapeutic interventions, or whether they need to refer clients on to more specialist agencies. In addition, accurate assessment minimises the risk of false positive or false negative diagnosis.

 Top tip
Assessing for dissociative symptoms as part of the initial assessment can help to manage the challenges of dissociation in the therapeutic process.

There are a number of scales that practitioners may find useful ranging from self-report life events and traumatic experiences scales, to symptom checklists and structured and semi-structured interviews. Some of these are relatively general and easily available in the literature, through specialist organisations such as the International Society for Traumatic Stress Studies (ISTSS) and the International Society for the Study of Trauma and Dissociation (ISSTD) or trauma related websites (www.istss. org, www.isst-d.org, www.traumacentre.org), whereas others are more complex and can only be administered and scored by specifically trained clinicians (see Box 5.2).

Box 5.2 Clinical assessment scales

TRAUMATIC EVENT SCALES

- Life Events Checklist
- Traumatic Events Checklist (TEC), Nijenhuis *et al.*, 2001
- Trauma History Scale (THS)

PTSD SCALES

- Clinician-Administered PTSD Scale (CAPS)
- Post Traumatic Symptom Scale – Interview Version (PSS-I)
- Post Traumatic Stress Disorder Checklist (PCL)
- Acute Stress Disorder Interview (ASDI)
- Acute Stress Disorder Scale (ASDS)

DISSOCIATION SCALES

- Dissociative Experiences Scale (DES), Bernstein and Putnam, 1986
- DES-Taxon
- Somatoform Dissociation Questionnaire (SDQ5), Nijenhuis *et al.*, 1996
- Somatoform Dissociation Questionnaire (SDQ 20), Nijenhuis *et al.*, 1996
- The Dissociative Questionnaire DIS – Q Vanderlinden *et al.*, 1993
- Multidimensional Inventory of Dissociation (MID), Dell, 2006
- Structured Clinical Interview for DSM-IV Dissociative Disorders – Revised (SCID-D-R), Steinberg, 1994, 1995
- The Dissociative Disorder Interview Schedule (DDIS), Ross *et al.*, 1989; Ross *et al.*, 1990

As many clients are not aware that they dissociate, counsellors may consider incorporating a number of simple questions to identify dissociative symptoms as part of their initial general assessment of all clients, not just those that have experienced trauma. The Dissociative Events Scale (Bernstein and Putnam, 1986) is particularly useful in formulating questions around the core dissociative symptoms such as loss of time and memory, estrangement from self or their surroundings, and the presence of separate self-identities. Assessing dissociation can be critical in alerting counsellors to some of the challenges that might emerge when working with dissociative clients (see pp.51–54).

Assessment needs to be on-going throughout the therapeutic process. This helps the counsellor to keep track of emerging symptoms or difficulties and the consolidation and integration of newly acquired knowledge and skills. To engage clients with this and to highlight the importance of collaboration, it helps to invite clients to assess progress every six weeks in terms of symptom reduction and what is most helpful in the therapeutic process and what is less helpful. This reduces the power dynamic in the therapeutic relationship and allows clients to feel more in control and to take ownership for their recovery and healing. To support this, counsellor and client need to review regularly the learning and consolidation of skills and keep track of the trajectory in terms of achieving agreed therapeutic goals. Assessment is also necessary when deciding whether survivors could benefit from group therapy as an adjunct to individual work and when to move through the three stages of trauma therapy (see pp.89–92).

Top tip

On-going assessment by both client and counsellor allows survivors to feel more in control and take ownership of their process of recovery and healing.

THE ROLE OF PSYCHOEDUCATION

An important part of recovery and healing from complex trauma is to make sense of traumatic experiences and reactions in order to restore a sense of control. This can be facilitated through psychoeducation. Psychoeducation involves sharing information to enhance awareness and improve cognitive understanding. When clients are equipped with knowledge about the impact of trauma and the process of recovery they can develop reflective function and meta-cognition to make more sense of their experiences. In gaining greater understanding clients are able to normalise their reactions and begin to take more control rather than being embedded in or flooded by emotions. This enables them to create some order over what has felt chaotic or overwhelming. Knowledge and reflection can help to stabilise trauma reactions to acquire the necessary skills to allow survivors to have more choice over emotional and behavioural responses.

Top tip

Psychoeducation is empowering for clients in helping them to feel more in control over symptoms and the process of healing.

To maximise the effect of psychoeducation, practitioners need to be mindful of how knowledge is conveyed so as not to patronise or overwhelm the client. The information provided has to reflect the client's need at a specific time and be accessible without being condescending. Counsellors need to guard against 'lecturing' the client and emphasise the sharing of information. It is helpful to ask clients whether they would find information helpful rather than bombarding them. To this effect the information has to be relevant and presented in such a way that is manageable for the client. This has to be carefully paced and counsellors must guard against appearing 'all knowing' or 'too expert' as this may create a power dynamic that is reminiscent of the abuse experience.

To facilitate learning and consolidation it is more effective to provide information in a format that the client can take away to digest, re-read and reflect on in between sessions. This is particularly the case with survivors who are dissociative. Ideally the mode of presentation should reflect the client's learning style and can be provided in a variety of ways including verbal instruction, in written or auditory form, or through self-discovery and practical exercises (see Box 5.3).

Box 5.3 Tips for psychoeducation

1. Verbal instruction
2. Handouts on trauma symptoms, grounding exercises such as breathing and useful techniques
3. Directed reading – articles, books, educational as well as first-hand accounts
4. Audio CD, MP3 player, smart phone
5. Experiential exercises
6. Watching relevant films, documentaries
7. Homework – keeping a journal, exercises, regular practice to gain mastery, review of skills
8. Skills based courses such as assertion training, social skills training

---

Psychoeducation is particularly useful for those clients who have not had the opportunity to develop life skills and those with acute or chronic dissociation. As dissociative clients are often not present, or switch between conscious awareness and dissociation, they have difficulty in receiving, processing and storing information. This is especially the case when exploring experiences that are threatening or painful to the client as they are more likely to tune out, rendering the information meaningless. More importantly, they may forget ever receiving the information which can hinder learning. Some survivors who hold rigid, dichotomous beliefs will resist challenging these and either dissociate or distort and misinterpret incoming information to protect themselves. Counsellors will need to monitor to what degree information has been absorbed, consolidated and integrated at regular intervals. This can be done through homework exercises and a regular review of skills.

AREAS OF PSYCHOEDUCATION

Although psychoeducation is an on-going process, much of this will take place in the early stages of therapy. In order for survivors to feel more in control of trauma reactions and the therapeutic process it is critical that practitioners explore the nature and impact of trauma, the process of recovery, the therapeutic process and the therapeutic relationship as the crucible for change. In addition, psychoeducation needs to include information on specific areas of difficulty that the client is grappling with. Commonly these include dissociation, shame, self-harm, self-medication, substance abuse and sexuality (see Box 5.4) all of which can be supported with practical exercises as presented in Part 3 of this handbook.

THE THERAPEUTIC PROCESS

There are a number of therapeutic factors that counsellors need to consider when working with survivors of complex trauma. Given the betrayal of trust and disruption of attachment bonds it is critical that a safe and secure base is created in which the survivor can work through traumatic experiences and to which the therapist can bear witness (Herman, 1992b). Practitioners will need to provide a genuine presence in which they are fully engaged and to act as an active participant. It is only within a human relationship that the dehumanising effects of complex trauma can be reversed (see p.71). As traumatic experiences are associated with abandonment and aloneness, counsellors must guard against being too distant, clinical or protocol driven and need to listen with both head and heart to provide an engaged therapeutic stance (see Box 5.5).

Box 5.4 Areas for psychoeducation

1. Nature of traumatisation, impact of trauma, trauma symptoms, role of dissociation, role of attachment

2. The process of recovery and post-traumatic growth

3. The therapeutic process – contract, duration, the nature of therapy, theoretical orientation, therapeutic goals, phase oriented treatment

4. The therapeutic relationship and the role of collaboration

5. Trauma and trauma symptoms – emotional immune system, resetting of the alarm system, affect regulation

6. Acquisition of skills and the role of practice to gain mastery

7. Life skills to enhance well-being and life balance such as role of nutrition, sleep, rest, exercise, relaxation, play

8. The role of boundaries, safety rather than control, being able to say no, assertiveness

9. Relationships and relationship skills, balance between dependence and independence

10. The role of shame in complex trauma and current difficulties

11. Specific problem areas such as self-harm, self-medication, substance misuse, sexuality and sexual functioning

12. The role of empathy and compassion for self and others

13. Traumatic loneliness

To facilitate this they will need to create a safe and secure setting in which the hidden, vulnerable, authentic self – what Winnicott (1965) refers to as the 'self in cold storage' (p.145) and what Nijenhuis, et al., (1998) calls 'the scared self' (p.257) – can emerge and be affirmed. When such safety is provided, survivors can begin to explore their traumatic experience, integrate and make sense of these to regain control over their lives.

Box 5.5 Therapeutic stance

- Honest and transparent – counteract secrecy
- Explicit to counteract implicit nature of abuse and avoid need to mind-read
- Do not make promises that can't be kept
- Collaborative
- Non-judgemental
- Genuine interest in helping and be able to convey that to the client
- Warm, human and caring
- Attuned
- Validate experience
- Well bounded
- Flexible approach – not rigid but what works best for individual
- Allow survivor some control, e.g. pacing, not forcing, rushing
- Don't make assumptions

CREATING A SAFE THERAPEUTIC SETTING

As trauma compromises survivors' sense of safety, it is essential that practitioners create a safe therapeutic setting which will act as a secure base for clients. Counsellors need to provide a predictable and consistent therapeutic space to reverse the unpredictability and inconsistency associated with complex trauma (see Box 5.6). In addition they must ensure that the therapeutic space is safe from intrusions or loud or unexplained noises to minimise trauma reactions. It is also important that survivors are familiarised with the location of exits and relevant facilities should they need to leave the consulting room. Ideally survivors need to be able to see the door and know that they have unobstructed access to the exit. This will make them feel safe and contained, and reduce the need for hyper-vigilance to focus on establishing internal safety.

Box 5.6 Creating a safe therapeutic setting

- Safe and calm setting with no external distractions or loud noises
- Attachment dynamics
- Clients need to see exit, access to facilities, comfort breaks, refreshment
- Power and control needs to be restored to client to encourage self-agency
- Boundaries: confidentiality, length of session, out of session contact, duration of therapy, touch, self-disclosure
- Pacing of sessions needs to be client led, do not pressurise to talk
- Starting and ending
- Secure base of the therapeutic relationship that is well bounded and genuinely warm and human, predictable and consistent

---

Survivors will also need to know that they can go to the cloakroom during the session if necessary. Counsellors need to be mindful that re-experiencing trauma can revive terror states in which the survivors will be overcome by nausea or the need to evacuate their bowels. Survivors need to know that this is permitted as the fear of vomiting in session not only increases anxiety, but also prevents attending to and processing any therapeutic input. In addition, anxiety often leads to an increased need to go to the lavatory and survivors will need to know that they can take a comfort break during the session (Sanderson, 2010a).

 Warning

Terror states induce states of nausea or need to evacuate the bowels and survivors will need to know that they can take a comfort break during the session. Counsellors must not mis-interpret this as resistance.

Alongside this, anxiety and elevated stress reactions lead to respiratory difficulties and a dry mouth. Counsellors will need to be explicit in terms of access to water, or bringing drinks and refreshments into sessions. They may also consider placing a bottle of water and a glass in the consulting room and inviting clients to help themselves if necessary. Practitioners will also need to consider whether they will offer tissues to the client, or whether they are expected to help themselves. It is worth remembering that survivors of complex trauma are generally terrified of expressing needs and will often endure physiological discomfort rather than ask for help. As a result they become so immersed in the alleviation of their unexpressed needs that they are unable to engage in the therapeutic process.

Counsellors will also need to be aware of personal space and create an optimal space which is not intrusive or invasive, and yet not too distanced. Ideally they must also guard against creating such barriers as taking notes or taping sessions as these are often experienced as intrusive, which makes the survivor more self-conscious and hyper-vigilant, which in turn can impede the therapeutic process.

Box 5.7 Attachment dynamics in the therapeutic process

- Power and control
- Trust – inability to trust vs. indiscriminate trust
- Fear of dependency needs
- Fear of intimacy
- Fear of rejection
- Insecure attachment style – approach and avoid behaviour
- Interplay of client and counsellor attachment style
- Idealisation or vilification of counsellor

ATTACHMENT DYNAMICS IN THE THERAPEUTIC PROCESS

As relationships are experienced as dangerous rather than a source of pleasure, counsellors will need to monitor any attachment dynamics that might emerge in the therapeutic process (see Box 5.7). Issues around power and control, trust, fear, intimacy, dependency and rejection will create therapeutic challenges that will need to be addressed (see p.93). In addition the ability to connect will be hindered by insecure attachment patterns and approach/avoid behaviours. Counsellors will also need to monitor their own attachment style in response to the survivors and how this influences the therapeutic process. This will help enhance awareness of the therapeutic dance between the client's and counsellor's perspectives as well as understanding and managing such dynamics as idealisation or vilification of the counsellor.

POWER AND CONTROL

To support the sense of safety, counsellors will need to pay particular attention to power and control dynamics, and ensure that these are minimised. Survivors know all too well what it feels like to be controlled by someone else, and to feel that they have no control over their body, feelings, thoughts or actions. Counsellors need to be mindful of this and ensure that they restore power and control to the client and encourage self-agency. To facilitate this, counsellors will need to provide opportunities for survivors to regain control by providing a genuinely collaborative therapeutic alliance in which survivors are able to take ownership of their healing. This is best achieved by encouraging clients to set personally meaningful goals and to pace the therapeutic work.

To avoid recreating abuse dynamics, counsellors will need to be client led rather than imposing a rigidly held theoretical orientation or prescribed therapeutic techniques. Counsellors need to be mindful that 'Theory is merely a guide not God' (Kohut, 1972, p.67) and be flexible in how they work with survivors. They may have to consider making reasonable adjustments to incorporate client needs rather than working in a rigidly prescribed way. In addition, emphasis must be placed on establishing a mutually respectful relationship in which clients feel valued and validated rather than pathologised or infantilised. To this effect survivors need to be seen as individuals, not just as survivors of complex trauma, to avoid making trauma the central organising principle of the client's self-identity as this reinforces the sense of victimisation.

 Top tip

The most powerful instrument for healing traumatised clients is the therapeutic relationship and counsellors need to be mindful that ' …therapy should not be theory-driven but relationship driven' (Yalom, 2008, p.204).

It is critical that all communications are explicit, and if necessary reiterated, so that survivors are clear and not left to 'mind read' implicit messages as they needed to during the abuse. This is especially the case with survivors who dissociate and may have no recollection of what has been said. In such instances it is helpful to provide important information either in written or auditory form so that survivors can remind themselves. Counsellors will also need to be interactive in engaging with survivors to check meaning and note points for clarification. This is best achieved by making the client visible without being voyeuristic, or scrutinising them, and finding a healthy balance between being emotionally available without being too intrusive.

BOUNDARIES

To balance safety needs with restoring control to survivors, counsellors will have to pay particular attention to boundaries as these act as an ' …envelope of trust' (Brown and Stobart, 2008, p.36). Survivors will have strong reactions to the setting of boundaries, with some welcoming them while others will feel controlled by the counsellor. In being abused survivors will have experienced numerous boundary violations and counsellors must make sure that they set appropriate boundaries to keep both client and counsellors safe. Ideally they need to be well bounded and flexible when appropriate. This is best achieved by setting agreed boundaries with clients which are subject to review throughout the therapeutic process (see Box 5.8).

 Top tip
Counsellors need to be well bounded and flexible to balance client needs with providing a secure base.

Many survivors have a distorted view of boundaries and see them as a form of control by more powerful individuals who can impose restrictions and yet also violate personal boundaries. In addition, survivors have not been allowed to defend boundaries, or say no for fear of further abuse or punishment. It is for this reason that counsellors need to provide psychoeducation around boundaries and encourage the survivor to set healthy boundaries of safety rather than control. The more they feel involved in the process of establishing agreed boundaries the less controlled they will feel.

Box 5.8 Core boundaries in trauma therapy

- Explicitness
- Boundaries of safety
- Confidentiality
- Duration of therapy
- Length of session
- Out of session contact
- Touch
- Self-disclosure
- Pacing

To this effect counsellors need to be explicit in stating agreed boundaries and if necessary provide these in written or auditory form. In addition they must devote time throughout the therapeutic process to check that these boundaries remain intact and do not collapse. Survivors may challenge boundaries and counsellors must not shy away from addressing such challenges and managing these appropriately. To aid them, counsellors will benefit from assessing their window of tolerance for flexibility. While ethical and professional boundaries such as confidentiality, safety, and not entering a personal or sexual relationship with clients are non-negotiable, there may be some that can be negotiated. It is crucial that counsellors consider and identify the degree of flexibility they feel comfortable with as a matter of principle rather than agree to something that they are not able to tolerate or manage.

Common areas for consideration include duration of the therapeutic process, session length, outside session contact and writing of reports.

Duration of therapy

Recovery from complex trauma takes time and is rarely achieved in short term, time limited therapy. While survivors will vary in terms of length of therapeutic intervention, most benefit from a minimum of two years of psychological support. Counsellors will have to assess whether they can commit to long-term therapy and that they have the stamina and resilience to manage such therapeutic work. If clients need more than one session a week they will also need to assess whether they can provide this. As the therapeutic process is not linear and has relapses and crisis, counsellors need to assess to what degree they can offer extra support, including outside of session contact.

Length of session

One other boundary that needs to be addressed is the length of each session. Survivors vary in attention span and their ability to concentrate and remain in the present, and this will need to be considered in terms of optimal length of therapeutic session. Some survivors may only be able to manage 30 or 40 minutes, while others benefit from an hour and a half. It is helpful during the initial assessment stage to consider what is most beneficial for the client. Individual needs have to be balanced with what counsellors are realistically able to manage. Irrespective of length of session, the agreed length must be discussed and agreed with the client as part of the contract, rather than varying session length on an ad hoc basis.

Out of session contact

Survivors in crisis often benefit from telephone support in between sessions and counsellors will need to decide whether they can offer this. Some counsellors find that brief check-in calls that offer psychological support rather than therapy can help in stage one until the client has developed the skills to regulate unbearable internal states. Such phone calls need to be well bounded in terms of frequency, availability and length of time. Most importantly, they must be focused on helping clients to implement grounding and affect regulation skills. Any such arrangements must be explicitly stated as part of the contract and counsellors need to check that they have been understood by the client. During such crisis, or when survivors are feeling suicidal, counsellors may use this as a basis for formulating a safety contract.

Alongside this counsellors need to be explicit around how to manage chance meetings outside the therapeutic setting and specify whether they will say hello, nod or refrain from any acknowledgement. Furthermore, counsellors will need to be clear that they cannot enter into any dual relationship and give the reasons why. It is always helpful to support such decisions with some psychoeducative input so that survivors do not feel rejected or ignored.

Touch

Physical contact between client and counsellors is generally to be discouraged, especially when working with survivors of complex trauma, and boundaries around this must be explicitly stated as part of the contract. However, some counsellors do use touch in the therapeutic setting with good effect (Hunter and Struwe, 1998). Touch should never be used without considerable thought and evaluation of the benefits and dangers of touch. A guiding principle is if in doubt don't, and only ever if it is in the genuine interest of the client. Sexual touch is never acceptable under any circumstances.

Self-disclosure

When working with survivors of complex trauma it is important to be authentic and transparent, which usually requires an element of self-disclosure. Ideally, these should be confined to immediate bodily or sensory reactions in the moment, although at times these can be supported by an open discussion about the therapeutic relationship and level of connectedness. Counsellors will need to be honest and authentic in their responses rather than hide behind a façade of professional distance. In the case of personal questions, counsellors must use their judgement as to the degree to which they wish to answer these and if they feel uncomfortable doing so, support this with an explanation rather than be evasive. What is essential is that self-disclosure must be brief, in the interest of the survivor as an aid to understanding, and must not be used to shift the focus away from the client.

Pacing

The pacing of the therapeutic process is crucial so that survivors do not rush into the trauma narrative before they have acquired the necessary skills to manage trauma reactions. Survivors often want to 'rush through' exploring traumatic experiences, much as they did when they were abused, so that they do not have to feel. Such rushing prevents the reflection on and processing of feelings which means they cannot be integrated. Before exploring traumatic experiences, survivors need to acquire skills to manage these so they are not re-traumatised.

Counsellors will also need to pay close attention to pacing sessions to allow survivors to go at a pace that is manageable for them. Some survivors will want to start the session as soon as they enter the room while others need time to settle in. Generally speaking survivors tend to prefer time at the beginning to settle in and feel comfortable under the counsellor gaze. They need to check that the counsellor is still a secure base in being present and engaged. Many survivors use this time to check the emotional availability of the counsellor before lowering any defences that have built up in between sessions. Counsellors need to respect this settling in period and not pressurise survivors to talk and allow them to set the pace.

The ending of the session also needs to be carefully paced. To ensure safety when leaving the session, survivors will need time to prepare to leave. This is especially the case when the session has revived painful memories and feelings, or if the survivor has dissociated or is disoriented. Ideally counsellors need to ensure that the last ten minutes of the session are devoted to containing the client so that they can manage the transition between the safety of the therapeutic setting and the external environment.

Throughout the therapeutic process counsellors must balance respect for the client's pace and when to be more proactive. Rather than direct intervention counsellors can use non-verbal interventions such as tone of voice and speech rate to moderate the pace and intensity of emotions. Counsellors may also need to consider integrating short breaks in the session for containment and rest to modulate the work. This will ensure that survivors are not overwhelmed by emotional states and are able to stay 'in mind'. In helping clients to regulate emotional states they will facilitate the acquisition of skills to self-regulate. It is this interactive process in which the client's pace is prioritised and balanced with gentle guidance that survivors can regain control over trauma reactions and learn to be present in the safety of a secure relationship.

SAFE TRAUMA THERAPY

Pacing the therapeutic process is one of the most essential ingredients of safe trauma therapy as it promotes client safety and minimises re-traumatisation. It is crucial that counsellors do not explore the trauma narrative until the survivor has acquired sufficient skills to feel more in control of trauma symptoms, and there is an improvement in daily functioning. This enables survivors to manage the primary symptoms of trauma such as hyper-arousal, intrusive re-experiencing and avoidance and to learn vital skills to reduce secondary symptoms such as self-harm or self-medication. Research has shown that safe trauma therapy is best conducted in three stages (Chu, 2011; Herman, 1992; Rothschild, 2010; van de Hart *et al.*, 1993, see Box 5.9) and that such a phase-oriented approach can be incorporated into an individual counsellor's theoretical orientation and preferred treatment modality.

Box 5.9 Stages of trauma therapy

Stage 1: Establishing safety and control, psychoeducation, developing skills to manage symptoms, improve functioning and everyday life, support network, building the therapeutic relationship

Stage 2: Processing the trauma narrative, integrating trauma experiences and traumatic memories, and associated abuse dynamics, loss and mourning, challenging distorted core beliefs and restoring reality, grief and mourning

Stage 3: Reconnection to self and post-traumatic growth, increased vitality and engagement with the world

---

Stage 1 focuses on establishing safety and restoring control over trauma symptoms, and a reduction in symptomatology. The emphasis is on increasing everyday functioning and improving daily life. This is best achieved through psychoeducation and the acquisition of necessary skills to manage trauma reactions to contain traumatic re-experiencing. These skills will also reduce activation of less adaptive ways of managing trauma reactions seen in secondary symptoms. In providing a safe secure base, clients can learn that overwhelming internal states can be managed and controlled through affect regulation (see Chapter 11, pp.169–173). breathing, and grounding exercises. As survivors restore control and learn to self-regulate they are more able to reflect. Such reflection enables survivors to move from being embedded in trauma reactions to make more sense of their experiences. Restoring internal safety needs to be supported by external safety in building a healthy support network and by learning the requisite skills to improve daily life by balancing work, exercise, rest and play.

This is also the stage in which to establish and build the therapeutic relationship which will be essential in providing a secure base in which to explore attachment and dependency fears. The stabilisation of trauma symptoms is critical before exploring the traumatic experiences. Survivors need to gain more control over internal states so that they can manage traumatic re-experiencing that may occur when exploring the trauma narrative and traumatic memories.

Warning
To minimise re-traumatisation counsellors must focus on safety, stabilisation and symptom reduction prior to exploring the trauma narrative.

In Stage 2, once stabilisation and affect regulation has been mastered, survivors can begin to explore the trauma narrative safe in the knowledge that they have sufficient skills to manage any increase in re-experiencing of trauma reactions. It is during Stage 2 that the unprocessed emotional and somatosensory traumatic memories can be unlocked, processed and integrated. The preparatory work in Stage 1 is built upon refining skills and applying these to the range of secondary symptoms. This is also the stage in which a range of dynamics associated with the trauma can be explored such as shame, self-blame, idealisation of the abuser, traumatic rage and loneliness, the sense of betrayal, loss of trust and attachment difficulties. From this, survivors can also begin to challenge distorted core beliefs, restore their reality and continue to make sense of their traumatic experiences.

Counsellors will need to continue to build upon the therapeutic relationship to facilitate a learned secure attachment so that deeper attachment difficulties can be worked through, including fear of dependency, intimacy and attachment loss. In order to fully integrate the impact and long-term effects of complex trauma, survivors will need to grieve the range of losses incurred. It is through the process of grief and mourning that the survivor can move into Stage 3 and experience post-traumatic growth. Pacing is crucial during this stage and some survivors may need to return to Stage 1 in order to acquire or master more skills to ensure restore stabilisation and control.

The focus in Stage 3 is on consolidating skills and integration to enable survivors to reconnect to self and others. As they come out of survival mode they can begin to embrace life and re-engage with the world with renewed vitality and experience post-traumatic growth. As survivors begin to heal the wounds of complex trauma and feel more in control of their life they can begin to make more positive choices about their future. This is also the stage in which survivors prepare for the end of the therapeutic process. This needs to be sensitively handled by ensuring that fears around dependency, attachment loss and termination are worked through. It is critical that the ending phase is sensitively managed with a gradual reduction in sessions, and the opportunity to maintain the secure base with some supportive contact when needed.

A sensitively managed therapeutic process which is phase oriented is essential in recovering and healing from complex trauma. Counsellors need to be mindful that the therapeutic process is not linear and that there will be relapses, diversions and innumerable challenges. The following chapter will look at the range of demands and challenges and how these can be managed.

6

THERAPEUTIC CHALLENGES

While working with survivors of complex trauma can be hugely rewarding, it can also be extremely demanding and challenging. To ensure that practitioners are not overwhelmed it is essential to be aware of some of these challenges in order to be prepared and develop strategies for how these can be managed. Commonly therapeutic challenges cluster around professional issues such as knowledge and self-awareness; challenges in the therapeutic process such as testing boundaries; challenges that occur in session such as silences and dissociation; and how these impact on counsellor responses and the therapeutic relationship. This chapter will explore some of these challenges in more depth so that counsellors are more equipped to manage challenges and to minimise 'burnout' or vicarious traumatisation.

PROFESSIONAL CHALLENGES

Professional challenges tend to centre around knowledge and understanding, not only about the nature and impact of trauma, but also self-knowledge and awareness (see Box 6.1). Keeping abreast of the latest research in trauma and clinical issues can be difficult in terms of time and availability of continuous professional development (CPD) opportunities. Practitioners often find it difficult to balance a busy practice and work commitments with additional training, or scheduling time to read current research or clinical literature. This reduces access to innovative therapeutic interventions which potentially limits the range of skills in the counsellor's repertoire. Counsellors also need to familiarise themselves with, and feel comfortable talking about, difficult or taboo subjects such as sex, sexuality and shame. If counsellors retreat from or are embarrassed about discussing such topics they will reinforce survivors' perceptions that these are shameful or dangerous and they will close down all further communication. In addition, if practitioners lack knowledge and skills they are more likely to feel deskilled and risk being overwhelmed which can lead to 'burnout' or STS (see Chapter 24, pp.279–82).

Box 6.1 Core challenges for professionals

- Adequate training
- Knowledge and understanding of nature and dynamics of complex trauma
- Enough time to read and engage in CPD
- Enough time to reflect
- Awareness of power dynamics, both client and counsellor
- High level of self-awareness – own abuse, especially attachment, shame, sexuality, gender
- Feeling comfortable talking about trauma, sexuality, shame
- Acquisition and mastery of additional skills to manage the work without becoming overwhelmed
- Cultural sensitivity
- Socio-political context
- Integrating trauma therapy with existing therapeutic approach
- (Dis)courtesy stigmatisation
- Tolerating and managing uncertainty
- Understanding impact of vicarious traumatisation and secondary traumatic stress
- Counsellor self-care

In-depth knowledge of the nature and dynamics of complex trauma allows practitioners to place the abuse of the most vulnerable into a socio-political context in which the abuse of power is perpetrated and maintained by those who have power and authority over them. Alongside this, practitioners will need to explore their own beliefs around gender, ethnicity and culture to ensure these do not contaminate the therapeutic process. Survivors need to be understood within their cultural framework and counsellors will benefit from a good understanding of cultural differences. This is especially the case when talking about abuse outside of the community and the role that honour plays in some cultures and how this can make disclosure dangerous. It is essential that counsellors balance cultural sensitivity with acknowledgement of abuse and explore the most beneficial options for each individual survivor rather than impose their own cultural view (Sanderson, 2010a). In addition, they need to be able to integrate the principles of trauma therapy with their existing therapeutic approach.

Counsellors also need to make time to reflect on the work and their reactions to understand any counter-transferential reactions and how these impact on the therapeutic process. Good reflective function aids self-awareness and understanding of what counsellors bring to the therapeutic encounter. It is crucial that practitioners are aware of their motivation to work with survivors of complex trauma and how this might link to their own experiences. This can alert them to potential triggers that revive their own exposure to trauma, or invalidating experiences and associated dynamics, such as the need for power and control, attachment needs and fears, gender or cultural stigmatisation, unresolved shame and sexuality. These can be triggered by exposure to survivors' experiences, but may also be elicited through being stigmatised by others. It is not uncommon for professionals, colleagues and friends to question the practitioner's interest or partiality in working with survivors of abuse. Many people cannot comprehend why anyone would want to bear witness to horrendous acts of brutality and violation and thus tend to devalue such work, through what Mattley (1998) has called '(dis)courtesy stigmatisation'. This can undermine practitioners' professional status and leave them feeling isolated and beleaguered (Sanderson, 2010a).

Such isolation can lead to increased vulnerability to vicarious traumatisation. It is crucial that counsellors do not overcompensate for this vulnerability to avoid grandiosity and distorted views about their omniscience or omnipotence (Sanderson, 2010a). This will prevent them from being enticed by '...the three most common narcissistic snares... to heal all, know all and love all' (Maltsberg and Buie, 1974, p.627) and allow for the development of a more human therapeutic relationship, in which power dynamics are minimised and not exploited (see Chapter 7, pp.119–121). To reduce the misuse of power, counsellors must ensure that they do not impose their theoretical orientation and remember that '...theory is merely a guide, not God' (Kohut, 1972) and that they need to prioritise the survivor's individual experience rather than reshaping it to fit their own beliefs.

Counsellors must be mindful that they are not all knowing, especially when working with complex trauma which is fraught with uncertainties and 'not knowing'. To manage this, counsellors must guard against their own need to know and be able to hold the not knowing rather than rushing to premature answers or solutions. It is in not knowing that clients can explore their full range of experiencing and create meaning rather than jumping to conclusions. This necessitates containment for both client and counsellor, as well as patience and an investment of trust in the process. This will require stamina in remaining engaged despite not knowing and uncertainty. As this therapeutic process takes time practitioners will need to have a high degree of resilience, which is best maintained through good self-care, in which their own well-being is prioritised.

CHALLENGES IN THE THERAPEUTIC PROCESS

The therapeutic process presents a number of challenges, especially as it is not linear and resembles an endless rollercoaster ride (see Box 6.2). Managing the many obstacles and diversions requires an enormous amount of patience and flexibility. Many survivors have difficulties around trust and will constantly test whether the counsellor can be trusted through the testing of boundaries. This is commonly seen in boundaries related to outside session contact, time keeping, cancelling or missing sessions or not paying bills. In addition, survivors will test the counsellor through re-enactments of approach and avoid behaviour, or by being hostile and rejecting. Counsellors must guard against personalising such behaviours and understand these as efforts to balance the need to be close with the fear of being close or being abandoned. As trust is not finite such testing can persist throughout the therapeutic process as a test of the counsellor's stamina and commitment.

To manage such testing, counsellors will need to remain well bounded yet flexible and contain any re-enactment of abuse or acting out and understand these within the context of betrayal of trust. In order to establish trust, counsellors must be attuned to survivors' needs, not retreat or disengage, and be authentic and explicit in their responses. Survivors will be highly sensitised to being judged, patronised or dismissed and counsellors will need to respond openly rather than defensively, or hiding behind a professional mask.

Box 6.2 Core challenges in the therapeutic process

- Power and control – client and counsellor
- Patience
- Approach and avoid behaviour
- Maintaining boundaries despite testing of these through re-enactment, acting out
- Managing emotional volatility, dependency needs, rejection, hostility, rage
- Authenticity and explicitness
- Containment
- Attunement
- Balance between empathy and not being too intrusive
- Flexibility of approach
- Uncertainty

 Top tip
Too much empathy can be experienced by some survivors as dangerous and intrusive.

This is especially so in the case of empathy, which must feel genuine and real rather than artificial. Many survivors will react strongly to highly empathic responses as they are not familiar with such empathy, or because these are associated with enticement by the abuser. Counsellors will need to be mindful of not being overly empathic as this can make survivors feel extremely uncomfortable or highly suspicious (see Chapter 7, pp.110–11). While too much empathy can feel intrusive, too little empathy can be experienced as cold and clinical. Counsellors will need to regulate the expression of empathy throughout the therapeutic process and within each individual session.

CHALLENGES IN THE THERAPEUTIC SESSION
There are a number of challenges in the therapeutic session most of which centre around pacing. To avoid the re-playing power and control dynamics associated with abuse (see Box 6.3), it is important that survivors feel that they have some control over their healing process. Counsellors

can facilitate this by encouraging survivors to take more control in the therapeutic process; by pacing the session; and by letting the client lead in terms of starting and ending the session and talking or not talking so that they do not feel rushed. Counsellors will need to balance this by pacing exposure to the trauma narrative in a way that is truly manageable by the client. Counsellors will need to reassure clients that they will not be pressed into going into traumatic experiences until they have more control over trauma reactions and have mastered emotional regulation skills.

Alongside this counsellors will need to face challenges around boundaries in session such as time keeping and making sure that traumatic material is left to the last few minutes of the session with not enough time to process it. While there are good reasons for doing this, it is critical to explore it as it impedes the therapeutic process. In addition, counsellors will need to understand, yet gently and firmly challenge, extreme acting out or hostility. Rather than personalising hostility it is more helpful to focus on how it prevents connectedness, making it harder to engage with each other.

 Warning

Silence can be the most dangerous place in the world and needs to be managed sensitively.

Box 6.3 Core challenges in session

- Pacing
- Beginning and ending
- Managing boundaries
- Managing silence
- Balance between knowing when to put brake on and when to accelerate
- Need to remain contained and containing
- Remaining engaged and not distancing
- Not being too intrusive or voyeuristic
- Asking too many direct questions

As in the overall therapeutic process, a constant challenge in session is balancing when to accelerate and when to put the brake on. This is particularly the case in the presence of silence. Silence in session is natural and necessary for staying in the present, experiencing feelings and to allow time for reflection. However it can also be dangerous as much of the abuse will have been committed in silence. In addition, the survivor will have been silenced in not disclosing the abuse and prolonged silence can trigger the powerful feelings of being voiceless. Silence may also be a sign of dissociation, avoidance or unexpressed anger. Counsellors will need to monitor the function and meaning for the silence and whether it is reflective, hostile or dissociative.

To manage silence, counsellors will have to find a healthy balance between holding and breaking the silence. In holding the silence they will need to remain present and embodied. It is critical to remain focused on the client rather than drifting off or thinking about other demands or activities. It helps to focus on the survivor by observing their somatic and non-verbal changes such skin tone, breathing, eye gaze, facial expression or motoric behaviour. This can help in understanding what the silence represents and to reflect back to the client to bring them back into the room. Rather than questions, it is more helpful to say what can be observed or noticed such 'I can see that really touches you.' This helps survivors to feel seen and acknowledged. It is important that this is not intrusive or voyeuristic and represents bearing witness to the hurt and pain rather than ignoring it as it was during the abuse. It is also important to remain present and convey empathic understanding. In this the counsellor maintains the secure base in which silence is no longer dangerous.

One challenge when making clients visible is to ensure that the practitioner is not overly intrusive or voyeuristic. This can be excruciating for the survivors as such scrutiny will trigger shame and fear of exposure. To minimise being intrusive, counsellors will find the use of reflection a much more effective tool to elicit information rather than asking direct questions. Too many questions can create a distance in which the survivor feels like a specimen for analysis rather than a human being who craves connectedness. Similarly, too much counsellor interpretation can be experienced as intrusive or seductive which can lead to the client disconnecting or disengaging (Sanderson, 2010a).

CORE CHALLENGES DUE TO DISSOCIATION

As seen in Chapter 3 dissociation gives rise to a number of challenges, some of which become manifest in the therapeutic session (see Box 6.4).

When survivors dissociate they lose focus by entering into another state of consciousness in which they screen out the present moment and as a result do not hear what is being discussed. This can lead to misinterpretation and miscommunication which create significant barriers in the therapeutic relationship such as mis-attunement, defensive reactions, criticism, projection and negative transference and counter-transference reactions (see p.117). Many of these occur because in tuning out survivors are not able to attend to, process or recall what they are experiencing or what is happening.

This reinforces time loss, memory lapses and confusion about what has been discussed. The memory loss means that clients are not able to retain information or recall it fully. This can lead to memory gaps which they will try to fill in through confabulation. As a result clients will have very different recollections of sessions and interactions than those of the counsellor. Dissociation can also lead to selective abstraction in which only those things that resonate positively or negatively are remembered. Commonly survivors will only recollect a part of what transpired or what was said and jump to conclusions, which will colour the whole therapeutic encounter.

 Warning

Dissociation can lead to confusion in both survivors and counsellors and create ruptures in the therapeutic relationship.

In dissociation survivors may remember only negative aspects of the therapeutic encounter and be unable to contact the positive aspects. This is often seen in the expression of empathy which the survivor cannot tolerate or blocks out, thereby misperceiving the counsellor as cold or distant. As a result crucial aspects of the therapeutic process may be mis-remembered, mis-understood or misinterpreted, which can lead to ruptures in the therapeutic relationship (see p.117). This can create considerable confusion within and between client and counsellor which can lead to distortions in reality for both. It is not uncommon for some survivors to leave sessions feeling misheard, rejected or judged while the counsellor feels that they have offered empathic understanding and reflection.

 Top Tip

To keep client focused and present during the session it is helpful for them to hold a 'tangle-toy' to ground them (see p.173).

Box 6.4 Core challenges due to dissociation

- Client not present
- Client not receiving information
- Loss of memory recall – partial, total, confabulation to fill in gaps
- Misinterpretation
- Selective abstraction
- Confusion
- Ruptures in the therapeutic relationship
- Inability to reflect
- Rigidity of thinking
- Counsellor's dissociation

Dissociation also reduces survivors' ability to reflect on their experiences, feelings and thoughts. As they retreat and disengage from overwhelming feelings they are not able to process them and as a result become embedded in them. Lack of reflection further compromises clarity of thinking with survivors resorting to rigid thinking patterns. These thought patterns are often characterised by extreme polarised thinking, which is based on distorted cognitions, assumptions and expectancies. Such rigidity of thought can be difficult to challenge as it acts as a protection from doubt and uncertainty and taking risks. While counsellors need to understand the function of rigid thinking patterns and their link to dissociation, they will also need to encourage survivors to challenge these.

Counsellors will also need to be mindful that bearing witness to complex trauma can be traumatising which can lead to dissociation. In witnessing unbearable emotional states counsellors may also feel overwhelmed, which might activate dissociative responses. Alternatively they may react to the survivor's dissociation on a sensory or bodily level by tuning out, feeling heavy and tired or retreating into a more distant, clinical therapeutic stance. To manage such dissociative reactions counsellors will need to identify triggers to dissociation and ensure that they are able to ground themselves back into the present.

CORE CHALLENGES TO COUNSELLORS

The demands of working with complex trauma can create a number of challenges to counsellors in how they respond to survivors and their material (see Box 6.5). Exploring abuse experience can trigger counsellors' own abuse experience(s), especially if these have not been fully processed. It can also revive feelings of being invalidated in early attachment relationships and associated feelings of helplessness and powerlessness. Bearing witness to brutality and dehumanisation can shatter assumptions about the world and how people relate to each other. At times this can elicit overwhelming emotions such as anger, rage and terror. If these are not regulated or moderated, counsellors can develop 'burnout' and the symptoms of vicarious traumatisation.

Feeling overwhelmed can also lead to disbelief and doubt, which can result in being judgemental of survivors for not having dealt with the abuse, or being so helpless and dependent. Listening to traumatic experiences can elicit feelings of powerlessness in which anger and rage cannot be expressed at the abuser and which may therefore be displaced on to the survivor. Alternatively counsellors may experience witness guilt (Herman, 1992a) in which they feel guilty for not having experienced such trauma. In combination such powerful feelings can lead to emotional overload and a need to withdraw either through disengagement, distancing or dissociation.

The doubt and uncertainty when working with complex trauma can lead to counsellor self-doubt in which they begin to question their ability to manage such work. This is especially the case when the trauma is so deeply entrenched that survivors feel hopeless about their recovery or healing. This sense of hopelessness can be infectious whereby the counsellor experiences similar doubts leading them to try harder and to overcompensate for feeling deskilled. Such overcompensation leads to increased working hours, higher caseload and not taking breaks, which increase counsellor stress levels and likelihood of burnout.

Stress levels are further heightened when counsellors react in ways that elicit shame and guilt. A common example is when counsellors become aroused by trauma narratives, especially if the arousal is erotic or sexual. Counsellors will need to explore such arousal within the context of fear responses which have become eroticised. They will need to discuss this with their supervisor and under no circumstances attempt to act upon these. Such arousal is not uncommon and need not be a source of shame.

It is critical that sexual or erotic arousal is discussed with a supervisor or trusted colleague so that this can be understood and worked through rather than acted upon.

Box 6.5 Core challenges to counsellors

- Destabilisation – own abuse/attachment experiences, shattered assumptions about the world
- Feeling overwhelmed by the material and vicarious traumatisation
- Anger and rage
- Disbelief, doubt, judgemental
- Feeling overwhelmed
- Hostility
- Witness guilt
- Wanting to withdraw, disconnect, dissociate, create distance, retreat, disembodied
- Feeling aroused – sexually, or by violence
- Shame
- Self-doubt and feeling deskilled
- Overcompensation
- Counter-transference – over identification, negative counter-transference reactions (CTR), somatic, bodily

---

 Warning

Sexual arousal when listening to trauma narratives is not uncommon and primarily represents fear responses that have become eroticised. Counsellors must take this to supervision and under no circumstances act upon it.

This is also the case in the range of CTR. Counsellors can experience both positive and negative CTRs and need to be aware that these represent the interplay between the client's projection and the therapist's own psychology (Sanderson, 2010a). It is important to remember that CTRs provide an opportunity to deepen understanding of both client and self which can enhance the therapeutic relationship (see Chapter 7, pp.123–26).

While the challenges can at times seem overwhelming, counsellors can become more sentient practitioners providing they are able to manage their own responses. It is crucial that they remain grounded and contained so that they can reflect on their responses. They must be honest about their limitations and remember that emotional responses can enhance their practice. To this effect they need to remember that emotional responses are integral to the work and they are a powerful resource for expanding insight into the realities of complex trauma. They also offer an opportunity for reflection, which enhances self-awareness and understanding. When equipped with this, counsellors are able to truly engage with survivors and provide a secure base in which to build a healthy therapeutic relationship. Given that this is the most powerful instrument in healing complex trauma, the following chapter will explore how to establish and maintain the therapeutic relationship.

7
BUILDING AND MAINTAINING THE THERAPEUTIC RELATIONSHIP

The repeated betrayal of trust characteristic of complex trauma makes it extremely hard for survivors to seek professional help. This is especially the case when all relationships, including professional ones, are seen as dangerous rather than a source of comfort. To risk connection despite repeated betrayal takes courage and is an indication that hope has not been extinguished. Counsellors must honour this in providing a warm, authentic, and sensitively attuned therapeutic relationship in which the survivor can restore relational worth. It is only in the presence of a human relationship that the dehumanisation all too often seen in complex trauma can be undone.

There is considerable evidence that the secure base of the therapeutic relationship can lead to both neuronal and relational changes which allow survivors to develop a more coherent internal relationship and more growth promoting relationships with others (Bromberg, 2011; Cozzolino, 2010; Schore, 2012). In addition, the constancy and consistency of the therapeutic relationship are crucial in providing the necessary safety to acquire the skills for emotional regulation to restore control over unbearable internal states and trauma reactions. As survivors begin to reconnect to the self and to trust again they are able move from isolation toward reconnection with others. Thus the therapeutic relationship becomes the crucible for post-traumatic growth in which relationships and connection with others become a source of comfort and pleasure in which human experiences of humour, laughter and joy can flourish.

This chapter will look at the importance of the therapeutic relationship and the qualities needed to establish and build a secure base in which trust can be rebuilt. This can be difficult as clients may create barriers to building a relationship which will need to be explored and processed.

Survivors frequently test counsellors' constancy and commitment through challenging behaviour and boundary violations which need to be understood within the context of complex trauma rather than rejecting the survivor. You will need to manage ruptures and repairs sensitively in order to remain engaged and to maintain the therapeutic relationship. The chapter will also highlight some of the challenges in the therapeutic relationship such as the interplay of survivor and counsellor attachment style, transference and counter-transference reactions and how these influence the quality of the therapeutic relationship. In managing these and restoring relational worth survivors will be able to leave the safety of the therapeutic relationship and be able to establish nurturing bonds with others as they reconnect to the world.

THE ROLE OF THE THERAPEUTIC RELATIONSHIP

Research into the effectiveness of psychotherapy consistently shows that the therapeutic relationship is the most powerful instrument for healing and change and that therapist warmth, understanding, trustworthiness, genuineness, validation, acceptance and positive approach far outweigh theoretical orientation or specific techniques (Lambert and Ogles, 2004). As a result many clinicians have emphasised the centrality of the relationship with Glaser (2008) proposing that 99 per cent is due to the relationship and only 1 per cent is everything else, while Kahn (1997) argues that 'The relationship is the therapy' (p.1) and Yalom (2008) asserts that the '...antidote to much anguish is sheer connectedness [and that] the relationship heals' (p.205).

When working with survivors of complex trauma you will need to build a '...relational bridge' (Blizard, 2003, p.38) in which internal and external relational changes can take place to allow for the development of alternative models of relationships and learned secure attachment. This helps survivors to develop a new internal standard for assessing closeness, intimacy and healthy relationships and to acquire relationship skills to enhance future relationships. As survivors begin to trust their inner experiencing and develop an internal locus of evaluation, they stop overvaluing the perceptions of others and move from extreme dependency needs or fierce independence to more healthy interdependence and an autonomous way of being.

The therapeutic relationship is not static and evolves over time to address and satisfy a range of needs. Clarkson (2003) proposes five components of the therapeutic relationship which are necessary for effective change. The first of these is the working alliance which is essential in establishing a collaborative framework in which client and counsellor work together and are committed to sustaining the relationships even when there are ruptures. Unconscious forces in the therapeutic relationship are understood through the transferential/counter-transferential relationship in which unconscious needs, wishes and fears are transferred onto or into the therapeutic relationship whereby the counsellor is seen as rescuer or abuser. To counteract damaged early relationships counsellors must incorporate the ingredients of the reparative/developmentally needed relationship by providing a reparative, corrective and replenishing relationship in which they provide what was missing in childhood. To ensure that clients are able to be, and relate, in the present it is crucial to foster the real here-and-now, person-to-person relationship and the healing aspects of the spiritual or transpersonal relationship.

When working with survivors of complex trauma all of these relationship dimensions will need to be incorporated alongside a warm, emotionally available, engaged and interactive style in which survivors are seen, validated and respected. In addition, to counteract the duplicity and distortion of reality prevalent in abuse, you will need to be honest, authentic and genuine in providing a human to human relationship rather than hide behind a professional mask.

BUILDING THE THERAPEUTIC RELATIONSHIP

When survivors of complex trauma enter therapy they are a taking a huge risk, which must be honoured by the counsellor. To risk connection after being repeatedly betrayed is a signal that hope has not been extinguished. However, the fear of intimacy and closeness can create challenges when building the therapeutic relationship. You will need to understand these within the context of complex trauma and work towards providing a '...bridge from the world of trauma where needs were desperate and life threatening to a world where needs can not only be modulated, but also fulfilled' (Cohen, 1985, p.118).

 Warning
Trust is not finite and will fluctuate throughout the therapeutic relationship and you will need to monitor the degree of connectedness.

To build such a bridge takes time and must be sensitively paced (see Box 7.1). Ideally it helps to let the survivor lead in building the relationship rather than rushing or forcing it. In trying too hard to build trust you may unwittingly recreate abuse dynamics in which trust, care and affection masquerade as abuse. While some survivors who enter therapy will be overtly suspicious, hostile and reluctant to engage, others will trust too quickly. You must be mindful that trusting too quickly can mask a fear of rejection and attachment loss. Either way, survivors will need time to settle into the therapeutic relationship and take their time to build trust. It is important to remember trust is not finite and will fluctuate throughout the therapeutic relationship. Survivors will commonly test to what degree trust has been established causing ruptures in the relationship. You will need to see such tests as a way of developing deeper trust and not see these purely as a breakdown in the relationship but as opportunities for repair and deeper connection.

Box 7.1 Establishing and building the therapeutic relationship

- Establishing the relationship – warm, human, authentic, engaged, connected, responsive, genuinely caring, compassionate, sensitively attuned, empathic, affirming, validating, respectful, attentive
- Trust not finite
- Honour the client's courage and hope
- Provide a secure base and holding environment
- Psychoeducation – normalise responses
- Be visible and make client visible
- Restore relational worth, connection to self and others

As the therapeutic relationship takes time to develop it is important to focus initially on establishing a therapeutic alliance in which there is an agreed willingness to engage and to work collaboratively. This becomes the basis for a secure base in which survivors feel accepted and supported and in which they can experience a genuine and authentic relationship. It is crucial to stress that this is a collaborative process in which both parties need to engage, rather than something being imposed or enforced upon them. To facilitate this it helps to use inclusive language such as 'we will explore' rather than 'you must…' or 'I will…' Such collaboration encourages self-agency and allows survivors to feel more in control of developing the therapeutic relationship.

COUNSELLOR QUALITIES

The working alliance is most easily achieved when counsellors possess certain qualities (see Box 7.2). It helps to be calm and containing so that survivors can explore their often overwhelming feelings without fear. In addition you will need to be authentic and transparent and not hide behind a façade to counteract the subterfuge and distortion of reality experienced during the abuse. This requires genuine, congruent and explicit responses so that survivors do not have to 'mind-read' or be forced into deciphering mixed messages. Many survivors are highly adept at reading non-verbal cues and will be able to spot incongruities in counsellor responses. The more congruent and genuine the counsellor is the more the survivor will feel safe to trust.

To counterbalance the dehumanising abuse experience, you will need to be human in your responses rather than clinical, cold or distant. It also helps to acknowledge that you are human, and that you are not all knowing and make mistakes. It is critical that you can show humility and be honest about admitting any mistakes so that survivors can learn that making mistakes are opportunities for learning rather than a sign of inadequacy. To be actively engaged in the therapeutic process you will need to be prepared to take risks and come out of your comfort zone rather than disconnecting. In addition it is essential that you are respectful, non-judgemental and accepting of survivors' striving for autonomy.

To reduce survivors' fear of intimacy, you must be genuinely comfortable with closeness and intimacy. It is essential that you feel secure enough to be able to connect to others without fear of enmeshment or feeling threatened by either powerful 'developmental dependency' needs (Steele *et al.*, 2001) or extreme, dismissive self-sufficiency. Ideally you will need to have a secure, autonomous attachment style and feel comfortable in connecting to survivors rather than rebuffing them. In addition, try to guard against being too charismatic or overshadowing the survivor much as the abuser did. It is only through making survivors visible that they can come out of hiding to risk connection and intimacy, and begin to relate more authentically.

Box 7.2 Counsellor qualities

- Calm and containing
- Authentic, transparent, honest
- Ability to be human and show humility
- Respectful, non-judgemental and accepting of survivor autonomy
- Warm empathic attunement
- Actively engaged
- Well bounded yet flexible, firm yet gentle
- Genuinely caring and concerned, empathic, compassionate
- Secure autonomous attachment style, able to connect to self and client
- Not defensively dissociated, or embedded
- Ability to tolerate uncertainty

EMPATHY

The therapeutic alliance can only be established in the presence of empathy and empathic attunement. The need for empathic attunement is heightened in survivors as they will rarely have experienced this. Some survivors feel extremely uncomfortable in the presence of empathic responses as they misread these as being pitied. You will need to be careful when conveying empathy so that survivors do not feel patronised or overwhelmed by empathic responses. Much like trust, some survivors will need time to receive empathy without recoiling or disconnecting and this must not be forced. Coming out of 'cold storage' can be extremely painful and it takes time to thaw out.

 Warning
Some survivors feel extremely uncomfortable in the presence of empathic responses as they misread these as being pitied and will need time to receive empathy without recoiling or disconnecting.

You will need to balance empathic attunement with setting appropriate limits and boundaries for yourself and the survivor. Being overly empathic toward clients can feel threatening as their image of the abuser is challenged and some survivors will react defensively to this as they try to hold onto the good in the abuser. You will need to manage this carefully so as not to create a power struggle between the client and the abuser. In addition, it is important to acknowledge your limitations without feeling inadequate or ashamed of these. It is not possible to know all or heal all and you must be able to tolerate doubt and uncertainty without feeling overwhelmed or deskilled. Boundaries are needed to keep you and the client safe, and you will need to be gentle and firm without being so rigid that you appear cold and unfeeling. It also helps to know when to be flexible and to extend your window of tolerance around boundaries without fearing a collapse of these.

Well balanced empathic attunement will gradually enable survivors to develop empathy and compassion for the hurt child or adult rather than deflecting empathic responses. It will also help them to become aware that their lack of self-empathy represents internalised hostile, dismissive and critical messages that they received from their abuser and how these create obstacles in relationships. As they become aware of how hostile behaviour alienates others they begin to recognise that they do have an impact on others, and that relationships are based on mutuality and reciprocal influence. In being more able to receive empathy and develop self-compassion they begin to develop genuine empathy for others and see how bi-directional empathy enhances relationships, including the therapeutic one (Sanderson, 2010a).

BARRIERS TO BUILDING THE THERAPEUTIC RELATIONSHIP

The repeated betrayal of trust will make it very difficult for some survivors to enter into the therapeutic relationship. As relationships are seen as dangerous and exhausting rather than sources of comfort, survivors will erect seemingly unassailable barriers. It is essential that you understand these as protective strategies rather than conscious resistance or hostile defensiveness. You will need to persevere in enabling the survivor to feel safe enough to slowly dismantle these barriers rather than attempt to bulldoze them. Forcing the survivor to breakdown barricades can lead to a power struggle in which the more the survivor is pushed to do something they are not ready to do the less safe they will feel, and the more they will need to keep the barriers in place.

Most barriers crystallise around the fear of losing control, re-experiencing abuse and re-traumatisation (see Box 7.3). This is compounded by anxieties about disclosure and being judged, or not believed, due to uncertainty, fragmented memories or not being able to provide a coherent trauma narrative. Disclosure means exposure and this will evoke a crippling sense of shame and a need to hide. The paradox in complex trauma is that being visible is dangerous as it leads to abuse, while being invisible threatens the survivor's very existence. You will need to find a balance between making the survivor visible without being intrusive, and not rendering them invisible.

The biggest obstacles in building the therapeutic relationship are fear of attachment, including fear for dependency, fear of attachment loss and fear of security. Many survivors are terrified that when entering any relationship they will be controlled, manipulated or exploited. This leads some to be as compliant and submissive as they were forced to be during the abuse or to be controlling, hostile or dismissive. Survivors who are compliant often trust too quickly as they need to please the counsellor in order to have their dependency needs met and present as what is generically known as a 'good client'. Such clients appear eager to engage and seemingly connect easily and quickly. It is important not to be lulled into believing that such survivors do not struggle with relational difficulties. Such compliance commonly masks a range of relational difficulties which you will need to explore.

In contrast some survivors enter therapy overtly hostile, aggressive or dismissive, and fiercely self-sufficient. This creates enormous barriers to building the therapeutic relationship as such survivors reject any attempts at empathy and compassion and attempts to connect. It is critical that you do not personalise such behaviours and see them as self-protection strategies to keep you at bay and to hide shameful dependency needs. In essence such behaviours are tests to see how you react and manage negative emotions and it is important that you are able to remain present and engaged and don't enter into a power struggle to regain control. It is crucial not to overcompensate in trying too hard or to mask your own anger by being overly empathic so that boundaries can be established in which both you and the survivor feel safe.

Even though survivors will relentlessly challenge these, it will help you to regard such testing of boundaries as a fundamental part of building of trust. It is critical that you do not interpret these as a personal attack or rejection of you but see them as opportunities for strengthening the therapeutic relationship. Some survivors test boundaries by switching between compliance and dominance, which can be confusing and exhausting. In the presence of such erratic and self-sabotaging behaviours it is essential that you remain constant and consistent in your response to ensure that the survivor feels accepted.

Box 7.3 Barriers to building relationship

- Belief that relationships are dangerous rather than sources of comfort
- Fear of re-experiencing abuse, re-traumatisation
- Fear of losing control
- Fear of disclosure, being judged or not being believed due to lack of trauma narrative
- Fear of exposure – visibility vs. invisibility
- Shame
- Uncertainty
- Fear of attachment, dependency and attachment loss
- Attachment style of survivor and counsellor
- Fear of security
- Therapist stance, responses and emotional availability

Remember

Testing boundaries is a survival strategy to aid protection and must not be interpreted as a personal attack or rejection of you and you must remain consistently connected and available to the survivor.

THE ROLE OF ATTACHMENT STYLE IN THE THERAPEUTIC RELATIONSHIP

To help you understand and manage some of the complex relational dynamics in the therapeutic relationship it is helpful to be aware of the survivor's and your own attachment style (see pp.57–61) and any associated difficulties. It is important that you are aware of how your and the survivor's attachment might collide, which can create additional relational difficulties. While each survivor is unique in terms of how their attachment style is affected and what is brought to the therapeutic relationship, there are some commonalities that might help to equip you in managing these.

Anxious-preoccupied attachment style in therapy

Survivors with an anxious-preoccupied attachment style tend to be over-focused on their relationships, including the therapeutic one. They commonly have high dependency needs and seek a lot of attention and reassurance. This usually manifests in testing boundaries around contact. They often want to increase or bring appointments forward, or request permission to phone or text in between sessions. Alternatively they present as the 'good or perfect' client in order to please and be liked by you. However, when faced with rigid boundaries they can become critical or threaten to harm themselves. They are usually quietly demanding but can switch into emotional outbursts when you resist their demands.

As they are hyper-vigilant they are constantly monitoring your responses and the slightest perceived sign of not being fully there for them can lead to an onslaught of criticism. Such survivors crave connection as they are terrified of being alone, and yet they are equally terrified of being too close in case they are abandoned. As a result they tend to feign intimacy and closeness as a cover-up for unbearable fears of rejection and abandonment and turn into relationship chameleons. The danger of constantly adapting to whatever they believe the other person wants them to be is that they can never be authentic enough to develop a deeper relationship or connection. In addition they are so preoccupied with presenting themselves in a certain light that their narrative is often confused, inconsistent and unfocused. Survivors with this attachment style benefit the most from a relational approach in which they can learn to be more authentic and autonomous (Bateman and Fonagy, 2004).

Anxious-avoidant attachment style in therapy

Those survivors with an anxious-avoidant attachment style commonly avoid sessions by being late or not turning up. In session they tend to be hostile, dismissive, confrontational and demanding. Their avoidance is further mediated by dissociation and disconnection in which the emotional impact of the trauma is minimised. Anxious-avoidant survivors tend to avoid emotions as these are overwhelming and exhausting and are particularly uncomfortable in the presence of empathy and empathic attunement. As they have dissociated from the emotional aspects of their traumatic experiences they are unable to connect to their vulnerability or dependency needs and so cannot feel empathy or self-compassion. Survivors with this attachment style will often have unacknowledged anger and rage which is displaced and projected onto the counsellor making it very difficult for you to connect. Initially such survivors respond best to a cognitive-behavioural approach until they feel safe enough to embark on more emotionally charged or relational work (Bateman and Fonagy, 2004).

Disorganised attachment style in therapy

The attachment style most associated with complex trauma is the disorganised attachment style as it replays many of the dynamics experienced during abuse. It is fraught with uncertainty and storms of emotions which alternate with total shutdown. As a result survivors with this attachment style find it difficult staying in the present and remaining contained. In addition, they are often highly resistant and chaotic, and attack with no conscious recognition of what they are doing. This is often due to dissociation where they split off from inner experiencing making it hard to recall the content of sessions or therapeutic interactions. This generates high levels of arousal and stress which are often expressed through a resurgence of PTSD and complex trauma symptoms. As the default setting on the alarm system is so high, survivors with disorganised attachment style are easily catapulted back into the traumatic past making it hard to stay in the present. Survivors with this attachment style will require a lot of focus on acquiring and mastering skills to manage and control trauma reactions before building the therapeutic relationship. You will need to be sensitive to this so as not to rush the therapeutic relationship by remaining patient, calm and contained. While the focus is initially on the acquisition of skills once these have been mastered it is essential to concentrate on building relational worth.

Warning

The therapeutic relationship is bidirectional and will consist of interplay between your own attachment style and that of the client.

COUNSELLOR ATTACHMENT STYLE

The therapeutic relationship needs to be a reciprocal one and as such is bidirectional. You will need to be mindful of your own attachment style and how this collides or melds with that of the survivor. Ideally you will have developed a learnt secure attachment style through your own personal therapy and training. However the challenges when working with survivors of complex trauma can revive dormant earlier insecure attachment patterns. If you are not sure of your attachment style you might consider some of the exercises in Chapter 4 (see p.58) or answer some of the questions in Box 7.4.

Box 7.4 Counsellor relational dynamics

1. How do you feel about being in intimate relationships?

2. How comfortable do you feel being close to your clients?

3. How do you feel about being in a position of power?

4. How do you feel when you are in control? How does that compare to when you are not in control?

5. How do you feel when you are in an asymmetrical relationship? How does that differ from symmetrical ones?

6. How do you feel when you are the object of another's intense preoccupation or adulation?

7. How comfortable are you when cast in the role of 'parent'?

8. How comfortable are you knowing your clients?

If you have an anxious-preoccupied attachment style you may have unfulfilled dependency needs which will manifest as a need to be mirrored and admired by your clients. You may find yourself looking to your clients for reassurance and affirmation from them, and become preoccupied with what they think of you and how important you are to them. This can lead to enmeshment and over-identification and a collapse of therapeutic boundaries, especially if the survivor is avoidant, dismissive or hostile. The more you need the survivor to satisfy your unmet needs the more you will come to resemble the abuser who prioritised their needs over the survivor's. This will undermine the survivor's sense of safety leading them to withdraw.

Conversely, if you have an anxious-avoidant attachment style you may unwittingly evoke the survivor's unmet dependency needs. If you are too distant or too much of a 'blank slate' the survivor will feel rejected and abandoned leading to the activation of powerful dependency needs. The more they express a need to be close, the more you feel the need to withdraw, the more the survivor craves closeness. This leads to an endless cycle of withdrawal in which the survivor's needs are not met and a therapeutic relationship cannot be established. To ensure that the therapeutic relationship can be established and flourish, you will need to examine your own fears around closeness and intimacy and any tendencies toward either enmeshment or aloofness. It is critical that such attachment patterns are explored in supervision or personal therapy and linked to your own experiences of trauma or abuse, or unhealthy need for power and control.

MAINTAINING THE THERAPEUTIC RELATIONSHIP

As the barriers to establishing the therapeutic relationship are explored and start to dissolve you will need to focus on strengthening and maintaining the therapeutic relationship. This will not be without challenges (see Box 7.6) as survivors continue to test boundaries. Although such testing behaviour diminishes as the therapeutic relationship strengthens you must be prepared for mis-attunement and ruptures. These are normal and not a negative reflection of you. Ruptures are a powerful way for survivors to discover that relational conflict does not lead to annihilation of self or other and that relationships can be repaired. Similarly, mis-attunement can be healthy as it provides opportunities for rapprochement and self-soothing which encourages self-agency and self-efficacy. These are all essential relational experiences that will help survivors to develop skills that will equip them in how they relate to others and approach future relationships.

 Remember
Mis-attunement or ruptures are opportunities for rapprochement and developing self-agency and self-efficacy.

MEASURING CONNECTEDNESS

Given the potential for ruptures and fluctuations in connectedness you might find it useful to track this on a session by session basis. You could do this using a standard session rating scale such as Johnson, Miller and Duncan (2000; see Box 7.5) which the survivor can fill in at the end of each session or you can check with the survivor during the session how connected they feel. You will also find this a useful tool to monitor your own level of connectedness to ensure that you remain engaged and present. It might help to have a small visual rating scale of one to five for each session in your notes so that you can track your relational reactions to the survivor and the material being explored.

Box 7.5 Measuring connectedness (adapted from Johnson *et al.*, 2000)

Make time during the session, perhaps at the end, to check how connected the survivor feels. This can be done by asking them to rate the following questions on a scale of one to five with one being not very and five very. Examples of useful questions are, on a scale of one to five:

1. How comfortable do/did you feel in the relationship today?

2. How close do/did you feel today?

3. Do/did you feel heard and understood today?

4. Do/did you feel respected?

5. How do you rate the level of empathic attunement?

Remember to ask yourself the same questions to score your rating in your notes.

 Top tip

Checking degree of connectedness is a powerful way of monitoring the strength of the therapeutic relationship.

CORE CHALLENGES IN MAINTAINING THE THERAPEUTIC RELATIONSHIP

The core challenges in maintaining the therapeutic relationship centre around the re-enactment of power, control, enmeshment, distancing, transference and counter-transference reactions (see Box 7.6). As they manifest in the therapeutic relationship you will need to address them and link them to complex trauma in which survivors learn that relationships are a source of danger and terror rather that a source of comfort. It is also critical to explore how trauma has impacted on relational worth and a deeply felt sense of shame, which has reduced opportunities to develop or practise essential relationship skills making it harder to connect to others.

Box 7.6 Core challenges in maintaining the therapeutic relationship

- Continued testing of boundaries
- Mis-attunement and ruptures
- Fluctuations in trust and connectedness – approach/avoid, disconnection client and counsellor
- Issues of power and control – submission or need to dominate
- Enmeshment and distancing
- Transference – both negative and positive
- Counter-transference – both negative and positive
- Somatic counter-transference – managing somatic symptoms
- Erotic transference and erotic counter-transference

POWER AND CONTROL

The lack of control and sense of powerlessness in complex trauma strips survivors of any sense of autonomy, self-agency and self-efficacy. This compels some survivors to become compliant and submissive, while others need to be in control at all times, or switch between the two. These early destructive relational bonds can be re-triggered in present relationships and re-enacted in the therapeutic relationship especially when it intensifies or when exploring traumatic experiences. These re-enactments need to be managed sensitively without being seduced into a battle for power and control. This is especially the case when you feel challenged or overwhelmed by the survivor's helplessness or hostile projections.

Submission and compliance

Survivors who have been over-controlled by others find it extremely difficult to assert themselves for fear of rejection, punishment or lack of skills. They commonly surrender all control to others and present as submissive and compliant. They often lead highly chaotic lives in which they are unable to set healthy boundaries or say 'no', which makes them vulnerable to further abuse. In surrendering control they let others make decisions for them and find it impossible to establish structure in their lives, hold down a job or pay bills. As a result they are often attracted to people who find it easy to take control, or who are controlling. This makes them vulnerable to re-victimisation and accounts for the high tolerance threshold for abuse in relationships. As they are unable to trust their own instincts and are out of contact with their inner experiencing, they tend to be numb and emotionally empty to the point of invisibility, and seem to disappear from life by retreating into an alternative world through dissociation or fantasy to escape their unbearable reality.

As the survivor surrenders all responsibility to others, including you the counsellor, their sense of helplessness and powerlessness is heightened leading to intense fantasies of being rescued. As the survivor projects such fantasies on to you, you will need to monitor your reactions to avoid eliciting your 'helper script' or becoming the rescuer (Sanderson, 2010a). This can be difficult to resist especially if you cannot satisfy the survivor's needs. The survivor will experience this as abandonment leading to a reactivation of the abuse experiences and cast you into the role of the abuser. To protect themselves they will deny their needs, suppress their anger or rage and become overly-compliant.

Submissive and compliant survivors resist connection in more subtle ways such as by being overly-charming or by shifting the focus of attention away from the self onto the counsellor. As a result they can be highly seductive and charming in their attempt to become the 'perfect client'. Such survivors have learnt from the abuser how charm can entrance others and lure them into a relationship and once captured, to control and manipulate them. To achieve this they may bestow you with compliments or appear over-solicitous in wanting to take care of you. It is crucial to resist such seduction and shift the focus back onto the survivor's feelings and needs.

Alternatively, if you are repulsed by the survivor's helplessness you will need to examine your reaction to avoid disconnection. It is crucial to check to what degree such helplessness is expressed outside as some survivors are more functional than they appear in session. This will help you in encouraging the survivor to regain control through a collaborative therapeutic relationship in which they can learn to self-regulate and restore self-agency and self-efficacy.

Dominance and control

Conversely some survivors fear attachment or merger as they fear being abused again. As a result they set very rigid and controlling boundaries to ward off closeness. They often present as extremely dominant and critical especially of any attempts at connection. These survivors tend to be rejecting of any therapeutic interpretations or interventions, and constantly challenge the counsellor's capabilities and credentials. It is critical that you do not take this personally and see such hostility as attempts to ward off connection. It is also worth remembering that beneath such dismissive behaviour is a desire to connect otherwise they would not have entered therapy.

Some survivors alternate between surrender and domination, which can be extremely confusing for both client and counsellor. Such alternation is associated with dissociation and a disorganised attachment style. In such cases survivors appear helpless and wanting to be rescued, and yet when that is responded to, they switch into rejecting any offers of help or attempts at connection. This effectively creates a rupture which then has to be repaired. Other survivors who initially appear hostile and dominant and push you away switch into helplessness and dependency. You will need to be alert to such alternating behaviour and try to identify patterns that trigger the switch so that these can be explored. To manage such alternations it is crucial to remain steadfast, constant and consistent in your responses.

It may be helpful to spend some time looking at survivors' experiences and core beliefs around self-soothing and relational soothing. Asking them to describe how they comfort or reassure themselves when they are alone, and whether there are times when they prefer to be soothed by others can help them to find a better balance between self-soothing and relational soothing. It also enables survivors' to identify what is they would like from others rather than surrendering themselves or rejecting all attempts at connection. Ultimately re-enactments of power and control dynamics are a rich source of understanding complex trauma and transference, and CTR.

TRANSFERENCE

Irrespective of which therapeutic approach is used the therapeutic relationship will elicit strong emotional reactions in survivors of complex trauma. Some of these will be a replay of past relationships and conflicts with significant others, especially the abuser or non-protective carer, and some will be in response to the counsellor and the therapeutic relationship. You will need to be able to differentiate between re-enactments of abuse and what are realistic responses to what you bring to the therapeutic relationship (see Box 7.7). Some survivors will also use projective identification as a form of 'psychic surgery' to transfer unbearable feelings and impulses onto the counsellor.

Box 7.7 Common transference reactions

- Child or infantile ways of relating
- Counsellor as idealised parent
- Counsellor as rescuer
- Counsellor as hostile parent
- Counsellor as perpetrator or abuser
- Erotic in which counsellors is seen as idealised lover
- Reaction to therapeutic relationship
- Interplay of client and counsellor attachment style
- Reactions to counsellor CTR, or demands of therapeutic approach child/parent

---

Transference reactions can be either positive or negative and commonly consist of childlike patterns of behaviour in which the counsellor is seen either as an idealised or hostile parent. As idealised parent the counsellor is expected to nurture, nourish and rescue the survivor while the hostile parent is perceived as the abuser who means them harm. This leads survivors to displace their rage on you as a test to see if they will be punished. In contrast, some survivors will feel compelled to parent you by protecting you from the traumatic experiences, much as they protected the non-abusing carer(s), while others will be consumed with erotic transference reactions in which the counsellor is seen as an idealised lover with strong sexualised fantasies and seductive behaviour.

Transference reactions need to be worked through and linked to early attachment patterns and abuse experiences. This will enable both you and the survivor to better understand the meaning of the projected feelings and expectations and re-enactments. It will also help you to identify specific challenges and barriers that prevent connection and engagement, and how these impact upon you and elicit counter-transference reactions.

COUNTER-TRANSFERENCE

According to Maltsberg and Buie (1974, p.110) transference can elicit '…
the three most common narcissistic snares in therapists…the aspirations
to heal, know all and love all'. While some of these are undoubtedly your
reactions to the survivor's transference and projective identification, you
will need to be mindful that some CTRs represent your own feelings,
projections, expectations and relational attachment patterns. Some CTRs
may also reflect realistic responses to the survivor's hostile behaviour or
your current personal circumstances (see Box 7.8). You will need to be
mindful also of how your CTRs impact on the survivor's transference
reactions. To manage these challenges most effectively, you will need to
scrutinise and monitor your own as well as the survivor's responses as
to whether your CTRs are a true reflection of transference or your own
needs and expectations. You will need to be honest in assessing these to
ensure that destructive re-enactments by either you or the survivor are
minimised and contained.

Box 7.8 Counter-transference responses

- Realistic responses to survivor's here-and-now behaviour such as hostility, criticisms or threats making counsellor feel unsafe or scared
- Responses to transference such as being flattered or excited by survivor's seductive feelings and behaviour
- Responses that reflect counsellor's own psychology, personality or typical responses such as need to be liked, admired or able to fix things
- Responses that reflect counsellor's current circumstances or material that is troubling them such as relationship break up, illness, emptiness, loneliness

---

Counter-transference responses can evoke a range of feelings, thoughts
and behaviours in the counsellor which give rise to considerable challenges
in the therapeutic relationship (see Box 7.9). In response to overpowering
feelings of helplessness you may feel ashamed or vulnerable and begin
to become preoccupied by your own narcissistic needs in which you can
no longer see let alone respond to the survivor's needs. Feeling vulnerable
can elicit your own sense of inadequacy, shame or dependency which you
may try to cover up by becoming inauthentic or controlling. If survivors
are hostile or dismissive you may find yourself feeling less compassionate
and increasingly more judgemental. This can elicit appeasement behaviour

in which you overcompensate for your lack of empathy and try too hard to rescue the survivor and become the 'perfect counsellor'.

Any of these CTRs can lead to either enmeshment or distancing (Steele *et al.*, 2001; Wilson and Lindy, 1994). If you find yourself pitying or over-identifying with survivors, unable to set boundaries or limits, or becoming over-involved in their daily life, you may be becoming enmeshed. This is a signal that your own dependency needs are being triggered which you will need to keep in check. If these are not contained you are likely to be seduced into attempts to fix or control the survivor as a means to satisfy your own needs.

Box 7.9 Counter-transference reactions

- Enmeshment and over-identification
- Distancing, disconnection, dissociation
- Dependency needs which have to be covered up
- Rescuer, abuser/torturer, witness guilt
- Overwhelming feelings of anger, rage, fear, terror, anxiety, frustration, confusion, sadness, judgemental
- Loss of control, powerlessness, uncertainty, self-doubt
- Narcissistic responses
- Appeasement and overcompensation
- Shame
- Somatic counter-transference
- Erotic counter-transference

Your dependency needs may also underpin any tendency to recoil from the survivor or set excessive limits and rigid boundaries. This usually represents your shame about your own unresolved dependency needs which you project onto the survivor. In not being able to face dependency you may judge or shame and punish the survivor for expressing such needs, and force them to become entirely self-reliant, self-sufficient and independent. As the intensity of dependency needs threaten to overwhelm you, you will be tempted to withdraw and distance yourself by avoiding feelings and retreat into intellectualisation or a cold, clinical stance in which the survivor feels abandoned. In this you also abandon your own needs and vulnerabilities and avoid seeking professional or personal support.

Avoiding dependency needs means that these cannot be processed, which locks both survivor and counsellor into a spiral of shame and abandonment. To process dependency needs and minimise negative CTRs you will need to find a balance between being empathically attuned and emotionally available to the survivor without being overwhelmed and retreating. If your own unresolved dependency needs resurface, it is essential that you seek supervision or return to personal therapy so that these do not contaminate the therapeutic relationship. This will facilitate caring about the survivor rather than caring for them and getting enmeshed (Steele *et al.*, 2005). As CTRs can manifest throughout the therapeutic process, you will need to monitor these as the therapeutic relationship develops as they will provide valuable insights into both the survivor's and your relational growth.

Somatic counter-transference

Valuable insights into CTRs can be gained from somatic counter-transference reaction as this provides you with a sense of the survivor's bodily state (Shaw, 2004). Like CTRs, somatic counter-transference is an interplay between the survivor's inner state and the counsellor's own somatic reactions. Much of somatic counter-transference is a resonance of the survivor's unexpressed emotions or preoccupations and the counsellor's sense of these within the body. Common examples of somatic counter-transference are dissociative symptoms, exhaustion, unbearable terror states, self-harming impulses and unexpressed sexuality.

To make use of somatic counter-transference the counsellor will need to be embodied and be able to use their body as an instrument to pick up what the survivor cannot verbalise. You will also need to be able to differentiate between what the survivor is emanating and your own internal state irrespective of that. This is especially the case if your body is reacting to the survivor's dissociative states such as lapses in consciousness, numbing or depersonalisation, which you are likely to experience as tiredness, disruptions in attention and concentration, or restlessness (Sanderson, 2010a). If you do start to feel yourself drifting, feeling heavy and sleepy, or restless it is crucial that you discuss this with the survivor so they understand this as somatic CTR rather than you being bored or disinterested.

Erotic counter-transference

The intensity of the therapeutic relationship will invariably elicit erotic transference and counter-transference reactions. While these are present in most therapeutic relationships they are elevated when working with survivors of complex trauma. Erotic transference can be a replay of traumatic experiences in which the survivor has learnt to be seductive to ensure their survival. This is especially the case when working with survivors of CSA or sexual exploitation who only know how to relate to others sexually. Erotic transference also represents a separate yearning for love and intimacy which can become sexualised and projected onto the counsellor. You will need to be clear to what extent your reactions to such projections are a response to the survivor's transference, or whether they contain elements of your own erotic desire. Listening to accounts of trauma, violence or sexual abuse can be highly arousing in eliciting fear reactions which can become eroticised. In addition you or the survivor may conflate intimacy with erotic or sexual desire.

Whether it is the survivor's erotic transference, erotic CTR or you own erotic desire you must never act upon them. In order to manage erotic reactions you will need to seek supervision to assess how this can be managed most effectively. If it is not possible to work through it then you must consider referring the survivor to another counsellor in a sensitive way so that they do not feel rejected or abandoned.

MAINTAINING THE THERAPEUTIC RELATIONSHIP

Challenges will continue to persist throughout the therapeutic relationship and you must not recoil from these and see them as opportunities for growth for both you and the survivor. As the therapeutic relationship intensifies and trust is established some survivors will become increasingly fearful of betrayal or abandonment, As they become more attached the more they will fear the loss of attachment. This can re-activate the same defences and challenges seen in the early stage of building the therapeutic relationship. To prevent sabotaging the therapeutic bond you will need to understand these defences as a fear of attachment security, and that the survivor still fears abandonment. You will need to take these seriously and continue to encourage the survivor towards learnt secure attachment.

ENDING THE THERAPEUTIC RELATIONSHIP

Fears of ending the therapeutic relationship can also produce challenges which must be addressed. Many survivors will fear the loss of such an important attachment and may resist its ending. It is critical that you and the survivor assess readiness to end therapy and identify any resistance. Ending needs to be gradual and it is helpful to provide opportunities for the survivor to practise newly learnt skills. This needs to include graduated exercises around exposure to new situations, managing change, and healthy risk taking. You will need to encourage survivors to transfer the relational skills learnt in the therapeutic relationship into other relationships in which they can set healthy boundaries and balance dependency needs with independence.

As you start to work towards ending it is essential that you are explicit about this process and setting of boundaries. You will need to discuss how to move towards a gradual ending. Commonly, survivors benefit from a gradual reduction in contact so they can practise skills safe in the knowledge that their secure base is still there. For example, weekly sessions can become bi-monthly and gradually reduce to one a month or every six week, or occasional telephone support. Whatever is decided you must be clear about what you can realistically offer and how this will be managed. Finally, in honour of the therapeutic relationship it is important to allow time for both you and the client to review the relationship and how this has impacted on you both. It is helpful to perform a ritual about ending the relationship to allow for mourning so that the survivor can embrace their new beginning. With this the survivor can reconnect to others and the world equipped with the necessary skills to feel more in control of their life.

8

THE PROCESS OF RECOVERY

The process of recovery is unique to each survivor and varies from person to person. The journey can be gruelling at times with stops and starts, massive obstacles or blockades, or detours and diversions, as well as miraculous breakthroughs. It is made up of a continuous chain of small achievements rather than big leaps. For your clients to restore control and take charge of their lives and future it will require patience, stamina, hope and commitment. One way to help them take ownership of their recovery is to get them to create a metaphor or symbol that represents their healing process.

To help survivors to capture the process of recovery it helps to discuss a metaphor or symbol that illustrates how they see their recovery, including obstacles and setbacks as well as progress. Advise your clients that they could use an actual journey that consists of both difficult terrain and diversions as well as clear, straight roads. The metaphor that works best for them will be one that reflects their interest or hobby such as playing a musical instrument, managing a sports team, repairing or building something, or tidying up an overstuffed cupboard. They could use the image of the warrior within that has protected and fought for them so far, or the analogy of nurturing their inner child.

 Top tip
Discuss a metaphor that illustrates their healing process and use this to prepare for their journey to recovery.

Some survivors find a gardening metaphor useful as it includes a number of factors needed for growth, for example light, nutrients in the soil, fertiliser, regular watering and protection from extreme weather. To truly thrive and flourish the garden needs regular attention through adequate drainage, watering, and feeding, as well as weeding and pruning to maintain the best environment for quality growth.

Exercise
Using a metaphor
Invite the survivor to reflect on what metaphor is most useful for them and write this down in their journal. Get them to focus on the roles of commitment, dedication and practice, setting goals, and achievements as well as pitfalls and setbacks. Remind them to consider the feeling of triumph and growth that they will have at the end of their recovery and include that in their metaphor. The metaphor not only prepares your client for the hazards and delights of their journey, but will also help them when they feel discouraged during the process of recovery.

Before your client sets out on their journey you need to prepare them for any potential hazards and ensure that safety structures are in place. It is important for your client to identify and recognise their existing strengths and resources that have helped them to survive so far.

Exercise
The warrior within
Invite the survivor to identify what has helped them to get this far, including their strengths, inner resources and coping strategies. Encourage your client to access their warrior within and list how they have fought to protect them. As they list their strengths and resources in their journal make sure that you get them to celebrate these. Next, ask them to review their list and consider how they can build upon these and what might help them in that.

Top tip
Assist your client to acknowledge their warrior within by making a list of their strengths and resources that have helped them to survive.

IMPORTANCE OF A SUPPORT NETWORK

To aid survivors' recovery you will need to make sure that they have a good support network of people they can trust. This can include family and friends as well as professionals such as yourself or other key workers. They can also extend their support network to include other survivors by joining a support group. Make sure that they note the contact details of everyone in the support network and that they speak to at least one person for at least five minutes every day. If they can't meet up then make sure they phone, text or email them daily.

REGAINING CONTROL

To help them through recovery and allow them to come out of survival mode your clients will need to regain control over any traumatic reactions and symptoms. Research has found that control and a sense of purpose are the two most positive factors in recovery from trauma. Regaining control over distressing and overwhelming reactions allows them to process feelings and experiences which will help them to take charge of their current everyday life. It will also enable them to manage stress, restore healthy sleeping and eating patterns, and generally improve their quality of life.

To help your client restore control, read the sections on grounding and control (pp. 171–4) and how to manage emotions (pp. 167–71). Make sure they practise grounding techniques on a daily basis so that they gain mastery over them. They can also take control by creating a sense of achievement, even in such routine tasks as ironing or tidying up. This can be done by injecting fun and pleasure into the tasks such as listening and dancing to favourite music while performing these mundane activities.

Top tip
The most positive factors in recovery from trauma are control and a sense of purpose.

SENSE OF PURPOSE

Your client's commitment to their recovery will give them a powerful sense of purpose which is the second most important factor in recovery from trauma. Remember the focus and primary purpose in recovery is improving the quality of their lives. This sense of purpose will restore meaning to their life and allow them to live more honestly with a greater sense of vitality. Central to this is the setting of personally meaningful goals that are realistic, achievable, and measurable. To maximise achieving these goals it is important to check that your client will not be hampered by such restrictions as time, money, and access to resources.

Exercise
Personally meaningful goals

In your client's journal encourage them to list their personally meaningful goals for recovery and then rank these in order of priority with the most urgent at the top and the least urgent at the bottom. Go through the list with them and highlight those goals that they want to focus on immediately and rank these in order of importance. Starting with the most important, ask them to identify all the steps that are needed to attain this goal. Highlight the steps they have already taken and list those they need to take next to achieve the goal. Once you have identified their goals, they will need to reduce these down into small manageable steps and ask themselves what step they can take today to achieve their goals. Ensuring that they work at their own pace, help them to work through each step until they achieve their goal. Remind them to validate each step that they accomplish and keep a record of achievements to chart and monitor their progress.

To reach goals they might need to experiment with different ways of achieving each step, and their ultimate goal. For example if they are afraid to sleep in the dark, put a light on. If they are afraid to sleep in the bedroom tell them to allow themselves to sleep on the sofa. Encourage them to take their time and try different methods so that they find the right steps to reach their goal.

Remember

If a task is too difficult or upsetting for your client ensure that they stop, take a break from it, and make a commitment to return to it at a later point.

PACING

It is crucial that survivors do not rush their recovery and that they go at their own pace. To help your clients pace themselves it is important to break down the process of recovery with them into small manageable steps. This allows them to practice new ways of being, and to think about their accomplishments. It is important that they savour their achievements and take pleasure in their accomplishments. In doing this survivors are more able to see that goals are attainable which gives them the courage to continue.

It is important not to rush your client's recovery as rushing increases the likelihood of setbacks. For example, they may want to be hugged, but if this is still too overwhelming they might dissociate which will increase anxiety and even make them fearful of being hugged. This will set them back rather than help them to move forward. In addition, rushing may be reminiscent of the abuse experience. To get through the sexual abuse they may have 'rushed' through the experience in order not to feel or be upset. Rushing recovery will mean that your client will not process their experience of healing and find it harder to value their achievements.

Slowing down also reduces trauma cues and gives the mind and body time to embed new ways of being. It is much better to start slowly and consolidate each step than to leap forward only to stumble backwards or relapse. You might find that slowing down frustrates your client at times but it is worth persevering as they are more likely to achieve and ensure a better guarantee for future success.

Remind your client

It is important to go at their own pace as this is the one that gets them to their goal in a time frame that is right for them. Make sure that nobody, not even you, is rushing them.

CELEBRATING ACHIEVEMENTS

Central to recovery is celebrating achievements. This is crucial in validating the survivor's courage, and in restoring self-confidence and self-esteem. It also reminds them of their sense of purpose and progress. A good way of rewarding themselves as they achieve their goal is to make a 'cookie jar'.

Exercise

Making a 'cookie jar'

Instruct your client to write down positive things about themselves on small strips of paper. These could include their positive qualities, compliments people have paid them or their accomplishments and achievements. Ask them to find a nice jar or container, or customise an old jam jar. Next get them to roll each strip into a ball and place them inside your 'cookie jar'. Tell your client that whenever they feel the need to reward themselves, or remind them of positive things in their life, they should take out a ball of paper and read out loud what it says.

Top tip

It is important for your client to reward themselves as they achieve their goals. Suggest making a cookie jar.

COMING OUT OF SURVIVAL MODE

Regaining control, finding a sense of purpose and valuing achievements will help survivors to come out of survival mode. While in survival mode they are constantly alert to danger, and will tend to focus exclusively on potential threat and negative aspects in the world. This leaves no energy or mental space to notice positive things in their lives. As they begin to feel more in control and move from survival mode to feeling more alive, they can begin to incorporate more of the positive aspects of the external world. Gradually this allows them to balance negative feelings and experiences with positive ones. While this will not cancel out the negative, or undo their experiences, it will create a better balance.

Such balance opens up opportunities to make meaningful choices rather than being controlled by negative thoughts, feelings or abuse experiences.

Remind your client

When they are in the middle of feeling low they cannot focus on positive things.

As your client recovers they will free up trapped energy and notice the difference between surviving and living mode. This extra energy will enable them to engage in more pleasurable activities that are nurturing and growth promoting. As your client experiences more positive things in their life, the quality of their life will start to improve, allowing them to live their lives as they want to live it.

CHANGING CUES FROM THE PAST

To aid your client's recovery you will need to get them to counterbalance their traumatic experiences by re-introducing pleasure into their lives. A good starting point is to find a way for them to replace the negative cues present during the abuse with more positive ones. For example, if the abuse took place indoors in a darkened room then make sure they keep curtains and windows open to let light and air into their room. If they were abused in silence, then make sure they have music playing, or have the radio or television on. In the case of unpleasant smells advise them to replace these with pleasant ones such as scented candles or incense. If they were abused in a clerical context remind them to beware as incense could trigger negative memories.

Exercise

Changing sensory cues

Invite your client to reflect on their abuse experience and then attempt to identify as many cues associated with the abuse. For example, did the abuse occur indoors, at home or on other premises such as a church or youth club, or outside in a car, tent or field? Get them to list some of the most powerful cues such as whether it was light or dark, quiet or noisy, cold or warm, tidy or messy. Also encourage them to recall any smells associated with the abuse and their ability to breathe. For instance, if they were restrained or pinned down during the abuse this would have restricted their breathing. Help your client to link these cues to how they affect their mood and sense of well-being. As you work through this with them, have them start to list opposite sensory cues and experiment with these. For example, if they felt unable to breathe ask them to see how it feels to open the windows and allow fresh air to circulate. Get them to notice and record any changes in how they breathe, and how it feels to inhale fresh air rather than stale air, and how this affects their well-being and mood.

Changing sensory cues from the past can seem unfamiliar and strange at first but it is worth your client persevering to change as many of the negative cues as they can so that there are fewer reminders of the abuse to haunt them. As they replace negative sensory cues with more positive ones they will find that their sense of well-being will improve. They should also find that they will want more positive experiences in their life.

RECLAIMING PLEASURE

Letting go of negative cues from the past allows survivors to seek out more enjoyable activities that give pleasure and meaning to life. For instance, if your client felt silenced as a child then they need to sing, shout or scream. If they were constrained then they should move around, dance or swim. If they were prevented from playing, help them find a hobby that allows them to play or spend time with friends in fun activities. If they were isolated they will want to seek out and develop friendships. If they find it hard to trust people then they need to find other sources of trust such as animals or nature.

Exercise
Activities that give you pleasure

Encourage your client to make a list in their journal of pleasurable activities and things they enjoy including good people they like to be around. Also encourage them to list the treats that they find positively rewarding and nurturing. They will need to include calming and soothing as well as invigorating and stimulating activities, alongside inspirational and creative ones. They might also reclaim a hobby or passion they had in childhood and pursue this again. They should make a commitment to build these into their weekly schedule of self-care.

Top tip
Singing, talking and writing are ways for survivors to reclaim their voice, while smiling and laughter are ways of reconnecting with others.

LIVING IN THE PRESENT

The more survivors engage in pleasurable activities the more they override negative childhood experiences and live in the present. Try to get your clients to simplify their lives by refining routine chores, making these more fun and reducing their work load and commitments. This means they need to learn to set boundaries and be able to say 'no' without feeling guilty. Remind them that the goal is to reclaim pleasure without guilt or fear of it being wrenched away. They can maximise this by performing daily positive acts such as smiling, singing or being in contact with trusted friends.

Gradually survivors should achieve increasingly longer periods of calm and contentment. This will make it easier to manage the difficult times with more energy, vitality and renewed optimism. Your client will be able to enjoy living in the present rather than being catapulted into their past, which will lead to greater stability and contentment.

RENEWED ENERGY

As your client becomes less haunted by the past and feels less threatened and controlled by it, they will be able to release trapped energy in their body. This renewed energy can now be directed towards enjoyable physical activity such as dancing, swimming, walking or other forms of exercise. This can renew vitality which helps them to wake up with enthusiasm for the day ahead rather than dreading it. It will also allow them to become more relaxed and empowered rather than being flooded with fear and anxiety.

RECLAIMING THE SELF

Recovering from abuse is not just about survivors reclaiming the self, it is also about building a more complete person for the life that they want. It is about writing their own life script rather than have someone dictate and control it. Use a metaphor to illustrate this: liken their life to a book. While the early part of their life, or chapters, were directed and written by someone else such as their abuser, future chapters will now be written by them.

Remind your client that they can control whether to throw away earlier chapters, rewrite new ones, or build on earlier chapters by changing the course of future chapters. Help build the idea that they are the author and as such they have complete control over changes that they want to make and how to live the rest of their life.

Remind your client

The past no longer needs to dictate the present and how they are. They can now choose pleasurable and positive experiences that enliven them and bring them joy.

While your client cannot undo what the abuser has done to them, they can reclaim who they are and create their present and their future in the absence of abuse.

Exercise

Hopes, dreams and goals

To help your client reclaim themselves have them list how life would have been if they hadn't been abused. What were their hopes, dreams, goals, values? Remind them that these were stolen and can be reclaimed. Examine this list with them and compare it with their goals for recovery and see how they compare. Get them to make a second list, in order of importance, of what they wish to reclaim and the steps needed to achieve these.

In reclaiming their self, they will promote a more positive focus for the future as it will allow for post-traumatic growth and a return of vitality and spirituality. They will be able to reconnect themselves, others and the world. Letting positive things into their life will help them to take care of, and nurture themselves.

RECLAIMING POSITIVE ASPECTS OF LIFE

In order to reclaim positive aspects of life your client will need to identify all the things that they have in their life for which they are grateful. This will form the basis of their 'gratitude journal'. Research has shown that keeping a 'gratitude journal' can improve happiness and satisfaction. It also enables survivors to make a conscious effort to 'savour' all the beauty and pleasure in daily life no matter how small.

Exercise

Writing a gratitude journal

Your client should divide off a section in their journal, or find a new small notebook in which to record all the things in their life for which they are grateful. This could include their health, their children, their friends, their family, their pet(s) as well as the things they appreciate in life such as nature. Help your client to become more conscious of the good things in life. They will need to make time to listen to the sound of birdsong, or the rustle of leaves, to notice the shimmer of sunshine, or autumn leaves turning into a riot of colour, or breathing in the tang in the air. Advise them to also consider writing a gratitude letter to someone important in their life, past or present, even if not alive, that they have never properly thanked.

Becoming more consciously aware of the good things in life not only helps survivors to stay in the present, but reminds them that they are a part of something bigger. This can go a long way towards making them feel good about being alive. Allowing positive things into their life will not take away or make up for the abuse, but it will re-balance their life.

Keeping a weekly record of all the good things in life and their achievements will provide evidence of your client's recovery and post-traumatic growth. Along with gratitude and humility it will make them more appreciative of their life which will help them to manage setbacks. And while they may not be 100 hundred per cent free of trauma reminders, their recovery and growth will help them to bounce more quickly and allow them to feel thankful for the gift of life.

Top tip
Get your client to recount three good things that have happened that day each day before going to sleep.

UNDERSTANDING OBSTACLES TO RECOVERY

Although recovery is liberating and empowering it is also scary. Change can be very stressful and stir up powerful emotions. While this is normal, you will need to prepare your client for this and check whether they are ready to take on additional stress.

Before your client embarks on their journey to recovery it is important to ensure that their support network is in place and they have a degree of stabilisation. This will help them to manage any obstacles along the way. Obstacles are a normal part of the recovery process and are primarily opportunities for growth. Encourage your client to embrace these opportunities for growth so that they will be less likely to fear that their journey will be in vain. Like the flower that closes at night for protection but opens the next day in all its glory, their recovery must include protection and willingness to risk opening up.

Remind your client
The circle of life is characterised by change and rebirth in which growth becomes more vigorous and resplendent.

CHANGE IS DIFFICULT

Change is always difficult as it is hard to give up habits and old patterns of thinking and behaviour. As habits they have become conditioned and deeply ingrained making it harder to imagine alternative ways of being. Survivors' reactions become automatic and seem to occur outside any conscious awareness. This is because their reactions are frozen in time and will need to thaw. As they gradually acclimatise to change and reduce their fear, they will be able to reduce the obstacles to recovery.

Many of the obstacles to recovery stem from the fear and stress of change. Each person has specific anxieties and concerns that are unique to them. Some survivors welcome the opportunity for change, while others are terrified. It is normal to have mixed feelings about change and it is helpful for survivors to acknowledge these.

 Exercise
Plan of action for overcoming obstacles
To identify your client's fears around recovery and change, invite them to make a list of all their worries and anxieties. These may centre on re-experiencing the trauma, increased emotional distress, increased need to self-medicate or the impact change might have on their relationships. Next ask them to make a list of how they numb their thoughts and emotions, such as food, alcohol or drugs, and help them to link these to potential obstacles to recovery. Once you have identified with them some of the obstacles, reflect on how they might overcome them. It also helps to discuss their concerns with a trusted friend to help them develop a plan of action to manage any obstacles.

A common obstacle to change is that it will stir up overwhelming emotions which feel unmanageable. Often fear will set off the survivor's alarm system making them even more anxious. As their focus shifts onto their internal state of anxiety they will be unable to balance this with their external reality. To manage these fears they might resort to old patterns of avoidance or emotional numbing through the use of alcohol, drugs, food, work, sex or self-injury. A return to self-medication will inevitably create obstacles to emotional processing and hijack the recovery process.

 Top tip
Identifying your client's fears is the first step to helping them overcome them.

Fear of regressing is a further obstacle especially if there is an increase in trauma reminders and symptoms. This can also trip the survivor's alarm, making change seem too difficult as the fear of re-traumatisation will outweigh any gains of recovery. This could lead to increased fear of failure and doubts about ever getting better as the damage is so great.

Such a spiral of fear is a good reason to discourage seeking quick, radical changes but to advise savouring and valuing each small step and achievement. Change which is more gradual and less noticeable will seem less fearful and be a more solid foundation for recovery.

Fears and anxieties can stop survivors from thinking and reduce their ability to make decisions. This can create further obstacles which will interfere with plans for change and recovery. Remind your clients that they need to calm and soothe these anxieties so that they free up mental space and energy to think clearly. The clearer their thinking the more they will be able to make informed choices rather than activating automatic defensive reactions.

Survivors' fears can lead to self-fulfilling prophecies. An illustrative example is a fear of not having a healthy relationship, or having children. This fear can be so paralysing that they avoid all opportunities to have a relationship just so that they can avoid this dilemma. Jumping to conclusions and projecting into the future are clear signs of developing self-fulfilling prophecies. In order to prepare themselves for their worst fear they 'predict' it will happen so that they can 'psych' themselves up for the worst case scenario. This can create significant obstacles to their healing.

Secondary traumas

Another common stumbling block is the fear of secondary traumas linked to sexual abuse. Survivors may fear that they have sustained irreparable physical damage, and therefore can't have children, or that their sexuality has been affected and they will never find a partner. Or they may have an aching feeling of emptiness and loneliness that can never be soothed, or a constant fear of abandonment. Or they may fear their neediness or dependency. All of these can lead to obstacles in recovery. It is important that your client recognises that all of these can be worked through and overcome.

Your client may experience trauma reactions such as flashbacks, nightmares and intrusive memories which can lead to exhaustion and lack of energy, presenting further obstacles to recovery. To minimise this encourage them to improve their pattern of rest, work and play, and to take regular exercise. It is also useful to regulate eating patterns and improve diet. To increase their energy levels it helps to reduce their caffeine, alcohol and sugar intake. This will help them to restore zest and vitality to their life, which can help them to overcome any obstacles to change.

Unexpressed anger

Feelings of anger can also become a stumbling block especially if they have been suppressed over many years and involve a range of people. Your client may feel angry with their abuser, their non-abusing parent(s), their family, social services, the church or the criminal justice system. Such powerful, unexpressed anger can become all consuming and prevent recovery. While such anger is natural, especially if the abuser has not been held accountable, it can become toxic. Intense, unexpressed anger can be hard to let go and prevent your client from moving forward.

If unexpressed anger is dominating their life you will need to help them find healthy ways of releasing this in a safe and secure environment, such as your sessions. Releasing this anger is the first step in letting it go, so that it no longer infects their life and allows them to move forward.

Shame and guilt

Shame and guilt can also create obstacles to recovery especially if the survivor blames themselves for the abuse. Self-blame prevents them from legitimising abuse and leaves them feeling responsible for their abuse. This is particularly the case when there has been a lack of recognition of abuse from others such as the abuser, family, friends or the criminal justice system. Self-blame reinforces feelings of shame as they falsely believe that they enticed or encouraged the abuser.

A further source of shame is if the survivor experienced pleasurable sensations during the sexual abuse, or sought contact with the abuser. It is critical that they understand that pleasurable sensations during sexual contact are normal and do not mean that you wanted the sexual abuse. Reiterate that seeking contact with their abuser, on whom they were dependent, is not evidence that they wanted or encouraged sexual abuse. Obstacles that derive from self-blame, shame and secrecy can seem insurmountable and yet can be worked through.

Lack of self-worth

A related obstacle is stigmatisation and the survivor's belief that they are 'damaged goods'. This leads to a false belief that they do not deserve, nor are they entitled, to better treatment or a better life. This can result in a crippling lack of self-worth which prevents them from being assertive or asking for their needs to be met. Over-identifying as a victim who has no voice or rights can lead to further negative self-beliefs which undermine their recovery.

The critical voice

The lack of self-worth is often supported by negative and critical self-talk in which they constantly put themselves down. This can sabotage their recovery as such negative inner dialogue affects not only their self-esteem but also their mood. Such critical messages act as internal saboteurs which become major obstacles to change and recovery.

Exercise

Identifying and changing the critical voice

To identify your client's critical voice and the impact of negative self-talk, get them to list all the negative messages they tell themselves. Next, get them to state one of these and tell them to be mindful of any sensations or emotions that arise in response to this critical statement. Next, ask them to say something positive or comforting and reflect on how that feels. If there is a noticeable difference, encourage them to try to balance or override negative self-talk with positive self-talk to fully aid recovery. You can also turn to page 192 for help in identifying their negative self-talk and how to replace it with more positive messages.

Current unhealthy relationships

These are often the most resistant obstacles. If your client is in an unhealthy or abusive relationship they may fear upsetting the other person for fear of rejection or abandonment. As unhealthy relationships are primarily conditional, your client will fear losing them if they begin to express the full range of their feelings and thoughts. This fear of abandonment or rejection becomes a powerful motivator to not make changes even if the relationships are unhealthy.

Remind your client

Partners, friends and family may feel threatened by the recovery process as this can reduce the power they have over your client.

This is made worse if your client feels they do not deserve, or are not entitled to, empathic understanding or to support when trying to make changes. This can be further complicated as partners and friends may have a vested interest in your client not making changes, especially if this threatens to reduce the power they have over them. Such partners or friends will not want your client to change as they will be less easily manipulated, or if it means your client will become less compliant, or dependent on them. The more your client's partner or friend feels threatened by the recovery the more they will sabotage any changes you make. In combination, this can undermine recovery and prevent your client from becoming free from the past.

Gains and losses of change

Recovery and change can generate both gains and losses, and it is critical that your client is aware of this so that potential losses do not become major obstacles. To prevent this it is better to prepare your client for any losses so that they can make informed choices as to which changes they can realistically make, at a pace that suits them.

Exercise
Gains and losses of change

Ask your client to draw two columns in their journal, one headed 'What I have to gain' the other 'What I have to lose'. Under each heading, ask them to list all relevant gains and losses in their recovery. Seeing these written down will enable them to clearly see why the process of recovery is so hard. It will also allow them to make realistic commitments to their recovery. Review the two lists with your client and ask them to think about what resources are available to help them tolerate losses and changes.

OVERCOMING OBSTACLES TO RECOVERY AND CHANGE

This means your client needs to pace themselves. Rushing can undermine recovery as they leap forward only to retreat back. Remind them that recovery takes time and slowing down allows your client to consolidate change. Getting them to accept a slower pace and not berate themselves that they are not moving forwards fast enough will remove one of the major obstacles. It is also normal for survivors to become despondent, or lose faith in themselves at times. Helping them to accept this rather than fighting it will be more beneficial. Do not let them allow loss of hope to become an obstacle by ensuring that they keep faith in their warrior within. Keep their inspirational anchors nearby to remind them that they can have a better quality of life and that it is possible to recover.

Remind your client

The willingness to believe that change can occur and that experiences, emotions and thoughts are not set in stone but are dynamic, will help them to embrace change.

Finally, be mindful that the journey to recovery is not a straight line and that it is normal to encounter obstacles that force your client to backtrack or make detours. They may encounter relapses which fuel despondency and can undermine their faith, hope and resolve. Examine Chapter 22 on relapse prevention which will give you advice to help them if they do have setbacks.

The essential thing is to help them recognise that relapses and obstacles are part of the process and that these provide endless opportunities for discovery and learning. It is important for your client to keep their faith and have the confidence to find their way back to their chosen path rather than abandon the journey altogether.

Part 3

SKILLS TO MANAGE COMPLEX TRAUMA SYMPTOMS

9
ESTABLISHING SAFETY AND CONTROL

The survivor's journey of recovery can be very traumatic and it is essential that they create as much safety as possible in their life. This protects them when they experience overwhelming trauma reactions and helps them to feel more in control over their trauma related reactions, physical sensation, and emotions. Developing safety will also help them to regulate their mood states so that they can improve their well-being and quality of life.

You need to work with the client to examine how safe they are to begin this journey. You will need to check to what extent they feel safe in their environment (external safety) and how much they are able to control trauma related reactions (internal safety). External safety is dependent on being in a safe place with access to the basic necessities critical to daily life. These include: a safe place to live, adequate food and clothing and good quality support from trusted others. Internal safety is when we experience a degree of control over our feelings, sensations and thoughts.

 Warning
If your client has uncontrollable and frequent thoughts of suicide stop them attempting their recovery journey until they feel safer and more secure.

Your client will not feel safe if they are still living with, or are dependent on, their abuser or abusers; are in an abusive relationship; or are totally isolated from others. If they are in an unsafe environment it will be important for them to seek additional support or help (see the resources list at the end of the book). Your client's internal safety is dependent on how well they are able to function and manage in their everyday life. If they are able to get up, perform daily tasks, have some control over their anxieties and intrusive memories and are able to regulate their mood, then they have a degree of internal safety. If however, they tell you that they feel out of control, at the mercy of intrusive thoughts, flashbacks, nightmares or panic attacks, or frequently dissociate, then they are not safe. They are also not safe if they engage in self-destructive behaviours such as self-injury or substance misuse to regulate their mood. While this handbook aims to give you skills that you can pass on to your client to establish internal safety, you might also consider suggesting they join a survivors group or organisation.

The skills in this books will give you ways to help your client manage both their external and internal safety, and enable them to develop additional skills to gain more control over their trauma reactions and regulate their feelings. To make this easier it is important for you to identify with your client those things that calm and soothe them that will prove to be invaluable on their journey to recovery.

 ### Exercise

Creating a mood basket

Often survivors find creating a mood basket or mood box a helpful way to regulate their feelings and mood. A mood basket is particularly useful as it is can be easily transported between rooms or locations, while a box with a lock will ensure greater privacy. Instruct your client to find a nice basket or box which they can customise, and place things into it that calm them, bring them pleasure or which they find inspirational. These can include calming images, cards, or postcards, meaningful pebbles, stones, or crystals, favourite photographs, flowers, or favourite music CDs. Other items could include a favourite DVD, book, poem or quotation, a calming scent or aroma, objects from a time or place associated with good memories, jewellery from a loved one, a piece of cloth or a soft toy.

What is put in the mood basket will be unique and meaningful to your client. The only guideline is that it must help them to change their mood when they are feeling sad, overwhelmed or anxious. Encourage them to start by creating the basket with items already in their possession and gradually add any other meaningful items that will help them on their journey. Ideally it helps to include items that stimulate all of the five senses: smell, sight, sound, touch and taste.

MUSIC

Music can be a powerful way to regulate emotions and feelings. Ask your client to consider making a number of music compilations to help them regulate their mood; including uplifting and energising music, as well as calming and relaxing music. These can be stored as playlists on an MP3 player or mobile phone so that they are easily accessible. The playlists can reflect a range of moods from calming, to energising and invigorating, to music that will channel anger. Perhaps making a memory based playlist will help them when recalling blocked memories.

Warning

Warn your client that it is not safe to play memory based music until they have mastered a range of mood regulation and grounding skills.

ANCHORS

In creating a mood basket your client will have identified some objects that can help to anchor them in moments of distress. Anchors are any objects that ground us and represent a feeling of safety such as a pebble, stone, coin or crystal. It is especially helpful if the anchor is associated with the present day and did not exist in the past when the trauma occurred. A good example of this is an iPod or mobile phone, which they would not have had when they were a child. These can be particularly helpful during flashbacks and dissociation to orient your client in the present. It helps if the anchor is portable so that they can carry it around at all times. Another powerful anchor is a comforting smell such as favourite scent, aftershave or aroma. Advise your client that the smell should remind them of a time when they felt safe and should be associated with comfort and well-being. They can release their comforting smell by lighting a scented candle, leaving spices in a bowl in their room or spraying the scent or aftershave onto a scarf or piece of clothing.

OASES AND SAFE PLACES

Two other powerful sources to help regulate mood are an 'Oasis' and a 'Safe Place' to which your client can go when they feel overwhelmed. These will be activities or places that will ground and soothe them.

Exercise

Finding an oasis and safe place

Ask your client to make a list in their journal of activities, people or places that are associated with pleasure and which have a calming and soothing effect. Also get them to include some that they find uplifting and invigorating and which restore a sense of well-being. These will form the basis of the Oases and Safe Place. They can collect images of these and put them into their mood basket to use as required. Their Oases could include activities that help them to relax such as: having a warm bath, massage, meditation, sitting in the sunshine in the park, reading, watching a film, listening to music, going to a concert, or watching or playing sport. Alongside this, ask them to identify a grounding position which is comforting such as: curling up, squatting, or lying down with a favourite blanket. They may find it uncomfortable to relax and instead prefer invigorating activities that are a source of pleasure such as swimming, exercising, playing sports, dancing, singing, going for a walk or running. Once they have listed these, encourage them to identify those that they could easily integrate into their lives, and make a commitment to engage in these activities regularly so that they become an established part of their daily life.

Next ask your client to think of a Safe Place past or present, which has been, is or could be, a site of protection. If there has never been a safe place in their lives, then help them to imagine one. Whether real or imagined, it is helpful to associate as many sensory cues as possible to this safe place – the smells, the sounds, the feel, the sights and the taste. By writing down as many things they can think of that can be associated with this safe place they should be able to enter it whenever they need to.

Once your client has identified their anchor, oases and safe place, they will be able to use these throughout their recovery. From now on they should be able to regulate their distress and uncomfortable feelings by using their anchor, oases or safe place to soothe and comfort them. Knowing how to counterbalance negative feelings with more positive ones will enable them to improve the quality of their everyday life. Passing on these basic skills will help your client to take more control of their trauma related reactions which lead to a greater sense of safety and stability.

Remind your client
If they get upset at any point while doing these exercises they should STOP. Instead get them to do something pleasurable and, when ready, resume the activity or reading.

LOSS OF CONTROL
A significant impact of complex trauma is the loss of control. This includes loss of control over feelings, thoughts and the body as well as actions and behaviour. In addition the survivors control over their autonomy and reality is reduced. Lack of control over these essential functions ultimately decreases the survivor's capacity to live their life to the full and make informed choices. A central aspect of recovery is to regain control over physical and emotional responses to complex trauma.

To gain control and mastery over sexual abuse, and to overcome the tyranny of trauma reactions, it is vital to reset the survivor's inner alarm system. This means making sure that the default setting is changed, and that the alarm is not so easily tripped. This will allow the hippocampus to come back on line to restore physical and emotional balance. To achieve this renewed control it is helpful to find ways to reduce daily stress levels, stabilise trauma reactions and restore a sense of inner safety.

Managing stress

The lack of control and range of trauma symptoms can intensify the survivor's stress responses. As the survivor is already on high alert and experiencing high levels of irritability any additional stress can feel overwhelming. To this effect the survivor can benefit from finding ways to manage stress reactions in the moment. The following exercise can aid the management of stress responses and restore control and safety.

 Exercise
Stress reduction

1. Find a stress ball and a small object that represents healing and calm.

2. Hold stress ball in non-dominant hand.

3. Squeeze as hard as possible, imagine letting all tension and unpleasant feelings from the body flow into your arm, hand, then the stress ball. Visualise it like a magnet, drawing all tension to it. With the ball, stay present and focused.

4. When the ball is saturated with stress, open your hand and let go of the ball, allow all tension to stay in the ball away from you to dissipate into air.

5. Practise several times until all negative tension is relieved from the body.

6. When you feel calmer and less stressed, place object (anchor) into dominant hand.

7. Imagine object holds all healing and well-being, safety, contentment, peace and calm, emotional clarity, free of tension and conflict.

8. Allow all these feelings to radiate and flow through body and mind, like heat.

9. With each breath in allow well-being to flow through, with each out-breath let any remaining tension go.

10. The more you practise the more able you will be to recall associated feelings whenever you wish to remind yourself of well-being. This will allow you to automatically recall feelings of the object, colour, shape, texture, temperature, so as to fully experience all the positive feelings associated with it.

Regulating emotions

Feeling more in control will help to regulate emotions and enable the survivor to feel more in control of them. This will also aid them in finding more healthy alternatives to manage trauma reactions. Physical exercise and grounding techniques will not only soothe them, but also help them to reconnect to their body (see Chapter 10). This will reduce the survivors reliance on external sources of comfort such as food, alcohol, drugs or other people to regulate their emotional distress. This can be extremely liberating for the survivor as they learn that by trusting themselves they can take direct control over bodily responses and quality of life.

 Remind your client

In complex trauma someone else controlled them, their body, thoughts, feelings and behaviour, as well as their reality, preventing them from acting autonomously. To recover it is vital to restore control over their emotions, body and life to make truly informed choices.

To begin to regulate emotions the survivor will need to identify their 'window of tolerance' for arousal (Ogden *et al.*, 2006; Siegel, 1999; van der Hart *et al.*, 2006). This acts like a bookmark that lets the survivor know that they are experiencing just enough sensory arousal and when they are at an optimal level and not overwhelming or too numb. This window of tolerance will vary from individual to individual due to inborn temperament, natural physiological reactivity and experience. Knowing optimal arousal levels prevents the survivor from becoming too agitated, anxious, tired, numb or shutdown.

Generally the regulation of emotion is learned in childhood through being soothed by the primary caregiver which then becomes internalised (Schore, 2001). In cases of abuse or trauma, significant others are terrifying so the survivor cannot learn to self-regulate. This leads to either becoming over aroused and out-of-control of emotions, or to shutdown whereby emotions are over controlled. This leads the survivor to seek out others to help them regulate their emotions, leaving them dependent and vulnerable.

If your client is dependent on others for emotional regulation, encourage them to make a list of those they can trust or rely on, but remind them that it is imperative that they learn the skills for self-regulation. To facilitate this you can help your client to identify their window of tolerance and then help them learn to stay within that window. Gradually they should learn to widen their level of tolerance so they can withstand a broader range of experiences without being overwhelmed (see Box 9.1).

Box 9.1 Window of tolerance

1. Encourage your client to list the indicators for their optimal level of arousal and how they know when they feel: relaxed, calm, alert, pleasant, energised, warm/cool in body, competent, with a quiet or active mind

2. Next suggest that they write down what feels like outside their levels of tolerance – markers such as body tension, disorganised thoughts, the mind going blank, hyperventilation, inner chaos, drowsiness

3. They will then need to draw an arousal Scale of 1–10

4. Ask the client to mark the range that is tolerable (subjective, no right or wrong answer) e.g. 3–7, 4–6

5. Mark points below or beyond which they don't want to go e.g. if 3–7, then 2–6 as signals to stop

Make a list of helpful tips that help cope with feeling too much, and when feeling too little to implement if outside the window of tolerance

---

As the survivor becomes more in control of their bodily responses they can begin to regain contact with their body, allowing them to become more in tune with it. This means they will feel more embodied and live in their body rather than trying to escape from it. This will reduce their body shame while increasing their capacity to contain arousal and stress responses. Regaining contact with the body can be further enhanced through physical exercise which allows the survivor to release trapped energy and shed its protective armour.

LEARNING TO BE PRESENT

As the survivor masters the skills of emotional regulation and embodiment they can begin to allow themselves to be more present. Many survivors avoid feeling and find it difficult to be present. To facilitate being more present you could encourage them to practise the following exercise.

Exercise
Learning to be present

1. Invite your client to look at three objects in the room, identify their main characteristics such as shape, colour, size, texture and say these aloud.

2. They should then notice three sounds and identify their main characteristics such as pitch, intensity, constant or intermittent, pleasant or unpleasant and say these aloud.

3. Then they touch three objects and describe their characteristic out loud such as rough, smooth, soft, hard, cold, warm.

4. Ask your client to focus on the objects and focus on the fact that they are in the here and now, safe with these objects.

5. This can be repeated several times or the client can find three items for each sense – sight, sound, smell, taste and touch.

Practise at least twice a day for a few minutes each time, for example when getting up or before going to bed.

 Remember

All exercises need to be practised when the survivor is at their best, preferably during daytime when light as this is more grounding and they are more able to learn.

To help the survivor to practise staying in the present they may need to identify anchors in their familiar environment such as home or the work place, so that they can feel safe in whatever room they are in. This is especially the case if they cannot find their personal anchor. The exercise below allows them to identify anchors to orient them to their present environment.

 Exercise

Identifying anchors to the present

1. Invite the survivor to find three anchors to the present in each room (kitchen, bedroom, bathroom, living room).

2. Ask them to focus on things that they can see, hear, smell, taste and touch (a picture, music, other objects).

3. Make sure the anchors are pleasing and connected to the present.

4. Invite the survivor to write down a list of these anchors in their journal or mobile phone.

5. Whenever things are difficult, they can use these anchors to stay in a safe present.

6. These can be extended to other places in which you spend time such as work, college, car, therapist office.

Warning

Objects or items from the past that remind the client of painful experiences are best put away if possible. Perhaps buy something to link to the present and have in a special place, for example statue, photo, poster, print, stones. Every time the survivor looks at it, is a reminder of the present.

THE ROLE OF REFLECTION

As the survivor gains more control over their body they can begin to reflect more and stay in contact with inner experiencing. Reflective function is a skill which can be learned. If the survivor can reflect they will feel more secure and be able to make sense of their own minds and the minds of others (Allen, Fonagy and Bateman, 2008; Fonagy, Gergely, Jurist and Target, 2002). Reflection can also add richness to their experiencing and prevents the survivor from becoming embedded in their feelings. This enables them to mentalise their experiences and respond more appropriately rather than being reactive. Moreover, mentalisation helps the survivor to evaluate their sensations, feelings, thoughts and emotions.

When learning to reflect, survivors will initially only be able to do this after the event. However with practice this will become easier and they will be able to do this in the present as they come in contact with their inner experiencing. It is critical for survivors to reflect that they are safe, calm, relaxed, and free from distractions. As they learn to reflect they will be able to understand their reactions to emotions and to identify triggers, thoughts and how these impact on behaviour. They will also be able to understand other people rather than attempt mind reading and predicting their thoughts or actions, which can lead to healthier relationships.

Exercise

Learning to reflect

1. Encourage the survivor to be in the present.
2. Encourage them to notice inner experiencing without judgement.
3. Encourage them to acknowledge and accept feelings and to become more empathic.
4. Suggest that they notice similarities and differences.
5. Encourage them to be empathic towards self and others.

RELAXATION

As the survivor is more able to be in the present they will be able to relax more. This is often very difficult because of hyper- or hypo-vigilance. As they master the skills of regulating their arousal they can begin to take more pleasure in their body and feeling alive. To help with relaxation the survivor could prepare a relaxation kit (see below) alongside their mood box and try some of the following relaxation exercises.

Exercise

Making a relaxation kit

Suggest that your client collect together music, CDs, relaxing videos, special bath salts, pleasant lotions, comfortable shawl, sweater, scarf, pair of old slippers, warm socks, candles, special teas, healthy snacks, good book, favourite photo, mementoes, anchors. List one or two new activities to try out for relaxation. Identify any obstacles to trying these activities.

Relaxation exercises

Equipped with their relaxation kit the survivor can now devote time to engage in some relaxation exercises. Feel free to change the setting, for example mountain, forest.

Exercise

The tree (adapted from Boon, Steele and van der Hart, 2011)

Invite your client to relax while you say the following:

> Imagine a quiet and safe spot in the open air with beautiful scenery and right temperature and season. See magnificent trees in resplendent green. Find a particular tree that appeals and focus on that tree – colour, shape, size, is it alone, young, firm, soft, its shape, the texture, the warm wood scent, the palette of colours, branches, spreading, its shelter. Capture to your memory the touch of the tree; run your hand over the bark, the knotholes, its hollows, embrace it, its branches, boughs, leaves, etc. The tree is a refuge to go to whenever you wish, giving strength and beauty, peacefulness, protection and sturdiness.

Exercise

Healing pool (adapted from Boon, Steele and van der Hart, 2011)

Invite your client to relax while you say the following:

> Imagine a beautiful pool of water in the quiet forest/mountain lake/middle of a meadow; the air is fresh, clean, the right temperature. It is your favourite season. The water is inviting, still, reflects the sky, surrounded by trees; there

is a flowing, bubbling, waterfall and flowers nearby; it is shallow or deep, pleasant, fresh, clean, joyful, smell. There are sounds all around – rustling trees, meadow grass, bubble and babble of water, birds. Notice the pool's surroundings: colour, smell, taste, sounds, light, warmth, etc., whether there are fish. Notice the colours: a shimmering blue, sparkling green, clear as crystal. Light dances, skips. Relax, absorb contentment and safety. Feel the healing water, it refreshes your worn out mind, acts as a balm for a wounded heart. Explore the pool, take in the healing energy by dangling your toes and feet. The water buoys you up so you cannot sink. It nurtures, soothes, calms, restores, filling you with peace and lightness – take into every nook and cranny of pain, fears, stress and sorrow. Let fear, shame and worries be drawn from you to the water and carried away. Water surrounds you, flows around you. Refreshing, relaxing. Feel it soothe the body, mind and heart. Stay as long as you like until you can feel the healing power from this wellspring of well-being.

Muscle tensing

Some survivor find it terrifying to relax as they feel out of control and are not able to monitor their environment for danger signals. In addition, they fear relaxation as this may slow their responses making them feel more vulnerable and at risk. This is exacerbated if the abuser instructed the survivor to relax as a prelude to the abuse. For those survivors who find it difficult to relax, it may be more effective to encourage them to tense their muscles and thereby improving muscle tone. This can restore control over their body and feel empowering in strengthening muscles and energising the body.

 Exercise
Muscle tensing

1. Invite the survivor to sit or lie comfortably.

2. Encourage them to take a deep breath through their nose to a slow count of three, hold for three counts and breathe out slowly for three counts.

3. Tell them to repeat this three times.

4. Ask them to take a deep breath and tighten every muscle in body as tight as they can from head to toe, hold to count of five and let go, breathing out as deeply as they can and intentionally relaxing muscles.

5. Repeat the three deep breaths at beginning of exercise.

6. The client should then breathe deeply and repeat the tighten exercise, followed by three deep breaths.

7. The exercise can be repeated until the survivor feels physically relaxed.

Many of these exercises can be introduced and practised in session initially. Once the survivor has gained mastery over them and feels the benefit they can adopt these outside of session to restore control and feel safer in their home environment. This will prepare them to manage a range of sensations and feelings through grounding exercise.

10

SKILLS TO IMPROVE DAILY LIFE

One way of achieving greater control over the quality of survivors' everyday life is to reduce daily stress levels by simplifying their life. It is essential for them to have some structure to their life to counteract the chaos associated with trauma. This can be done by ensuring regular routines and rituals around going to bed, eating meals, taking exercise and resting. Streamlining daily routines and rituals will help them to be more organised and give a structure to their daily life. In addition it helps to reduce sensory overload by switching off TV, radio, computers and mobile phones. It helps to pick up and respond to emails, texts and voice messages once or twice a day rather than as soon as they are delivered.

It also helps to have a regular routine. Survivors may need to be reminded that routines don't have to be boring and can create safety, balance and an element of control, as long as the survivor does not overdo it. The aim is to reduce stress in the here and now in order to make trauma reactions more manageable. You can encourage them to make routines more fun by listening to loud, invigorating music when they are cleaning, ironing or washing the dishes. To further tame their day-to-day stress levels they must set boundaries, and not take on additional responsibilities or demands. This means learning to say 'No' without feeling guilty.

Another way for survivors to take control over their lives is to ensure that they restore control over their eating and sleeping patterns. Eating regular, healthy meals can counter stress reactions and regulate the bodily functions. If they have suffered prolonged traumatic stress reactions it might be worth advising them to take vitamin supplements such as vitamin B and vitamin C, which are often depleted during stress. Increasing the intake of Omega-3 can also help to lower stress levels. Have your client discuss this with their GP so that they can replenish any vitamin deficiencies and restore energy levels.

THE ROLE OF SLEEP AND REST

A healthy balance between sleep, work, rest and play helps to restore out of control stress levels. Sleep is essential to rest the body and to aid the processing of emotional experiences and is critical in the formation, storage and consolidation of memories. Sleep is also necessary for inspiration and finding creative solutions to everyday problems. If your client is plagued by nightmares and finds it hard to get to sleep, get them to experiment with a range of strategies to help them to sleep. Regular bedtimes and regular waking times, as well as relaxation exercises, can all aid sleep.

Improving sleep

Common sleep problems include difficulty falling asleep, staying asleep, frequent waking or very early morning waking. A disturbed sleep–wake pattern and lack of sleep can cause excessive sleepiness and result in falling asleep during the day. Nightmares, night terrors, and sleep walking will also disturb sleep patterns as will sleep talking, teeth grinding, bedwetting, restless legs syndrome and sleep apnoea. This leaves the survivor feeling as though they have not slept deeply or well. Recurrent nightmares mean that the survivor is too afraid to go to sleep and postpones it. Sleeping during the daytime or narcolepsy further disrupt the sleep–wake pattern and contribute to further sleep problems.

To help the survivor to improve their sleep you can encourage them to make a sleep kit and ensure that they make their bedroom a place of safety and comfort.

 Exercise
Sleep kit

1. Encourage the survivor to make up a box or basket of nice comforting things that they can use before going to bed.

2. Suggest that they place anchors to the present either side of the bed, straight ahead, and on the ceiling.

3. Encourage the survivor to listen to relaxing music or sounds prior to going to bed and to place anchoring items such as a special pillow or blanket, night light, favourite piece of clothing, doll or stuffed animal, favourite book, photographs of people they care about and who care for them nearby. A photo of a safe and relaxing place, a list of pleasant experiences, and people to call during an emergency can all be included in the sleep basket.

4. If they have a pet they can spend some time stroking it before going to bed.

5. Remember to include their dream journal.

Making the bedroom safe

It is also important to make the bedroom into a sanctuary and pleasant place to sleep. To help the client with this they can do the following exercise.

Exercise

Making the bedroom safe

Invite the client to make a list of what they want to change in the bedroom to make it more comfortable, including listing any inner conflict around the bedroom. Remove or change anything that might trigger flashbacks such as colour, smell, objects, sounds (e.g. ticking clock) or smells. Make sure the lighting is different to when they were abused and that the temperature is comfortable and differs from the abuse. It is better to have the room cool with a slightly open window than too stuffy. Encourage the survivor to remove all stimulants such as TV, radio, mobile phone and video games. While some survivors do prefer background noise especially if the abuse took place in silence, it is best when it is muted and soft such as soft music or wind chimes. If the survivor prefers noise, white noise such as a fan is preferable to aid sleep. Survivors should also try to have things from the present to remind them of the here and now rather than the past such as the position of the bed, bed linen, blankets and duvets.

It is also important to ensure that the house is secure, that windows and doors are locked, pets are in or out and that the security system is activated. Some survivors find it comforting to have local emergency numbers pre-programmed into their phone, and to have this by their bedside.

Sleep routine

It is helpful to have a regular bed time and waking up time. To aid sleep survivors need to make sure that they rest and relax before bed by reading a book, taking a bath or shower, drinking a caffeine-free drink, or eating a small healthy snack before bed. Some survivors find hugging a favourite pillow or reading a favourite story comforting. It is important to avoid sleeping in day clothes and to change into night wear as a reminder of bedtime. If the survivor wore a nightdress when younger they may wish to wear the opposite now. It is helpful to listen to recorded sounds of nature, the ocean or birdsong to help with relaxation. If reading is a way of avoiding sleep then this is not advisable, and it is important for the reading to be pleasant rather than overly stimulating. Some survivors find meditation relaxing before bedtime while others find it helps to reflect on three things for which to be grateful, or to identify three good things that happened that day.

Box 10.1 Strategies if unable to sleep

1. Slow down thoughts, relaxation

2. Distraction – focus on another mental activity to stop worrying, count sheep, count backwards slowly from 100, if lose track go back to beginning

3. Stop sign – imagine a giant stop sign so when ruminating think of the stop sign and refocus attention on breathing breathe in count of three, hold for count of three, breathe out for count of three, repeat

4. Release thoughts – imagine thoughts flowing down a river, stream, one by one, no need to do anything just observe them flowing down stream

5. Get up and write down the thoughts that are bothering them and deal with them the next day

6. Containment – imagine putting the problem in a safe container, for example a box, bank vault, computer for the night, can return next day

7. Imagine warm white light enveloping you, or a beautiful balloon in which to blow all tensions and problems; when relaxed let the balloon float into the sky. If appropriate lean against a safe and caring person

8. If unable to sleep after reasonable time turn the clock away so cannot check time and make up for sleep the following day

9. Stop forcing sleep. It is better to get up, go to another room or part of bedroom, distract self with quiet activity, read a book, watch TV as long as not too stimulating, listen to peaceful music, do stretching exercises

10. Go back to bed when sleepy. Do this as often as necessary during the night

 Exercise

Bedtime routine

Invite your client to list activities to avoid before going to bed and to identify what sort of routine they would like such as meditation, breathing exercises, imagery, reading. Next get them to list optimal bedtime and wake time, and any obstacles to developing a healthy routine. Lastly make a list of anchors to have in the bedroom.

Strategies if unable to sleep

To prepare for the eventuality that your client is unable to sleep it helps to have some strategies in place (see Box 10.1).

Box 10.2 What to do after a nightmare

1. Calm down and self soothe

2. Get bearings in the present. Use anchors in the bedroom, talk to self quietly, and remind yourself where you are

3. Turn the light on and get out of bed, get a drink or find something to distract yourself

4. Splash cool water on your face, hands, back of neck to help stay present and awake

5. Do breathing exercises

6. Do gentle stretching exercise to reorient back into present

7. Stroke or cuddle pet, if appropriate

8. If physical symptoms, for example bad taste in the mouth, pain or discomfort, brush teeth, have a decaffeinated drink, suck a mint or hard sweet, massage painful muscles

9. Write down distressing dream if it helps, put it away, tear it up, and discuss in therapy. Do not go into the experience; this is just to contain it and leave for a later time

10. Change the nightmare: add a supportive person to the dream, plan an escape route, give yourself special powers

11. If paralysed by nightmare – look at visible anchors to present, on left, right, ceiling, straight ahead. (Even if too terrified to move the survivor can see. This can help shift from paralysis mode.) Try to make a small movement such as blinking eyes or twitching a toe or little finger; make light movement with a hand, foot, arm or leg; continue slowly until the entire body can move

12. Be careful with medication as these only provide short term and temporary relief and can cause dependency. Also try to avoid alcohol and drugs as they interrupt sleep patterns

In a similar vein the survivor can list what to do after a nightmare (see Box 10.2).

PHYSICAL EXERCISE

Physical exercise is especially important if your client adopted a freeze response during the abuse or finds it hard to relax. Relaxing can feel like giving up control and submitting, as they had to during the abuse, and can make them feel even more vulnerable. If your client finds it hard to relax, or if relaxation increases their anxiety, then physical exercise may be a better choice for them. In contrast to relaxation, physical exercise involves tensing muscles to give a sense of being in control and in charge of the body.

Both relaxation and physical exercise can help survivors to reconnect to their bodies, which is vital if they have become detached and out of contact with their bodies. Restoring control over the body is particularly important if your client felt betrayed by their body in responding to the abuse. It is essential that you work with your client to find what is best for them to remain in contact with, and in control of their body.

Releasing stress hormones

Physical exercise is an excellent way to stay in the present, or here and now, rather than focusing on the past. It is also a powerful antidote to the freeze response in discharging trapped energy, which sends messages to the brain to switch off the alarm system as the trauma is finally over. Not only is trapped energy discharged, but it releases built up stress hormones such as adrenaline and cortisol which have grown to toxic levels. As the built up stress hormones fade away renewed levels of energy are accessed to regulate current stress levels.

Increased muscle tone

As the stress hormones are released and your client exercises with new vitality they will discover a sense of well-being as feel good hormones, known as endorphins, are released into the brain. A further benefit of physical exercise is the increase in muscle tone. Research has shown that increased muscle tone is a much more powerful ally in trauma than relaxation, as it makes one physically stronger which in turn promotes greater emotional strength. Physical exercise also regulates breathing, which is another aid to reconnecting to and restoring control over the body.

As the freeze response prevents the discharge of trapped energy, the body remains frozen. If your client wants to start exercising it is better to thaw their frozen body slowly by engaging in gentle exercise. If they do this too quickly they can cause further damage so encourage them to start gradually and build up slowly. Moving the body slowly through carefully chosen exercise can cancel out the paralysing effects of abuse and help to regain control over the body. As your client begins to feel their body move, and shed its protective armour, they can build up to more strenuous exercise.

Warning

Before engaging in regular physical exercise advise your client to have a medical check-up with their GP or the practice nurse, especially if they have taken no exercise for some years.

Regaining contact with the body

Physical exercise not only allows survivors to release trapped energy and shed its protective armour, it also allows them to regain contact with their body, and to become in tune with their bodies. This means they will feel their body more, known as embodiment, and be able to live in their bodies rather than trying to escape from them. This will reduce their body shame, while increasing their capacity to contain arousal and stress responses.

To enable your client to feel more embodied start by encouraging them to become more aware of their body and to move whenever they feel themselves detaching from their body. It is better if they start gently by wiggling fingers or toes, moving their arms or legs, rotating their head, or standing up. Gentle muscle tensing in the legs, feet and back can also have beneficial effects. These activities can give your client improved balance and a sense of being grounded, while strengthening their body and increasing their sense of protection.

Remind your client that their body is a powerful resource as it provides important signals about their inner experiencing. As this will have been largely terrifying in the past your client will have shutdown these signals. While this may have felt like they were shrouding themselves in protective armour, it has put them at greater risk. Physical exercise can help by sending messages to the alarm system that the trauma is over and that freezing is no longer necessary. As their body thaws and the armour melts away, they will become more in tune with their body and bodily signals. This will help them to truly protect themselves and strengthen their bodily responses.

You will need to be mindful that strenuous physical exercise might not suit all survivors as increased heart rate, respiration, and sweating can mimic the arousal during the sexual abuse. If this happens, they will need to find lower levels of activity that do not increase heart rate or respiration such as slow weight training, muscle tensing, swimming or gardening. Remind them to experiment to find what works best for them. To help them choose which forms of exercise appeal to them the most, try the exercise below.

Exercise

Which form of physical exercise?

Encourage your client to list in their journal any physical exercise that appeals to them. A selection of options could include walking, jogging, step classes, cycling, weights, sit ups, push ups, ball games, Pilates, yoga, treadmill, swimming, tennis, golf, self-defence, boxing, kick boxing, martial arts, tai chi, riding, gardening or dancing. Ask your client to highlight those that appeal to them and which they would like to experiment with. Encourage them to make a commitment to try one at a time and be mindful of which is best for them. It is worth getting them to try out some slow, gentle exercise as well as some fast, high-paced exercise to see how they feel both during and afterwards.

Before your client decides, check with them how realistic the chosen physical exercise is. How much time can they realistically commit in terms of the frequency and duration of the physical exercise? It is also important to consider any financial costs such as class fees, gym membership and ease of access to the location. They will also need to consider whether they prefer outdoor or indoor activities, or prefer to exercise at home.

If your client is socially isolated they might consider pursuing group activities or team sports, or finding an 'exercise buddy' to keep them motivated. When they have tried a few alternatives settle on those that have been the most effective and that they can realistically manage. Remember you want them to reduce stress rather than increase it! Finally, it might help initially to use a reward system every time they take exercise to sustain their level of motivation. For example, they could put some money into a box every time they exercise.

Remind your client

Strenuous exercise which increases heart rate and respiration can mimic the arousal during sexual abuse which can trigger trauma reactions.

11

MANAGING SENSATIONS, FEELINGS AND GROUNDING SKILLS

Many survivors of complex trauma tend to avoid inner experiencing because their internal state is so overwhelming, or because they have received no guidance or reassurance in childhood on how to manage or regulate intense emotions. This lack of emotional regulation means that they cannot manage the intensity of their inner pain and fears. In not being able to regulate emotions many survivors either become stuck in a state of hyper-arousal or emotional shutdown, or hypo-arousal. Some survivors oscillate between the two in an attempt to manage their feelings.

Hyper-arousal is associated with experiencing too much and being plagued by flashbacks, panic attacks, intrusive memories, thoughts and feelings. These are often accompanied by out of the blue, unexplained sensations or pain with no medical cause. Survivors also report feeling as though they are being physically controlled by someone else, hearing voices commenting on their actions and behaviour or arguing and criticising them. This represents being stuck in the trauma and feeling as though it is still happening. As such the survivor is hostage to right brain activity in which sensorimotor and hyper-emotional states predominate. In contrast, hypo-arousal is characterised by emotional shutdown to numb all feelings. As a result the survivor is unable to feel any emotions or sensations. Both hyper-arousal and hypo-arousal mean that the survivor is in thrall to the past and finds it impossible to live in the present.

To encourage the survivor to be in the present they will need to learn grounding skills to help them manage their inner experiencing in a more healthy way and they will need to learn to stay in the present (see pp.153–54). This is best practised in session until the survivor can master these skills and use them in daily life.

LOSS OF CONTROL OVER FEELINGS AND THOUGHTS

Trauma symptoms represent the loss of control over physiological arousal and inner experiencing such as feelings, thoughts and body as well as actions and behaviour. In addition control over autonomy and reality is reduced. Lack of control over these essential functions ultimately decreases the survivor's capacity to live their life to the full and make informed choices. A central aspect of recovery is to regain control over the physical and emotional responses to abuse.

To gain control and mastery over complex trauma, and to overcome the tyranny of trauma reactions, it is vital for survivors to reset their inner alarm system. This means making sure that the default setting is changed, and that the alarm is not so easily tripped. This will allow the hippocampus to come back on line to restore physical and emotional balance. You can help your client to achieve this renewed control by finding ways of reducing their daily stress levels, stabilising their trauma reactions and restoring a sense of inner safety.

MINDFULNESS

To support greater awareness and control over their body and physical being, it is useful for survivors to develop mental strategies that track sensations, emotions, thoughts and feelings. They can achieve this through mindfulness which helps them to become more consciously aware of their current thoughts, feelings and surroundings. As well as increasing awareness of their experiencing, mindfulness encourages survivors to accept such experiencing without judgement. This helps survivors to keep an open channel of communication between their mind and body. As your client develops this they will become more aware of how their mind and body are linked, and their experiencing.

Mindfulness will also help both you and your client to monitor the impact certain foods and drinks have on them and their body. For instance, caffeine tends to increase physical and psychological tension, or hyper-arousal, whereas carbohydrates have a calming effect. This is useful to know so that your client can regulate their body by being more mindful of what they eat and drink. Test this out by getting your client to monitor their reactions to caffeine and carbohydrates in a more conscious way.

Becoming more aware through mindfulness of the impact of what we read or see, either on television or in films, or hear, such as music, or topics of conversation, can also help to regulate such stimuli. If your client's alarm system is already on high alert, or they find it hard to filter incoming stimuli, they will benefit from finding ways of reducing sensory overload. Advise them to try to find regular time to sit in quiet surroundings so that they can just focus on themselves and their experiencing.

IDENTIFYING TRIGGERS

Mindfulness can also help survivors to identify the triggers that cause intrusive memories, flashbacks, dissociation or panic attacks. In identifying these they will be able to understand which triggers they are sensitised to. This will help them to prepare for anticipated problematic reactions, as being forewarned means they are forearmed. To help your client with this get them to try the exercise below.

Exercise
Identifying triggers

Examine your client's list of trauma reactions with them and help them to identify as many triggers as possible that trip their alarm system. Remind them not to worry if they can only identify a few. As they work through their traumatic reactions using mindfulness skills they should be able to identify more triggers which can be added to the list. Next get them to grade the triggers on a scale of one to four, with one, triggers that are the least difficult to manage; two, triggers that they are not able to cope with yet but may be able to handle soon; three, triggers that are hard to control but they would like to master in the future; and four, those triggers that they will always wish to avoid for their own or others' safety. Starting with those triggers that are least difficult to manage, ask them to write down what happens, how they would like to control these, and how this can be achieved.

HYPER-AROUSAL

If the survivor suffers from hyper-arousal they will need to find ways of managing their overwhelming internal states through a range of methods such as temporary distraction, containment, calming and soothing and grounding techniques. This can be done through the following exercise.

Exercise
Managing hyper-arousal

1. Temporary distraction (not the same as avoiding) – to slow down arousal and to press the rest button. Always make a promise to return to what is overwhelming. The distraction has to be related to overwhelming emotion, for example for anger, a physical activity like walking, running or gardening. If the emotion is sad then a soothing activity such as watching a film or a favourite comedy show, reading a nice book, listening to soothing music, singing lyrics or going to a safe inner place could be chosen; or an activity could be chosen to match a feeling, to do something fun like a hobby, to talk to someone, to do concentration exercises such as a crossword puzzle or computer game, or laughter.

2. Containment – the survivor must contain, not ignore, and commit to return to the feelings at a later point when in better place or time. They can visualise a range of containers for their feelings such as a box on a shelf labelled with the distressing feelings, or imagine a bank vault, floating up in a balloon, a submarine, a computer file or video. Encourage them to write it down and leave it for later, or to draw the feelings.

3. Calming and soothing – soothe and reassure through empathic acknowledgement of feelings. Engage in calming breathing exercises, make use of anchors and safe place, or take time out to rest, slow down thoughts, get some rest, or listen to soothing music.

4. Grounding and reassurance – using all five senses, say out loud what can be seen, heard or smelled, slow down breathing. Remember that feelings have a beginning, middle and end and try to identify these or recall a time in the past when they ended.

HYPO-AROUSAL

Survivors who suffer from hypo-arousal will need to learn skills to manage these symptoms. While these are explored in more depth in the following chapter, it might help to practise the following exercises.

Exercises
Managing hypo-arousal

1. Physical activity – as soon as there is awareness of hypo-arousal survivors will need to resist the tendency to stay still and start moving using brief, vigorous activity that increases the heart rate such as star jumps, running up and down stairs, running, or running on the spot.

2. Visual stimulation – avoid focusing on one spot as this can induce a trance-like state. Visually scan surroundings and identify objects, colours, sounds, smells and say them out loud.

3. Mental stimulation – count backwards from 100 in threes or sevens, or count trees, cars or trucks if outside.

4. Physical numbness – notice where in the body it begins and ends and where it is completely numb. If there is an area where there is feeling encourage the survivor to touch this gently and say 'I am touching…' You could suggest that they scratch their back with a long soft brush, or hair brush, rub themselves against a door frame or tree or wrap themselves in a blanket to feel skin. If the survivor feels paralysed encourage them to make small movements with their finger, or blink their eyes, or touch their nose and try and get them to focus on moving as much as possible.

5. Emotional numbness – try to get them to notice the slightest emotion and plot these on a scale of 1–10. Encourage them to concentrate on their feelings and verbalise these. Even if only small try to visualise this as a teaspoon and attempt to hold on it for a specified period of time such as to a count of 5, then 10 seconds, then 30 seconds. Increase the amount gradually.

6. Temperature changes – if cold or freezing encourage the survivor to have a warm bath or shower, or snuggle under a blanket, put a hot water bottle on the stomach to warm the core, or have a warm soothing drink.

GROUNDING TECHNIQUES

One way of restoring control over triggers and traumatic reactions is to find grounding techniques that will allow your client to stay connected to themselves and their current reality. Grounding techniques will also remind your client that they are safe and no longer in danger. Grounding techniques are particularly useful to manage anxiety, intrusive memories, flashbacks, dissociation, panic attacks and self-injury.

Using all the senses

The most effective way for survivors to ground themselves is to connect to all five senses, sight, sound, touch, smell and taste, preferably with objects that represent their current reality. Thus it is better to focus on objects and stimuli in the present rather than the past. To make grounding techniques work, your client needs to personalise them by making them specific to them. They will also need to practise and rehearse these techniques so that they become familiar and automatic.

The first step for your client in grounding is to refocus attention to the present by concentrating on things around them. In this, they will need to focus on the physical space they are in and try to identify and name out loud as many objects around them as they can.

Grounding smell

Your client should already have identified some grounding techniques such as their anchor, oases and safe place. To these they can add their grounding smell such as a comforting or favourite scent or aftershave sprayed onto a scarf or fabric, smelling comforting spices such as vanilla or cinnamon, a lavender bag or a scented candle. Alternatively advise them to use stimulating smells such as lemon zest or pepper.

Grounding images

Suggest your client adds grounding images to ground themselves. If possible, get them to make this image interactive. For example they could use an image of a secluded garden and make it interactive by walking around it. Describe them strolling around, ask them to smell and name each flower out loud, listen to the fountain, and touch the leaves and grass. Alternatively they could create a luxury home and imagine themselves walking from room to room touching and naming all the beautiful objects they have. Or they could use a luxury car and imagine looking at and touching the interior, as well as the engine. The more pleasant the images are, the easier it will be to recall them. Advise your client to support their image by collecting relevant pictures from magazines or vivid drawings, that can be put into an album or collage. Remind them to practise their grounding images daily so that they become automatic and can easily be recalled when they are in crisis.

To help your client get to their grounding image or safe place, they need to create a 'bridging image'. For example their bridging image could involve imagining themselves floating away from the trauma or traumatic reaction to their safe place. Describe a trusted friend taking them there, or a door opening to reveal their safe place.

Grounding phrases

You can encourage your client to support the bridging image with grounding phrases such as 'I am ok' or 'I am strong, I have survived. I am safe.' Remind your client to personalise this phrase using their own unique voice. To help them remember their grounding phrase advise them to send themselves a voice message and store it on their mobile phone. Alternatively, tell them to write it on a post it note and stick it somewhere they can see it. An elaboration of this could be identifying a grounding song that symbolises their survival or courage which they can play and sing along to.

Grounding body position

It is also helpful to find a comforting or grounding body position in which your client feels safe and strong. This could be curled up in a comforting position with a favourite blanket, or standing up straight and tall with shoulders back to make them feel strong and powerful. Or they could tense their muscles and feel their strength course through their body. Get them to experiment with a number of positions to find which is the most comforting or empowering for them and encourage them to practise this whenever they can. Controlling their bodies in this way can be an effective way to regulate mood as well remaining embodied.

Grounding hobby

Finally, they could consider finding a grounding hobby in which they can immerse themselves such as painting, playing a musical instrument, doing the crossword or Sudoku, or collecting something meaningful to them. This will not only absorb them until the traumatic reaction subsides but it can also restore pleasure and fun in their daily life.

Keeping Minds and Hands Occupied

To keep focused and grounded it is helpful to keep the mind and hands busy. This can be achieved by manipulating sensory toys such as a tangle-toy, sress ball, handheld puzzles, or juggling balls, small bean bags or knitting.

With an arsenal of grounding techniques you can help your client to further equip the warrior within to help them face their triggers without detaching or engaging in self-destructive behaviours. This will allow them to move from avoidance which gives them the illusion of control, to truly being in control of their trauma reactions. Grounding techniques will also help them to regulate their mood and emotional distress and allow them to confront the unprocessed aspects of their trauma. Remind them that the more they avoid the traumatic experience the more intense their emotional distress, and the more likely they are to re-experience the trauma.

FEELING MORE IN CONTROL

Regulating emotions will help your client to feel more in control of them, This will also aid them in finding more healthy alternatives to manage trauma reactions (see pp.168–174). Physical exercise and grounding techniques will not only soothe your client, but also help them reconnect to their body and to themselves. This will reduce your client's reliance on external sources of comfort such as food, alcohol, drugs or other people to regulate their emotional distress. They should find this extremely liberating as they learn that by trusting themselves they can take direct control over their responses and quality of life.

Remind your client

In abuse someone else controlled them, their body, thoughts, feelings, and behaviour, as well as their reality. This prevented them from acting autonomously. To recover it is vital that they restore control to themselves so that they can choose what is right for them.

12
MANAGING FLASHBACKS, NIGHTMARES, PANIC ATTACKS AND DISSOCIATION

Flashbacks, nightmares and panic attacks can be extremely distressing as they seem to have a will of their own and can strike at any time without warning, which intensifies the sense of being out of control. The fear of flashbacks, nightmares and panic attacks can have a paralysing effect given that they can overwhelm at any time making it hard to leave the house or fall asleep. In order to manage their flashbacks, nightmares, panic attacks and dissociation, clients need to gain control over them. To help them in this they can use some of the skills you have taught them from earlier in the book such as regulating their breathing, monitoring their internal and external reality, and use those grounding techniques that work best for them.

FLASHBACKS

If your client is plagued by flashbacks it is essential that they recognise what they are. First and foremost, flashbacks are precisely that: flashbacks to the past. They are incredibly vivid and intense sensory memories of past experiences that have not been processed. They do not represent what is actually happening in the present. In essence they are signals that certain memories of the trauma have not been processed or integrated into the memory system.

 Remind your client
No matter how intense or how vivid and real the flashback feels it is a memory.

Managing flashbacks

To manage flashbacks your client will need to remember that they can feel terrified while not being in any actual danger, and flashbacks are powerful and intense internal experiences that do not reflect external reality (see p.34). While something in the external environment may have triggered the flashback, such as a smell, sound or visual stimuli reminiscent of past experience, this does not mean that they are in danger. To truly assess the actual danger, they need to monitor not just subjective internal sensations but also objective external reality. During flashbacks, your client may become over focused on internal cues rather than actual reality. As their alarm system is already on a high alert default setting, it fails to register whether the environment is hostile or safe.

Remind your client
If they cannot evaluate true safety, they also cannot evaluate actual danger.

In order to gain control over flashbacks your client will need to develop a protocol of how to manage them. This can be done prior to an actual flashback when your client is calm and relaxed, which they can then rehearse and practise on a daily basis so that it becomes automatic.

Exercise
Triggers to flashbacks

Invite your client to identify in their journal any triggers that have activated flashbacks in the past. Next ask them to write down the various ways that they can remind themselves that this is a flashback and keep them grounded in the present. Advise your client to write down a mantra such as 'This is a memory not a repeat of the trauma. I am remembering, it is not happening now. I am no longer in danger' or 'This is a flashback and this is a normal reaction to trauma. It happened in the past and the worst is over and it is not happening now.' Your client should keep their statements short to make it easier to remember them. It helps to leave out the details of the trauma as this can intensify the flashback. Get them to practise in order to find the words that work for them. When they have found a statement or mantra that suits them, ask them to write it down on a sticky note or piece of card. This can then be displayed as a reminder. Alternatively, your client can record it on an MP3 player or as a voicemail message on their mobile phone. Your client can also share these statements with a trusted friend or partner so that they can coach them or guide them through it.

Internal dialogue

During flashbacks your client may experience an internal dialogue in the present tense describing what is happening such as 'He is coming to get me. She is making me do things I don't like.' This self-talk in the present tense gives the flashback more power and makes it seem more real. The more it feels as though it is happening in the present, the more the alarm system will remain on high alert and set off the appropriate physiological responses. To reduce the power of the flashback tell your client that they will need to change the tense of the self-talk from the present to the past, such as 'I was attacked. I had to do things I didn't like.' This places the flashback firmly into the past.

Another technique to manage flashbacks is for your client to imagine that the images that they are seeing are on a TV screen and that they are holding a remote control which allows them to turn the sound down or up, to pause the image, or to turn the TV off so that the images fade away.

 Remind your client

They are not going mad. Flashbacks are normal and are a signal that your client is dealing with overwhelming experiences and trying to make sense of them.

Protocol to manage flashbacks

Alongside your client's statements, they will need to develop a protocol for managing flashbacks that also includes regulating breathing and some grounding techniques. Box 12.1 gives an example that might be helpful.

Your client should feel free to edit and experiment with the protocol to find what suits them best. They should get support if they need it by letting a trusted, designated friend know about the flashbacks and asking them for help. This help can involve talking to your client, holding them, or helping them to reconnect with the present while reminding them that they are safe and cared for.

Box 12.1 Suggested protocol for managing flashbacks

Give your client the following instructions:

- Breathe fully, with feet on ground (see p.157).
- Recite your mantra reminding you that this is a memory
- Check the date on your mobile phone, calendar or daily newspaper
- Find your anchor or object from the present and look at it, hold it, feel it, smell it – make sure you have access to your grounding smell
- Adopt your grounding position, or walk around
- Shift attention from internal to external senses and name them out loud, for example 'I see the sun shining, I can smell coffee, I can hear the news, today's date is'
- Look around the room and notice the colours, the shapes, the objects, the people and listen to the sounds around you – the traffic, voices or washing machine. Identify each sound and say it out loud
- Evaluate actual external danger by reminding yourself that this is a memory and not actually happening, and that there is no danger
- Stamp your feet or grind them on the floor to remind yourself where you are
- Consciously feel the boundary of your body and skin, the clothes you are wearing, the chair in which you are sitting, the floor supporting you
- Have an elastic band to hand (or on your wrist); ping it and feel it on your skin. This will remind you of the present and that what you are experiencing internally is in the past
- If you have lost all sense of where you end and the rest of the world begins, rub your body so you can feel its edges, or wrap yourself in a blanket or scarf, and consciously feel it as it surrounds you
- If you feel very unsafe call a trusted friend who knows the protocol

What to do after a flashback

As flashbacks are powerful experiences which drain energy, it is essential for your client to take care of themselves once the flashback is over. Advise them to have a warm relaxing bath or a sleep, a warm drink, or play some soothing music. They will need to take some quiet time for themselves, for instance by looking at the items in their mood basket, and generally nurture themselves. When they feel ready, get them to write down all they remember about the flashback and how they got through it. This will help your client to remember the experience, the triggers, the internal dialogue, and how they got through it. It is crucial for their healing to record how they got through the flashback and knowing that will help your client get through future ones.

Gaining control over flashbacks

To gain control over flashbacks your client will need to explore their content to identify specific aspects of the unprocessed memories (see p.194). Ask your client to keep a record of their flashbacks by logging the time and date, any internal or external triggers, and the duration and content of the flashback. To help your client to monitor their progress in managing the flashback and its intensity, it helps to rank the physical and emotional reactions to the flashback on a scale of 1–7, with one being mildly distressing and seven being highly distressing. The more your client monitors their flashbacks the more they will gain control of them and identify the traumatic memories and experiences that need to be processed.

NIGHTMARES

Like flashbacks, nightmares and recurring dreams are reminders of past experiences that need to be processed consciously so that they can be stored as memories. In essence, nightmares are flashbacks that occur while we are asleep. As such they have the same intensity and biochemical responses such as increased heart rate, sweating and palpitations as the actual experience in the past. In many ways, nightmares are more terrifying because the strategies that would help to control them when awake are 'off line'. In addition, the fear of nightmares can make it difficult to go to bed or fall asleep, leading to insomnia. Even if your client is able to fall asleep, the constant waking up from the nightmare makes for very fitful, unsatisfying sleep leaving them feeling exhausted.

Remind your client

Nightmares are the night-time equivalent of flashbacks and are the brain's way of processing experiences and filing them into the memory system. They are not dangerous.

The impact of nightmares

Lack of sleep is not only exhausting but also leaves the survivor feeling tired, irritable and lacking in energy. Fear of going to sleep means that there is no opportunity to recuperate or process new experiences. This can lead to poor concentration, confusion and a sense of not being able to manage even the simplest of tasks. To restore sleep and control over dreams and nightmares survivors will need to combine the management of their nightmares with improved sleeping patterns.

 Warning

Sleep exhaustion can tempt the survivor to use sleeping tablets. This can help in the short term but as they are highly addictive they can lead to dependency.

More importantly, sleeping tablets are merely aids to help someone to sleep which do not process the experience contained in the dreams. If your client has no alternative but to use prescribed sleeping tablets, then make sure they use these as a short term measure to relieve exhaustion. It is much better long term if you can help them develop strategies to aid sleep and manage unpleasant dreams.

Improving sleep patterns

To improve sleep your client will need to change their sleep schedule to regulate the sleep pattern. Encourage them to have a set, regular time that they go bed, along with a calming bedtime ritual. Keeping sensory stimuli in the bedroom to an absolute minimum aids sleep so they should avoid using a radio, TV or MP3 player while in bed. It is critical that your client makes the bedroom into a safe place, or sanctuary, especially if the abuse took place in a bedroom. Your client can do this by making sure that the sensory cues are different to those of the room in which the abuse took place. This could include the colour scheme, lighting, smell and type of bed clothing. It is also useful to have a comforter from the present, such as a special blanket or a stuffed toy, that can be used in moments of distress to soothe your client and remind them that they are in the present not the past (see p.149).

Sleep can also be more restful if your client eats regularly and at least three hours before going to bed as this aids digestion. It helps to be aware which food gives them heartburn or indigestion and which affects sleep and dreams. Heavy meals, spicy food and too much caffeine or alcohol can all interrupt sleep, as can smoking. Your client should not exercise before bed as their body needs to wind down rather than remaining on high alert. To help your client relax advise them to take a soothing bath with scented candles, wrap themselves in a warm towel or bathrobe, and rub their favourite scented moisturiser or body oil onto their skin. A soothing drink such as herbal tea can also help your client and their body to wind down.

 Exercise
Recording dreams

Encourage your client to find a notebook that they can use as a dream journal and keep this by their bedside with a pen. Whenever your client wakes as a result of a dream or nightmare, or when they wake up in the morning, they should record their dream(s) in their journal. They should try to include as much information and detailed content as they can, as well as how they felt. This will help your client to keep track of their dreams, and identify recurring themes with which to process and make sense of them.

Recording nightmares and dreams

Remind your client to record their nightmare, no matter how terrifying, before they try to go back to sleep. Falling asleep after a nightmare in the hope that the nightmare will not return is often futile. Remember if it has not been processed it is much more likely to recur. In recording dreams your client will be able to process their content consciously, and link them to the trauma experiences. This will make it easier to integrate them into their memory system, which in turn will reduce the nightmares.

Encourage your client to read through the nightmare or dreams during the daytime when your client feels safe and is in a calm state and consciously reflect on them. This will help your client to consider hidden or symbolic messages and what they mean. When they reach the terrifying or upsetting parts, they should write 'Stop. This is just a dream.' Ensure that they practise saying this as it will help them to say the same thing while they are asleep and stop the nightmare.

Alternatively ask your client to discuss their nightmare with a trusted friend or, upon re-reading it, imagine it as a fictional story. This will allow your client to try out two or three different positive endings, allowing them to re-write the outcome of the nightmare. These more positive endings can then be rehearsed and inserted into the dream or nightmare while they are asleep. It is useful for your client to rehearse their rewritten endings before going to sleep so that they can insert the alternative ending more easily.

Lucid dreaming

To further reduce the power nightmares have over them, suggest that your client practise lucid dreaming. Lucid dreaming means knowing that you are dreaming while still dreaming. Your client can achieve this by regularly recalling dreams, rehearsing alternative endings and practising auto or self-suggestion to remind themselves that they are dreaming. With practice your client will become more aware that they are dreaming and will be able to control how the dream develops and its ending. All these strategies will help your client to process the content of their nightmares and dreams and reduce their power to allow for more restful and satisfying sleep.

 Remind your client
Sleep has powerful restorative effects and can aid their recovery by integrating memories as well as inspiring insight and improve problem solving skills.

PANIC ATTACKS

Like flashbacks and nightmares, panic attacks are so overwhelming that they are appear life threatening making it hard to manage them. One way to help manage panic attacks is to understand the link they have to unprocessed feelings and experiences. It is also useful to identify any anxieties or areas of stress in life that trigger the panic attacks. In doing this your client can find alternative, more healthy ways of expressing their anxieties and feelings.

Mimicking sensations

A good way of learning to manage panic attacks is to mimic the sensations of the panic attack in a safe setting. This will show your client that the sensations in panic attacks are not life threatening and can be controlled. Suggest your client breathes through a straw to simulate panicky breathing, or tenses their muscles to resemble muscle tension, or spins in a chair to mimic the dizziness and disorientation that accompanies panic attacks. In mimicking these sensations in a safe setting and learning how to manage them your client can then transfer and use these skills in an actual panic attack.

Protocol for panic attacks

As your client mimics the sensations of a panic attack, they need to identify what helps to ground them and restore control. Ask your client to list all the things that help them and make sure that they are included in your client's protocol for managing panic attacks. Box 12.2 gives a suggested protocol for you to give your client that they can adapt or edit to include what is most helpful to them.

Box 12.2 Suggested protocol for panic attacks

- Stop, take a break and try to think about what it is that is making you panic
- Check and regulate your breathing by breathing fully and consciously
- If you are hyperventilating, hold each breath for three counts. If necessary use the paper bag technique (breathing into a paper bag can alleviate panic attacks)
- Touch your anchor
- Sit down somewhere comfortable
- Try to think positive thoughts
- Remind yourself that you are not going to die, that the attack is harmless and will soon pass and that you will be fine
- Rather than run away from the scene, tell yourself that you will stay for one or two minutes. When that time is up try to stay for another couple of minutes. If this proves too much then leave

---

 Remind your client
This is a panic attack. They are not going to die. The panic attack is harmless, it will pass and they will be fine.

DISSOCIATION

Dissociation is an adaptive part of the emotional immune system to protect us from traumatic experiences. When traumatic experiences, or memories of them, threaten to overpower your client, dissociating or 'tuning out' is a way to avoid being overwhelmed. To aid survival, dissociation also anaesthetises the intensity of both physical and emotional pain. While not all survivors of abuse dissociate, many do and yet are not always aware that they do. To check whether your client dissociates and how it impacts on them, use the exercise below.

Exercise
Identifying dissociation
Invite your client to ask themselves the following questions in their journal.

- Do you find yourself detaching?

- How frequently and when does this happen?

- Does dissociating concern you or cause you problems?

- Are you extra sensitive to certain topics or abuse related cues?

- What particularly upsets you?

- What are the triggers?

- What are the cues to dissociation?

Your client might also consider keeping a diary of dissociation, like the one for flashbacks, to record the triggers and cues for dissociation and the frequency and duration of dissociative episode.

It is helpful for survivors to begin to identify when they feel spacey, foggy or fuzzy and lose connection to the present, or are engulfed by negative feelings, thoughts and images, or are preoccupied with internal states. They need to learn to distinguish between being present yet not present and when they lose track of time, or 'blank out'. Although they may not be aware of this until afterwards it helps if they can become more conscious of when they avoid inner experiencing. This helps them to restore control over their internal sensations and prevents them from becoming a captive to them. This can help them to feel less vulnerable and enable them to integrate the full range of experiencing into unified, cohesive whole. As the sense of self becomes more cohesive they will feel more stable and in control.

Grounding strategies
As in flashbacks it is vital that your client grounds themselves, using as many sensory cues as they can as soon as they are aware of dissociating. Encourage them to reconnect to their body and the physical world by briskly rubbing their arms or legs, or by planting their feet on the ground. Alternatively advise them to touch or hold something cold such as an ice cold aluminium can or drink, or a packet of frozen peas. Suggest they also put their hand in a bucket of ice, or have a cold shower. Having a hot drink can also help, as long as you advise them to be careful not to burn themselves.

Eating or drinking something with a strong taste or texture such as chilli or lemon will also help to ground your client so that they feel bodily sensation. Alternatively they should eat something they enjoy such as a crunchy apple or something cold such as ice cream, or suck an ice cube. Ask them to notice how it feels as they chew it, or as it melts in their mouths and travels down their throat to their stomach. Remind them to avoid strong coffee or tea as this might increase arousal.

Remind your client to use their grounding smell, or smell something strong such as lemon zest or a strong spice. Reiterate though that the smell they choose should not remind them of the past, or be linked to their traumatic experiences. Energising or uplifting music can make them more alert, as long as it does not remind them of the past. To reduce disconnection from the body, your client could dance or do some light exercises such as sit-ups. Alternatively they can go for a walk or run outside to reorient them in their physical surroundings. If your client has prolonged episodes of dissociation they need to be careful; going outside may not be safe as they could get lost.

 Top tip

Get your client to record their voice on their mobile phone, or MP3 player, or send a voice message to themselves noting the date, their age, where they currently live and the names of family members, partner, children or pets. This will help your client to remember that they are not in the traumatic situation from the past, and that they are safe.

As in flashbacks, your client should look around the room and name each object as they see it. Hearing their voice out loud will help your client to remain connected to the present and increase their awareness of their surroundings. Alternatively, your client could read aloud to themselves, look at and describe their favourite painting or poster, or sing a song from the present day as loud as they possibly can. If possible your client should speak to someone who knows what they are experiencing and can help by talking to them. They can also remind your client of the present time and their location by holding your client's hand, and maintaining eye contact so that they can reconnect to their body.

If your client is sitting down, they should get up and walk into another room, especially if they are feeling paralysed or are out of contact with their external surroundings. Stepping outside for a minute can also help. If safe, your client should go out for a walk, go to a café, or go shopping where there are other people around. As they do this, ask them to make a point of noticing the ordinary things around them to remind themselves that the environment is not threatening. If the room your client is in when they dissociate is dimly lit, they should walk around and turn on all the lights. This is especially good if they get frightened at night.

When your client has reconnected to themselves and the physical world, get them to write down all they can remember about the dissociative episode, including any triggers. They can then keep a record in their journal to help them to monitor the triggers, frequency and duration of dissociative episodes. This can help your client to identify what is making them dissociate and how to manage and control these episodes. Ultimately it can help your client to reduce their frequency so that they remain more grounded in the present.

 Warning
Your client should be safe and should not drive, iron, or operate machinery if they suffer frequent bouts of dissociation. They should also makes sure any young children, pets or dependents are safe.

Medication to reduce dissociative symptoms

There are a number of opiate antagonists such as Naloxone which needs to be injected, or Naltrexone which can be taken orally, which block endorphins and reduce dissociation. While these can help in severe cases it is more beneficial if the survivor can learn and master grounding skills so that they can restore control over dissociative symptoms. This will allow them to accept and regulate their inner experiencing without judgement or splitting off.

13

MANAGING NEGATIVE THOUGHTS AND BELIEFS

We are all vulnerable to negative thoughts and beliefs but these can be inflamed by trauma and heightened anxiety. Being in survival mode can also result in more biased thinking. This makes us more vulnerable to misjudgements that tend to reinforce fears or anxieties and prolong pain and misery.

As biased thinking is often deeply embedded, it is critical for survivors to identify and challenge it to find alternative ways of thinking and to reduce being controlled by it. Survivors also need to understand the impact these thoughts have on them, and replace them with more objective beliefs. This will enable them to improve their self-esteem, their mood and their view of the future.

Distorted thinking usually consists of negative thoughts and beliefs about the self, others, the world, and the future. Sometimes these are so habitual that they become automatic and seem to occur outside awareness. Some negative beliefs are distorted perceptions inserted by the abuser which the survivor could not challenge as a child and therefore they have included them in their belief system. Negative self-beliefs such as 'I am to blame', 'I am bad', 'I am worthless' infect the developing self-identity. This ultimately leads survivors to filter the world through the abuser's eyes, voice and actions. As these become incorporated into the sense of self, survivors may not even be aware of their negative thoughts or how they impact on them.

Negative self-beliefs are reflected in the inner critical voice which constantly undermines survivors and acts as a saboteur, stripping them of self-esteem. They also lead to the false belief that they were to blame for the abuse and thus deserve all the bad things that happen to them. In contrast, negative beliefs about others centre around other people being untrustworthy, rejecting, or potentially abusive. Your clients' negative beliefs about the world focus on the belief that it is hostile and full of danger and disappointment. Such beliefs emphasise their lack of safety and trust which leads to defensive reactions such as disconnection from self and from others and the world. Negative beliefs about the future revolve around beliefs that they will be haunted by the abuse forever.

Distorted beliefs are also seen in the belief that feelings are facts and the more the survivor feels something the more real it must be. For example, because they feel flawed, they feel everyone else will think so too. This can lead them to believe that they will never be able to have a healthy relationship. Left unchallenged, negative beliefs can lead to pervasive anguish, despondency and thoughts of suicide.

 Remind your client
Negative beliefs about themselves may have been inserted by the abuser and do not reflect reality.

HELPING TO CHALLENGING NEGATIVE BELIEFS

To reduce the impact of negative thoughts and beliefs your client needs to recognise them along with any misinterpretations and misjudgements associated with them. Once recognised it will be possible to help them challenge these beliefs by asking them key questions such as: to what extent is your thinking biased? Is there anything to support these biases? What is the evidence against such biases? While this can be hard at first it is worth encouraging them to persevere. Once they have evaluated their negative beliefs, they can begin finding alternative thoughts that are more objective and not coloured by distorted perceptions. To explore any fears about changing beliefs your client needs to consider what the worst is that can happen in adopting new thoughts, and how they would manage these.

With focused practice your client will find it increasingly easier to create more balanced and objective re-statements enabling them to change biased thinking and beliefs to have a more authentic view of themselves. This will permit more realistic and positive self-appraisals which will reduce distress, regulate mood and facilitate healing.

COMMON BIASES IN THINKING

There are a number of common biases in thinking that support negative beliefs and it is worth considering each of these in turn.

All or nothing thinking

This is the tendency to only see extremes rather than the full range of possibilities. For instance the survivor may see themselves as either good or un-redeemably bad, brilliant or a complete failure. All or nothing thinking is usually directed at self-appraisals but can also be applied to others who are often seen as either totally trustworthy or totally untrustworthy, or to situations which are either a complete success or utter failure. Such thinking is self-limiting and increases anxiety and disappointment. Challenging such thinking can allow for a range of possible interpretations, reduce perfectionism and allow for opportunities for change.

Over-generalisation

Over-generalisation is when we draw conclusions based on isolated events and apply these to a wide range of situations. A common example of this is seeing one negative event as an indication of everything being negative and assuming that outcomes will always be negative. This is particularly seen in a survivor's false belief that because they were abused by a man all men are abusers and not to be trusted. This can undermine their trust in men and prevent them from having a healthy relationship with a man.

Mislabelling

Another form of over-generalisation is mislabelling which is the tendency to create a totally negative image on the basis of one single, minor deficiency. Thus one minor flaw or attribute is used to totally negate the whole person, or self. Linked to this is catastrophisation which is the tendency to predict and expect the very worst in any one situation based on one minor difficulty. While this is primarily used to prepare for the worst possible scenario to avoid disappointment, it leads to increased and unwarranted anxiety and worry.

Mental filtering

Another common thinking bias is mental filtering in which positive aspects of a situation are filtered out leaving no choice but to dwell exclusively on negative aspects. Filtering out all positive experiences, thoughts and feelings keep you locked into a spiral of negativity from which there seems to be no escape. This can lead to a very negative view of change and a better future.

Alongside mental filtering is disqualifying the positive in which a positive aspect of self, others or a situation is downgraded, rejected or dismissed as unimportant. This is often seen when you transform positive experiences or feelings into something negative, leading to distorted beliefs despite contradictory evidence.

Another aspect of mental filtering is magnification and minimisation in which negative events are exaggerated in importance and positive events are underestimated. In magnification survivors might exaggerate mistakes and deficiencies totally out of proportion to reality. With minimisation they play down positive attributes leading to negative self-image as the positive is always cancelled out.

Minimisation is also seen when survivors try to reduce the impact and effects of trauma by maintaining that the abuse was not that bad and had no negative effect. Such denial serves an important function in enabling them to manage the trauma experiences without having to work through them.

Jumping to conclusions

This is another common example of distorted thinking in which negative conclusions are drawn which are not justified by the facts. A common example is 'Because I feel ashamed and blame myself for the abuse, everyone will also blame me'. Two commonly associated aspects of jumping to conclusions are mind-reading and fortune telling.

Mind-reading

While mind-reading is in part a protective mechanism developed in childhood designed to predict the abuser's thoughts, feelings or behaviour, it is not always accurate. It tends to always assume negative reactions due to the heightened alarm setting. In addition, when survivors mind read they come out of their own frame of reference and enter the other person's. This further reduces the opportunity to monitor the full range of feelings or thoughts.

Fortune telling is a form of mind-reading in which we believe that we can predict all future outcomes. This is rarely based on objective evidence but is primarily driven by fear and projection. It is a form of 'psyching' oneself up for the worst case scenario so as not to be disappointed or to be prepared for the worst possible threat. This is an understandable defence mechanism which aims to predict and thereby control behaviour and outcome.

Emotional reasoning

Due to the intensity of their emotions survivors can be driven by emotional reasoning in which they assume that feelings are facts and an accurate reflection of reality and truth. This is based on a common assumption that the more intensely or vividly something is felt the more real it is. In the same way that thinking can be distorted, so can feelings, especially when your alarm system is constantly on high alert. Common examples of this are assuming that if they feel bad they must be bad, or because they feel guilty they must be guilty.

 Remind your client
Feelings are signals from the body and not necessarily facts.

Emotional reasoning can lead to personalisation in which survivors assume responsibility when there is none. A classic example is assuming that because they experienced an erection or an orgasm during the sexual abuse they must have wanted it. It is also seen in taking things very personally in assuming that bad or unpleasant experiences are specifically directed at them and must be their fault. Thus, if a situation doesn't go well it must be because of something they did or didn't do and they deserve to be punished.

Seeing themselves as the cause of bad events, and the belief that they deserve punishment, further fuels survivors' self-blame and self-criticism. They take responsibility for things that really are not their fault. Self-criticism is fuelled by a harsh, internal self-critic who labels them as 'useless' or 'stupid', or calls them names. Such name-calling may reflect criticism and negative beliefs inserted by the abuser which sabotaged the development of a more positive self-image. In combination, these all serve to maintain an already poor self-image.

Perfectionism

To compensate for any perceived flaws survivors may impose unrealistic expectations on themselves and become perfectionist in their thinking and behaviour. This is reflected in 'should' statements of how they should or ought to be or behave. As these expectations and criteria are unrealistic and virtually impossible to achieve these strivings are destined to failure. This in turn leads to a sense of failure, and even more guilt and self-criticism. This fuels low self-esteem rather than focusing on realistic and achievable ways of creating change.

Often survivors also have high expectations of others that are impossible to achieve, leading to a repetitive cycle of being disappointed in them. This confirms the belief that others will always let them down and cannot be trusted, leading to disconnection from others and further isolation and loneliness.

As can be seen negative thoughts and beliefs can have a huge impact on self-esteem and create obstacles to recovery and healing. To help your client identify their negative thoughts and beliefs give them the following exercise to reappraise their thoughts and find more accurate alternatives.

Exercise
Negative thoughts and alternatives

Explore the range of negative thoughts and beliefs presented above with your client and ask them to highlight which ones apply to them. Get them to list these in their journal along with an example of each negative thought or belief. Next try to identify with them any biases in their thinking and beliefs and how these shape their thinking and behaviour. Once they have identified biased thinking you can begin to help them challenge this by asking themselves 'Is there any evidence to support this thought or belief?' and 'What is the evidence that does not support this thought or belief?' As they write down the evidence for and against negative thoughts or beliefs begin to discuss alternative ways of thinking.

Next, encourage your client to write down any alternative thoughts or beliefs which more accurately reflect reality. Before putting these into practice and testing them make sure they ask themselves 'What is the worst that can happen if I adopt this alternative thought or belief?' and 'How would I cope if the worst happened?' By exploring their fears around changing negative thinking they should be able to anticipate obstacles and prepare for the management of alternative thoughts. Ensure that they take time to do this for each negative thought and belief and remind them to pace themselves when testing out alternative thoughts.

REAPPRAISING THOUGHTS

Over time your client will find that they are able to reappraise old patterns of thinking and beliefs, as well as new situations and experiences. They will also be able to check their thoughts for any biases more easily. This should enable them to navigate the world with more realistic appraisals and not be restricted by negative biases that serve to undermine their self-esteem and self-worth.

To support the reappraisal of biased thinking and beliefs your client needs to develop greater self-compassion and self-forgiveness. To facilitate this get them to see what happened to them through a child's eyes rather than filtering it through an adult perspective. In developing compassion for themselves they will be able to access empathy for the child they were. They will recognise that they were not responsible for their abuse and had no choice in their reactions and behaviour.

This reappraisal will help to minimise self-blame, guilt and shame by helping them recognise that their reactions were normal within the context of being abused. They will be able to forgive themselves and begin to let go of self-criticism and negative self-beliefs and thoughts. It will also allow them to redistribute responsibility for the abuse and reduce the tendency to take responsibility unnecessarily. This should free them up to only take responsibility for what is truly theirs.

Top tip

To help your client develop compassion for themselves try to make them see the abuse through the child's eyes rather than filtering it through an adult perspective.

Ultimately, identifying and reappraising negative thoughts and beliefs will enable survivors to take more control and remove obstacles to their recovery. They will begin to reconnect to themselves and others in a more authentic way, reduce distortion of reality and begin to accept who they truly are.

14

MANAGING
FRAGMENTED MEMORIES

Many survivors of complex trauma and abuse have unclear or fragmented memories of their abuse. Sometimes these are fleeting images, sounds or smells which lack context and sequential narrative or are detached from any meaning. The degree of memory recall will vary from person to person. Thus your client could have only partial memories, no memories at all, or full recall.

The overwhelming nature of abuse can make it hard to process the experience and integrate it into the memory system. If it is accompanied by dissociation or avoidance it may be even harder to store the experience. As a result the memories are stored and remain 'on line' at the same intensity as when first experienced. This can result in flashbacks, intrusive memories or nightmares.

 Remind your client
Experiences and memories that are suppressed are twice as likely to resurface.

HOW MUCH DO SURVIVORS NEED TO REMEMBER?
There is considerable debate about to what extent it is necessary to recall all memories. Focusing on full memory recall can create more pressure on your client. It is important that they have a choice as to what extent they want to recover memories. The dynamic nature of memory will limit full recall of every experience and event. Only your client can decide how much detail they wish to remember. Do not let them become pressurised either by you, themselves or other professionals.

Only your client can decide when they have enough memories to validate their experiences and work on processing them. They need to avoid searching for something that it may not be possible to recover.

Delving into past memories is only worthwhile if there is something to be gained, and must be paced to suit their stage of recovery. If your client has quite clear memories, although distressing ones, then it may not be the best use of their resources to continue to probe. Over-processing does not necessarily generate any real benefits.

If your client's memories are fragmented or sketchy and they want to improve recall then it makes sense to do some memory work to flesh these out. If, however, retrieving memories always destabilises, it might be better to leave memory work until later in their recovery.

If your client suffers from intrusive memories, flashbacks or nightmares which consistently make them feel worse, then it will help to process these. However, they will need to ensure they have mastered some of the grounding techniques and are more able to regulate their reactions.

If your client has no memories at all but senses that something may have happened, do not let them focus exclusively on searching for abuse memories. Doing so could lead to fabrication and leave them vulnerable to false memories. Try to keep them in the present and this will allow memories to emerge gradually rather than delving as this can have severe consequences. Do not try to persuade your client or let them be persuaded by others, including other professionals, that they must probe and find evidence through memories as this can be fraught with problems.

Warning
Work with the memories your client has rather than delve and risk false memories.

To help your client decide, they need to reflect on their goals for recalling memories. The exercise below can help you in this.

Exercise
Reflection on goals for memory recall
Encourage your client to take some time to reflect on their goals for recalling memories. Are they are plagued by intrusive memories, flashbacks and nightmares? Does your client want to improve the quality of their life? Do they need your confirmation of abuse? If so then processing and integrating memories may be invaluable as long as they do it at a pace that suits them.

THE DANGER OF OVER-PROCESSING MEMORIES

If your client already has clear memories and is not haunted by unprocessed memories, then it may not be necessary. Over-processing memories can lead to elaborated, distorted, and inaccurate memories which can result in further difficulties. If your client is searching for memories to gain clarity or make sense of their experiences then memory work will be beneficial. Try to ensure they avoid focusing on 100 per cent recall as this may not be possible to achieve.

It is worth noting that memories are not the only source of validation of abuse. If your client wants to recall memories to confirm their experience then you may need to help them set a limit on how much it is necessary to remember rather than keep searching. Memory recall is not always the best, or only, source of validation of abuse. Advise your client to seek out additional sources, such as others who have been abused by the same person. This is often the case in institutional abuse or clerical abuse. Remind your client that they need to trust themselves rather than trying to search for evidence to convince others.

 Remind your client
The dynamic nature of memory means that they may not be able to restore full memory so they need to set a gauge that is 'good enough' for them that validates their experiences.

Pressure to recall memories can risk a sense of failure and promote self-suggestion. In addition, pressure from others can lead to potential false memories. To prevent this it is critical that your client takes the pressure off and does not try to recall too hard. They need to allow memories to emerge when they are ready to manage them. Most importantly, remind your client that memory is subjective and dynamic and that we do not store or recall memories like a video recording. Commonly memory provides a general sense of what happened. This means it is often imperfect and contains gaps in the details, which we naturally try to fill to create a narrative.

THE RELIABILITY OF MEMORY

The reliability of memory is largely accurate but can be distorted or elaborated due to our attempts to gain meaning and fill in gaps. This is more likely if the memories are fuzzy or there are large pieces missing.

It is also more likely if your client has been taught to doubt their memory through denial or minimisation of the abuse.

Denial and minimisation can lead to having no recollection of the abuse at all, which is technically a false memory if abuse has occurred. Equally rehearsing, imagining, self-suggestion or suggestion by others can also lead to distortions and strengthen the imagined memory and risk of false memories. In addition, lack of detail does not invalidate memory either. It is much better to work with the content of what is recalled, even if these are embedded in intrusive memories, flashbacks or nightmares. Remind your client that these all represent unprocessed memories which signal parts of their experiences that need attention to be processed and integrated into their memory system.

The content of flashbacks and nightmares contains fragmented, partial or elaborated memories of survivor experiences which trigger the same physiological responses as when the trauma occurred. This is why they are so vivid and the survivor feels like they are re-experiencing the trauma. When survivors avoid them they remain more 'alive' demanding even more attention.

MANAGING AND PROCESSING MEMORIES

To manage and process memories your client will need to identify the content of any recollections and keep a record of these. This will be difficult if the content is intrusive and overwhelming, and they may need to leave in-depth memory work until some way into the recovery process. It is more effective to do this when they have mastered grounding skills and are more able to regulate their reactions. It is also more helpful to try to process memories when calm and relaxed rather than overwrought. Integration of memories is a process that persists throughout your client's recovery journey and is best when they feel more in control of their trauma reactions.

One effective way of processing traumatic memories is through EMDR. This can only be done with a practitioner who has been specially trained in this technique. This method helps to process the traumatic experiences through rapid eye movement and can reduce the intensity of feelings attached to the traumatic memory. While EMDR can be hugely beneficial, some survivors may wish to process memories using more conventional techniques. Advise your client of this technique and where they might find a practitioner, but determine which technique they feel most comfortable with. Remind them that it is important that they choose what is best for them.

CUES TO AID MEMORY RECALL

If your client has no memories of abuse they could try to recall other aspects of their life at that time. Ask them to remember a typical day and try to recall a day in their life around that time. Suggest that they might think about who woke them up, got them dressed, and took them to school. Get them to make a list of their friends and teachers at school, and their favourite lessons. Who picked them up from school, gave them tea, and got them ready for bed? Such everyday memories can help them to recall other associated memories.

Photographs of your client before, during and after the abuse can also aid memory recall. Ask them to put these into an album alongside photographs of family members, friends and the abuser, if they have any. Such visual cues can be quite powerful in helping them to recall memories and feelings that they felt at that time.

Drawing their childhood home can also aid your client's memory recall. Suggest they draw the house or flat in which they lived at the time of the abuse, including floor plans of the rooms and the layout of the room in which they were most often abused. Get them to include as many things as they can such as how the furniture was arranged, where windows and doors were, the colour scheme and any associated smells or feelings.

If your client visits the home and neighbourhood in which they lived when they were abused, this can also be a powerful aid to memory recall. As this can be potentially distressing it is helpful if they have someone they trust with them should they feel overwhelmed.

In combination these can all aid memory recall but they may need to be explored over time. Remind your client that the memories may not return in a rush but emerge gradually when they are ready to tolerate them. They might also recur through dreams or as flashbacks. Advise your client to view these as signals that a memory is returning that needs to be processed.

Warning

Forcing memory recall can cause additional problems such as a sense of a failure or guilt, or distorted or inaccurate memories.

Assessing whether, and to what extent, your client wishes to restore memory will mean exploring whether they want to have full, detailed memories. Is your client happy to have general memories that are 'good enough', do they need full recall or do they prefer not to delve into memories at all? Alternatively they might wish to put any memory work on hold for the moment and reassess at a later point when stability has improved.

 Exercise
Is memory work right for me?
To assess whether memory work is suitable for your client, get them to make a list of the advantages and disadvantages. This list of advantages might include their desire to improve the quality of their life by reducing intrusive memories, flashbacks or nightmares; to feel more in control; to undo the freeze response and release trapped energy; to clarify what happened; to give meaning to their experiences; to legitimise what happened; to change the way they think about themselves; to reduce self-blame; to understand the impact of abuse and trauma; or to restore reality and perception. Their list of disadvantages might include a decrease in quality of life; destabilisation if they cannot remember; a sense of failure or shame; or feelings of being paralysed or trapped by their need to remember. Ask your client to add any other advantages and disadvantages they can think of. Reflect on these with them to help them decide and continue.

PACING MEMORY WORK

Before starting memory work you need to assess your client's level of functioning to ensure that they will be able to regulate their feelings. It helps to review their list of triggers of flashbacks with them and then get them to make one for intrusive memories. It is also wise for them to avoid some of the most distressing triggers until they feel more in control of their reactions. Effective memory processing should proceed at a manageable pace for your client so they feel in control. It is best to work towards memory processing gradually when your client is calm and stable, and to reflect on their progress. If the memory work is too fast, or conducted during crisis points, it will become overwhelming and can increase post-traumatic reactions.

Whenever your client focuses on recalling a memory make sure they have a block of uninterrupted time to really engage in the process. Ensure that they do not rush this and allow themselves time to do this over several days. Also remind them to treat themselves to a reward afterwards.

RECORDING MEMORIES

As memories return ask your client to write down the general points rather than the details of the memory. If writing is difficult for them, ask them to find another way to record it such as painting or drawing, making a collage or sculpture, writing a song or poem that encapsulates the memory, or making an audio recording. Once the initial impression has been recorded, revisit the memory with your client to include more details, including as many sensory cues as possible.

Get your client to try to recall what they saw, sensed, smelt, heard, touched or tasted during the experience and their body position. Include the sequence of events, what happened, what they were doing and thinking, their reactions, their feelings and their physical sensations. They should reflect on what the experience meant to them, what the worst bit was, how it impacted on them then and their life since, and how it has changed them. They need to allow themselves to experience feelings and sensations without judgement. Consider the hardest part of the experience to get used to. What are they not able to do anymore and where are they stuck?

PROCESSING MEMORIES

As your client revisits the memory, more details will emerge which can be added into their account. Remind your client that every time they read, look at or listen to it and make amendments they are processing the memory and integrating it. This will help them to gain meaning and reduce flashbacks, nightmares and intrusive memories. When your client is happy with their account ask them to discuss the memory with someone they trust – you or a trusted other – and make any changes. Once they have an account that they are satisfied with, ask them to revisit it with self-compassion and empathy to allow the full range of their emotions to emerge without judgement. They may wish to put their account somewhere safe to look at whenever they need to.

 Warning
Don't force your client's memory, or let them force themselves. Advise them to stop if they feel overwhelmed. Get them to ground themselves and revisit the memory at a later point.

If despite such focused memory work no memories of abuse or trauma are recalled, or they remain fragmented or patchy, then you will need to help your client to work on tolerating uncertainty and encourage them to rely on what they do know. They should use their body as a resource and store of memory, rather than pursuing the quest for perfect memory recall.

HYPNOSIS

Your client may feel tempted to undergo hypnosis to help memory recall. While this can be helpful, there is no guarantee that recalling memories under hypnosis will be any more accurate than if recalled without hypnosis. If they do want to try hypnosis make sure you help them find a reputable practitioner who also has therapeutic experience and who can provide emotional support as memories return.

 Remind your client
Only they can choose to what extent they wish to engage in memory processing. Do not be influenced by others, including professionals.

DRUGS THAT BLOCK MEMORIES

There has been considerable research into developing drugs that can block memories at a biochemical level, which can be administered either pre- or post-trauma. While drugs designed to eradicate traumatic memories sound highly desirable it is vital that you inform your client that currently their effects are only partial and may not work for each individual.

More importantly they may have a negative effect as blocking memories which signal that something is wrong will prevent emotional processing. These drugs will merely block the memory without helping survivors to process their abuse experience. As such they may be most helpful in the short term to block intrusive memories until emotional regulation is mastered.

You will need to remind your client drugs that blocking memories will not integrate their experiences which could result in lack of continuity and confusion. Ultimately this could interfere with the recovery process and the potential for post-traumatic growth in which your client can truly triumph over trauma.

15

MANAGING SHAME, GUILT AND SELF-BLAME

Shame is like a virus that infects the soul and is a core symptom in complex trauma, albeit largely outside of conscious awareness. It is often entwined with guilt and self-blame and as it has no direct channel for release is experienced as profoundly paralysing. Unlike sadness which can be released through crying, or anger which can be discharged through physical exercise, shame remains trapped in the body. Furthermore, as shame is a social emotion it is difficult to talk about for both survivor and counsellor despite its pervasive quality in the therapeutic space. Practitioners need to understand shame and its impact even if the survivor cannot express or verbalise it and make sure that it does not become the elephant in the room. This chapter will explore the function of shame in complex trauma, how it impacts on the survivor and practitioner, its link to dissociation and how it can be released.

THE FUNCTION OF SHAME

Shame is a necessary survival trait as it alerts us to the fact that something is wrong about an experience or behaviour. It also acts as a prompt to seek help. Shame also guides behaviour so that we do not hurt others or ourselves, which aids living in groups to ensure social cohesion (Sanderson, 2010a). It is useful to distinguish between healthy shame which promotes good behaviour, supports values and the development of conscience, and traumatic or chronic shame which is a toxic infection that pervades the core being of an individual. Healthy shame allows for the development of morality and ethical values and is a positive influence in shaping self-identity as a good and valued member of a group. In contrast, traumatic or chronic shame is destructive as it attacks the self as being flawed, defective and unworthy of love or life. This can lead to a crippling sense of fear and vulnerability making the survivor withdraw and hide from others. So although 'Everyone needs a sense of shame, no one needs to feel ashamed' (Nietszche, 1886).

A further distinction needs to be made between guilt and shame. Guilt is much more conscious that shame, and is usually focused on a transgression rather than the whole self. In guilt the individual is ashamed of their actions or behaviour which motivates reparative responses such as an apology, confession or restitution. It is often accompanied by a sense of remorse or regret, or a fear of punishment. The advantage of guilt is that it allows for the expression of regret and making amends and does not necessarily affect the core identity.

This is in contrast to shame which threatens the individual's core identity and very existence. Although shame is largely unconscious or dissociated, it is pervasive in radiating a sense of failure or defeat in which the whole self feels wrong. It is often accompanied by a chronic feeling of being 'less than' and the impossibility of making amends. Unlike guilt, there is no direct channel for the release of shame and the only reparation is total negation of the self, and this can feel like a life sentence from which there is no respite or escape.

The inner experience of shame can be induced and reinforced by others through humiliation, rejection and blame. It can also arise in the presence of 'shameless acts' in which the perpetrator has 'split off' any feelings of shame which are then absorbed by the victim. Thus many survivors of complex trauma carry not only their own shame but also the shame of the abuser. This intensifies the sense of guilt, self-blame and responsibility for the abuse. Practitioners will need to enable survivors to separate their own shame from that of the abuser and others who have betrayed them. This can be difficult as talking about and working with shame can elicit your own experience of shame, which can impact on a therapeutic relationship. As the expression of shame can lead to embarrassment and awkwardness many practitioners may unconsciously avoid talking about shame and prevent the survivor from exploring one of the central components of their trauma. To ensure that the survivors' shame can be fully explored, practitioners need to explore their own sense of shame. To do this it might be helpful to carry out the exercise below.

Exercise
Counsellor awareness exercise: own experience of shame

- On a sheet of paper make a list of your experiences of shame in the past and present.

- Reflect on how these experiences affected how you feel about yourself, your body, and your sexuality.

- Next reflect on how this has impacted on your behaviour, how you relate to others, and beliefs about yourself.

- Make a list of what triggers your sense of shame in the present and how you manage this.

COMPONENTS OF SHAME

Shame is like a virus that invades and infects the psyche in which the central conflict is between '... the attempt to suppress the self and the wish to express the self' (Mollon, 1993, p.45). As a result survivors oscillate between the need for invisibility to protect themselves from further abuse or humiliation and the need to be seen to validate their existence. Not being seen can lead to existential angst and annihilation of the self yet visibility can lead to annihilation by others. This unbearable paradox is reminiscent of the freeze response during the trauma and has the same paralysing effect. Moreover, although the shame is initially induced in the presence of others it continues to persist as it forms an internal image of defectiveness and negative beliefs about the self.

Remember
A recurring conflict in shame is the need to be visible and the need to be invisible. This paradox of needing to be seen, and needing to withdraw from others is paralysing. The shame is further reinforced by negative, shame-based beliefs such as 'I am a bad or shameful person' or 'I am a mistake' or 'I am less than'.

As there is no channel through which to release shame, unlike sadness which can be released through tears, or anger which can be released through physical action, survivors become more vulnerable to dissociative states to numb the pervasive existential angst. The terror of being further exposed to shame and humiliation leads to the chronic avoidance of others thus reinforcing alienation and traumatic loneliness. As the survivor fears being judged, humiliated and shamed it is critical that practitioners provide an empathic therapeutic setting in which the survivor can reveal themselves without fear of being judged or shamed.

SHAME AND SELF-BLAME IN COMPLEX TRAUMA

Shame in complex trauma commonly centres on self-blame for not stopping or preventing the abuse, becoming sexually aroused and for going back to the abuser. It is critical that survivors come to understand that they were not able to stop the abuse, and that just because their body responded that does not mean that they invited the sexual abuse. They also need to have a full understanding of traumatic bonding and how this results in having to stay in relation to the abuser and that this is enacted not to be abused but for protection.

As the survivor explores their shame they will also begin to identify areas of self-blame. Like shame, it is important to recognise what they blame themselves for. If they blame themselves for not fighting back, or submitting to the abuse, it is vital that you challenge this and remind them that freezing is a normal reaction to overwhelming trauma. If the survivor blames him or herself for approaching the abuser, you will need to remind them that they did this to satisfy their need for human contact and connection NOT to be sexually abused. In addition, the client may have gone back to the abuser to have some control and predictability over the abuse. Approaching the abuser is a survival strategy that makes the abuse more predictable to enable the survivor to prepare and plan for the assault. This is a way for the client to protect themselves, which makes them feel less vulnerable. Similarly, reiterate to the client that if they were aroused, had an erection or orgasm during the abuse this does not mean they wanted to be sexually abused and that they are not to blame.

Remind your client

If they felt aroused or experienced pleasure or orgasm during the abuse this does not mean they wanted to be sexually abused. It is simply that their body responded naturally in the presence of certain sexual touch.

Self-blame can sometimes be used as a way of reducing feelings of helplessness. When the client blames themselves they can feel more power and control over the abuse, rather than feeling helpless. While this power is illusory it does help them to feel less overwhelmed. It also helps them to feel more hopeful of the future. If the survivor takes on some of the blame then that means in the future, providing they can alter their behaviour, they will be able to avoid being abused. While such thoughts and feelings protect the client from feeling helpless, they come at a cost as the toxic effects of self-blame increase the sense of shame and self-loathing. To reduce self-blame survivors find it useful to explore how and for what they blame themselves.

 Exercise
Reducing survivor self-blame

- Invite your client to make a list in their journal of how they blame themselves, and what they blame themselves for.

- Encourage the survivor to reflect on these and evaluate them by reminding them that they were a child and had no choice but to submit.

- Remind your client that their size and age would have prevented them from fighting or fleeing, leaving them no option but to freeze. They also had no knowledge or information of how to stop the abuse, or their responses to it.

- Invite your client to make a list of significant others who had a responsibility to them and who let them down. These others will need to bear some blame for not protecting them.

INDICATORS OF SHAME

To understand how self-blame and shame have impacted on the survivor you will need to identify the ways in which their shame manifests.

 Exercise
Identifying shame

- To understand how shame has impacted on your client, get them to make a list in their journal of how shame has affected them.

- The list should include how they feel about themselves and their body and how they feel in relation to others.

- Encourage them to think about how shame has affected their beliefs about themselves and how these have restricted their relationships with others, including their sexuality.

- This will help you guide them in identifying how shame has impacted on their sense of self.

Once the survivor has identified how they see shame has affected them it might be useful to compare these to the common indicators of shame.

This is particularly useful as much shame is unconscious and it will help to identify other emotional reactions, behavioural responses or cognitive appraisals (see Box 15.1).

Box 15.1 Indicators of shame

EMOTIONAL

- Fear
- Anger
- Disgust
- Contempt
- Fear of failure
- Self-hatred
- Envy
- Lack of empathy or compassion
- Avoidance of inner experiencing
- Repudiation of needs, vulnerability, dependency

BEHAVIOURAL

- Self-attack
- Attack others
- Hostility
- Withdrawal
- Invisibility
- Concealment
- Compensation – grandiosity, narcissism
- Submissive NVC
- Shame-lessness
- Secrecy
- Self-sufficiency

COGNITIVE

- Cognitive appraisal
- Negative self evaluation and other evaluation
- Self-denigration
- Construction of idealistic self-image
- Self-blame
- Social comparison
- Failure or falling short of standards
- Self-criticism

These indicators can be used by practitioners to get a sense of how shame has impacted on each individual survivor and what needs to be explored in order to release shame. In addition, it is useful to identify the focus of survivors' shame. This is commonly not only on the self and self-identity, but also on the body both in terms of control and the body in action as well as achievement failure and relationship dynamics (see Box 15.2).

Box 15.2 The focus of shame (adapted from Sanderson, 2010a)

- The self – self-identity, dehumanisation, self-loathing, inauthentic self
- The body – perfection, total control, or disfigurement, BDD
- The body in action – performance, conversation, social performance, eating
- Achievement failure – reaching certain standards, reduce expectation, make invisible
- Relational/relationships – disconnection, isolation, attractiveness (including associates)
- Affect – feelings of vulnerability, anxiety, contempt, excitement, anger, envy, neediness, dependency
- Group shame – source of racism, sexism, prejudice, honour killings, desire for revenge, stigma, stigmatisation

Shame attacks the very core of our being and threatens to destroy our self-identity through self-loathing. Survivors often describe intense feelings of self-hatred, a lack of dignity or honour, and state that they feel like 'damaged goods' or that they are so flawed that others will be repulsed by them. Ultimately many survivors feel as though they have no right to exist. This will increase the survivors' neediness and dependency on others to value them and support their self-esteem, which further reinforces a sense of shame.

Survivors of complex trauma also report that shame affects how they feel about their bodies (Sanderson, 2010a). Commonly they feel that their bodies have betrayed them, or see them as an object of scorn, which results in a feeling of revulsion and dislike of the body. This can lead to believing that the body is defective, or body dysmorphic disorder (BDD). To manage this body shame survivors often go to great lengths to cover up by hiding their bodies in shapeless clothing. Alternatively, some survivors display their body in sexually provocative ways to 'prove' that their body is attractive.

To try to reduce body shame, some survivors exercise excessively to re-sculpt their body or seek perfection through extreme cosmetic surgery. Male survivors may body build and use steroids to get the perfect physique, or to look stronger. Alternatively, survivors punish themselves with deliberate disfigurement, perhaps by starving themselves or gaining vast quantities of weight to hide behind. Shame can also lead to a denial of the body or any bodily pleasures, leading to sexual shame, making it hard to enter into intimate relationships.

The extreme self-consciousness associated with shame can also manifest in ordinary social situations. Hence many survivors feel extremely uncomfortable eating or drinking in the presence of others, or fear drawing attention to themselves in public which can lead to social phobia. As the survivor's default setting is that they are defective and a failure, they must therefore hide from others at all costs. This sense of failure prevents them from achieving a basic standard of acceptance, and reduces expectations of themselves or their lives.

DEFENCE STRATEGIES IN SHAME

Given the psychic devastation ubiquitous in shame, survivors engage in a range of protective strategies in relation to self and others. These are enacted both outside of the therapeutic setting and within the therapeutic relationship. Nathanson (1992) identifies four primary shame scripts which are used as defence strategies. These are focused on 'self-attack' strategies in which the survivor attacks the self through self-criticism, self-sabotage and self-destructive behaviours and 'attacking others' strategies which consist of aggression, humiliation and the shaming of others. In addition, survivors will use 'withdrawal strategies' in which they withdraw from others by making themselves invisible both physically and psychologically alongside 'avoidance of inner experiencing' such as dissociation to numb, unbearable internal states and developing a false self to mask and hide their shame (see Box 15.3).

Box 15.3 Defence strategies in shame (adapted from Nathanson, 1992)

SELF-ATTACK

- Turn anger, contempt, revulsion and disgust inward
- Accept negative beliefs about self without evaluation or reflection
- Inner belittlement, threats, self criticism
- Heightened awareness of all things done wrong – failures, faults, negative characteristics
- Self-harm, self-medication
- Deflection
- Dissociate from own shame

ATTACK OF OTHERS

- Project shame on to others to assuage own shame
- Anger, disgust or contempt directed away from self to others
- Externalise shame onto other to make self-superior and the other inferior (much like the abuser).
- Can be verbal or physical
- 'Triumph over trauma'
- Usually not conscious and lack of awareness of own shame

WITHDRAWAL FROM OTHERS

- Ensure others will not get close
- Renders self invisible
- Avoid being exposed to further shame or seen to have shame
- Limits shameful exposure – people, social situations, eating, new experiences
- Heightened awareness of discomfort with others, any shameful actions, faults, flaws, failures

---

- Preoccupation with assumed negative reaction from others
- Unconscious
- Traumatic loneliness which reinforces shame

As these defence strategies can manifest in the therapeutic setting, counsellors need to ensure that they provide a safe environment to work through shame. It is critical that practitioners avoid re-shaming the survivor no matter how provocative he or she may be. This is part of testing the counsellor to ensure that they are truly safe to be authentic. Counsellors need to acknowledge the survivor's needs and vulnerability and understand the function of these defensive strategies. The expression of rage, grandiosity and arrogance is a cover for the deep hurt and narcissistic wounds and are designed to keep the practitioner at a distance. In addition, fierce self-sufficiency and the repudiation of needs and vulnerability are ways of avoiding dependency and intimacy and must not be personalised.

Box 15.3 *cont.*

AVOIDANCE OF INNER EXPERIENCING

- Dissociation from feelings of shame or thoughts that may evoke shame
- Disowning shame
- Distraction from painful feelings through self-medication or self-harm, or seeking joy or excitement
- Minimise the conscious experience of shame to prove that shame is not felt by acting in a 'shameless' way

---

MANAGING SHAME IN THE COUNSELLING PROCESS

To manage shame in the counselling process, you will need to help the survivor to name and identify shame (see Box 15.2) and be aware of how this manifests in the therapeutic relationship, including power dynamics that can elicit shame. This is best done by understanding the defence strategies used in shame, and acknowledging that these are protective strategies to avoid further shame. It is crucial that you remain connected, empathic and compassionate and avoid becoming defensive, especially in the presence of narcissistic rage, hostility, or projected shame. You will need to ensure that when shame is elicited in you or your own rage is triggered, this is not acted out and that you do not re-shame the survivor. This can be re-traumatising and will reinforce the survivor's sense of shame and inferiority. If shame is evoked in you it is critical that you are able to identify and acknowledge this and work through this in supervision.

Top tip
Do not personalise attack strategies used in shame but understand them as a protective strategy.

HELPFUL THERAPEUTIC STRATEGIES

You need to be mindful at all times to acknowledge and articulate the survivor's experience of shame from an empathic and compassionate position. This involves mirroring in a non-shaming way and listening without judgement. You will need to remain sensitively attuned and offer understanding and encouragement with warmth and human responses. In being sensitive to the survivor's shame you will find it easier to connect to the survivor. This is essential as the antidote to shame is connection to others. In providing a human relationship that is genuinely caring and sensitively attuned it is possible to reverse the dehumanisation associated with interpersonal abuse. Sharing shame and becoming visible is a powerful way to release the survivor from their prison of shame.

Once the survivor is able to connect and becomes more visible you will be able to reframe the survivor's experience of shame. This will allow you to reduce self blame and cultivate self-acceptance and reduce the need for perfectionism mistakes. You can help the survivor to see that no one is perfect and that we all make mistakes. This will enable them to see that it takes courage to make mistakes and that these are an essential part of learning, creativity and curiosity. In addition, being present and accepting of the survivor enables them to develop compassion and empathy for self which allows them to openly express their needs and vulnerability without fear of ridicule.

A good starting point for working with shame is to invite the survivor to explore their experience of shame. It might be easier to do that using a recent event or situation rather than during the abuse so that it is not too overwhelming.

Exercise
Coping with shame

1. Invite the survivor to describe an event or situation in the present in which they felt shame.

2. Ask the survivor to list the thought(s) or beliefs they had during the felt sense of shame.

3. Invite the survivor to describe the physical sensations that they experienced when they felt ashamed (hot, cold, shaking, frozen, collapsed, holding your breath, feeling shutdown, tingly, rigid, butterflies in stomach, etc.).

4. Next encourage the survivor to write down some of the thoughts, negative self-belief and negative self-talk associated with the felt sense of shame. Together reflect on these and critically evaluate and challenge them. It is helpful to remind the survivor these beliefs and values were imposed by the abuser and are not an accurate reflection of who they are. Next, encourage the survivor to change this cognitive distortion by re-writing each of the negative self-beliefs and unwanted shame identities. A good example is, 'It is important to me to be perceived as _____ and I do not want to be perceived as_____.' This will enable the survivor to develop their own self-concept rather than be defined by external forces.

5. Next invite the survivor to make a list of any specific triggers they are aware of that evoke a felt sense of shame.

6. In reflecting on this exercise try to identify which of the four defence strategies (attack self, attack other, withdrawal/isolation, avoidance of inner experience) they tend to use when feeling ashamed.

7. Finally, to counterbalance the sense of shame, invite the survivor to make a list of some experiences in which they felt a healthy sense of pride, achievement, or accomplishment. Encourage them to write these down in their journal and to reflect on these.

As the survivor becomes more comfortable exploring shame, you can begin to look at the shame they experienced during the abuse. The exercise above can be used and modified for the range or experiences associated with the abuse so that the survivor can begin to separate out their shame and the shame that belongs to the abuser. It is important to remind them that the shame in abuse lies solely with the abuser and that because the abuser felt no shame, they had no choice but to take on the shame he or she should have felt.

Remind your client
The shame of their abuse is not their shame but the abuser's shame that they have taken on.

By taking on the abuser's shame, the survivor increases any shame they might have felt during the abuse. Many survivors experience shame for submitting to the abuse, for not telling someone about it, or for having an erection or becoming aroused during the abuse. Whatever the reason(s) for their shame, it is important for the survivor to recognise that responsibility still lies with the abuser for abusing them. Remind them that they had no choice or control over their reactions while being abused. In addition, the abuser may have deliberately ensured that the survivor felt pleasure so that they would feel too ashamed to tell. When you combine this with taking on their abuser's shame, it is not surprising that the survivors sense of shame is increased, making it even more crippling. This is why it is vital to help them to redirect their shame where it belongs: onto the abuser rather than themselves.

Exercise
Distributing shame

1. To help your client separate the shame they feel for themselves and their abuser, ask them to make two columns in their journal. Column one is for the abuser's shame and column two is for their own.

2. Encourage them to identify and list any shameful acts in each column. Examine these two lists with the client. You will probably find that their personal list contains relatively small amounts of shame, most of which will be as a result of acts forced on them.

3. Show them how their shame is tied to the shameless acts of their abuser.

4. Next explore with the survivor whether they feel there is anyone else who has behaved in a shameless way, or if they have taken on anyone else's shame. This could include other family members, or authorities who had a duty of care to safeguard them such as the police, social services, school or, in the case of clerical abuse, the church.

5. To give the shame back to the abuser, encourage the survivor to write a letter or a poem to the person(s), without sending it. Or encourage them to express this by drawing or painting, or by talking to a trusted friend.

Another powerful way to release shame is to talk to trusted others. Remind the survivor that shame is a social emotion which shapes and regulates social behaviour and that it is an essential part of social interaction which guides behaviour to make us accepted members of families, tribes, cultures and social groups. When we feel ashamed we feel excluded or isolated from others and feel compelled to withdraw, both physically and psychologically. It is critical that survivors understand that withdrawal goes against our basic human need to be connected to others and makes things worse as shame festers in isolation and is reinforced.

As human contact is the best antidote to shame it is important to enable the survivor to talk about their shame with trusted others. You will need to remind the survivor that being accepted, understood and valued by someone in a non-judgemental way will enable them to release their shame. In essence, sharing their shame will enable the survivor to come out of hiding and become more visible. To truly ease their shame, encourage them to explore it with someone they trust at a pace that is comfortable to them.

 Exercise
Talking about shame

- Invite your client to make a list in their journal of trusted people they could talk to about their sense of shame.

- Next, make sure they are ready to explore their shame. You will need to ensure that they have developed some control over their trauma reactions and feel relatively stable. You must also remind them of any potential risks involved.

- Encourage your client to write a list of the advantages and disadvantages of exploring their shame and how they can get appropriate support. It may seem easier for them to explore their shame early on in your sessions, or they may prefer to leave this until near the end of their recovery.

- If they wish to explore their shame with another trusted supportive person you will need to support this but keep tabs on how this is managed.

- To maximise their chances of being heard, remind your client to check with their trusted person whether they are happy to talk about shame to minimise the risk of rejection.

- Finally, invite your client to make a list of what they feel ashamed of, with the most shameful at the bottom of the list and the least shameful at the top. Start by talking about the least shameful things and gradually work down the list. Exploring shame in this order makes it less overwhelming and will build confidence when sharing shame.

To reduce shame and allow the survivor to develop a more empathic view of themselves they need to develop self-compassion. Self-compassion is a powerful tool to reduce self-blame by recognising that what happened to them was abuse. No matter how they responded, they were a vulnerable child who was manipulated and exploited by the abuser(s). Recognising and believing this will reinforce their compassion for themselves and help them to break the crippling effects of shame and self-blame.

 Exercise
Encouraging self-compassion

- Invite the survivor client to look at photographs of themselves as a child and encourage them try to capture how they felt. Photographs are powerful aids to recovering buried feelings and getting into contact with childhood feelings.

- Where possible, get the survivor to collect a number of photographs of themselves, their family and their abuser (if they have any) preferably from before they were abused, during the abuse, and after the abuse.

- Encourage them to make an album of these with notes about their feelings then and now. Seeing themselves next to adults is a way of recognising how small and vulnerable they were.

- Invite them to reflect and think about what they would like to say to the child, and encourage them to write a letter to them.

SELF-FORGIVENESS

Finally, shame and self-blame can be reduced through self-forgiveness. It can aid recovery to accept that the survivor had no choice in how they reacted, or responded to the abuse. Try to encourage the survivor to forgive themselves for doing things that they thought were wrong. It is essential that survivors remember that they were a child and did not know what to do in such a frightening, or confusing situation. If they have subsequently hurt others they may need to forgive themselves for this as well. The survivor may have harboured rage or vengeful feelings towards their non-abusing parent, siblings or partner, and they need to give themselves permission to forgive themselves for not being perfect. If possible encourage them to talk to any injured parties and apologise for any hurt they might have caused them. If this is not possible or too dangerous, get them to write and if appropriate, send a letter.

It is often much harder but more important for survivors of complex trauma to forgive themselves before forgiving others, including the abuser. Forgiveness is a very personal thing and should only ever be decided by the survivor, and you must not direct or coerce them to forgive. It is critical that you encourage them to make an autonomous decision and that they do not have to forgive to recover or heal. Only the survivor can decide that. Some survivors feel relieved in forgiving their abuser, while others believe that their abuse can never be forgiven. Yet others see forgiveness as an act of kindness to themselves rather than the abuser, as it permits them to let go of anger and hurt which allows them to grow. Whatever the survivor chooses will be right for them, and only them. It is important not to impose your own belief system on to them, and to support them in whatever they decide. It is in supporting them in their autonomous choice without judgement that they regain control and the self-agency which will release them from their prison of shame.

 Warning
Forgiveness, especially of the abuser, is a very personal thing and can only ever be decided by the survivor. Do not decide this for them, and remind them not to allow others to influence them in this decision.

 Top Tip
The toxic nature of shame can elicit shame in practitioners. It is important that clinicians are aware of their own shame and how this might be elicited in the therapeutic process so that they can practice ethically and effectively. To this effect practitioners may benefit from engaging in some of the exercises in this chapter to enhance awareness of their own shame reactions and how these manifest and impact on the therapeutic relationship.

16

MANAGING SELF-HARM

To manage unrelenting emotional pain, overwhelming thoughts and PTSD symptoms, your client may resort to self-harming behaviours. The spectrum of self-harm ranges from passive self-harm, such as not looking after themselves, through to active self-injury, including eating disorders and substance misuse. Passive self-harm includes lack of self-care, poor hygiene, self-neglect, lack of boundaries and not being able to say 'no' or express basic needs. It also includes the suppression of pleasurable feelings.

In contrast, active, deliberate self-harm consists of direct self-injury such as cutting, burning, self-mutilation or persistent suicide attempts. Or your client might manage their emotional pain, or regulate their mood through alcohol, drugs, food or addictive behaviours such as gambling, shopping or sex.

 Exercise
Identifying self-harming behaviours
Get your client to make a list in their journal of the ways in which they could be harming themselves. Be sure they include passive as well as active self-harm such as lack of self-care, inability to express their needs, poor diet, or lack of balance between work, rest and play. Make sure they include any addictive behaviour such as excessive use of alcohol or drugs, gambling, shopping or sex. Also ask them to include any behaviour that puts them at risk, as well as acts of deliberate self-injury. To keep track of self-harming behaviour, your client could monitor it by including any triggers to self-injury, how often this occurs, and the consequences of self-harm.

FUNCTION OF SELF-INJURY

Self-harm and self-injury can be used in a variety of ways. These range from a way to escape emotions, cope with crises, or to calm and comfort when overwrought. They are also ways to restore control or to justify self-nurturing through tending to wounds. Alternatively, your client may use alcohol or drugs to block out intrusive memories, control flashbacks, or to help them sleep or avoid nightmares. Or they may use self-injury as a way to manage tension or anxiety, or to numb themselves by anaesthetising their pain. Self-injury can also be used to bring them out of a dissociative state, and make them feel more real and alive. They may also use self-injury to confirm their existence, to externalise inner pain, to see blood or as a way to cleanse themselves from toxic feelings.

Over time self-injury can become compulsive and addictive whereby your client no longer has control over such behaviours. Whatever their reason for self-injury it is necessary to identify what function it has in their life.

 Exercise

Identifying the function of self-harm

Identifying the function of self-harm and self-injury in life is the first step in learning to manage these behaviours. Show the list above to your client and with them reflect on what purpose self-harm has in their life and how it regulates their feelings and mood.

CYCLE OF SELF-INJURY

Your client will also need to identify the cycle of self-injury behaviour. They may find that self-injury is preceded by feelings of being engulfed by mental pain, intense feelings of anger, sadness or despair, out of control physical sensations, or negative self-beliefs. As these threaten to overpower them, panic and terror take over leading to a compulsion to self-injure. As your client cuts or hurts themselves, the body's natural opiates, known as endorphins, are released which numb and deaden the pain and replace it with a sense of calm and relief. This release makes them feel more in control, or more able to cope or function.

Alternatively, your client may already be numb through dissociation, and to exit this state of deadness they self-injure in order to experience a sense of aliveness or euphoria. This confirms their existence and allows them to feel more grounded. Once the positive aspects of the self-injury have worn off, feelings of shame, guilt, self-hate and self-disgust begin to emerge, until the need to self-injure recurs.

To help your client stop the cycle of self-injury they will need to identify the triggers that lead to either emotional overload or dissociation.

Exercise
Identifying triggers
Get your client to make a list in their journal of the triggers that lead to either emotional overload or dissociation. These can be either internal or external, and can include trauma associated signals, as well as critical messages from others. Self-injury can also be triggered by a sense of rejection or abandonment. Making a list of triggers will alert your client to the stimuli that make them vulnerable to self-harm. With this awareness they can pre-empt when self-injury might occur and try to find alternative ways of managing emotional overload or dissociation.

Remind your client
The need for self-injury is a signal of unexpressed feelings which do not have to be acted upon.

ALTERNATIVE WAYS OF REGULATING EMOTIONS
In finding alternative ways of regulating their emotional states your client will be able to reduce the need to self-injure. These may be difficult to begin with as self-injury is hard to give up because it has been effective and worked well in the past. If your client finds it difficult to stop the self-injury then it is essential that you get them to minimise the harm to themselves until they are able to stop. If your client cuts themselves, ask them to make sure that the implements used to cut are sterilised. To reduce infection, ask them ensure that they clean and dress any wounds carefully. Also, to avoid further risk of injury make sure they do not drink alcohol or take drugs.

Useful strategies to reduce self-harm and self-injury include replacing blood with a red marker pen, or replacing the pain of cutting with snapping a rubber band on your wrist or ankle. In order that they can bring themselves out of dissociation have them try squeezing an ice cube, or holding a cold aluminium can. A cold shower or chewing strongly flavoured food stuff such as chilli, ginger root, raw onion or a lemon also ease numbing. To establish greater control and reduce self-injury your client needs to find the best way of grounding themselves.

GROUNDING TECHNIQUES
To help your client it is vital that you encourage them to employ the range of grounding techniques that they have already identified as effective for them (see pp.171–3). Advise them to make a list of which ones work best

for them and try to adapt the techniques to manage self-harm and self-injury. Remind them to use all five senses and to try to engage in the full range of their emotions. They should also try to connect with someone they trust by phone, email, text or face to face.

A good way for your client to stay in their present reality is to find something that keeps their hands and brain occupied and which allows them to become totally absorbed in a task. If they are haunted by their internal critical voice then ask them to engage it in a dialogue to challenge negative messages and replace them with more compassionate ones.

Your client can also try the 15 minute technique in which they delay self-injury by 15 minutes by distracting themselves through doing a crossword puzzle or Sudoku, or writing in their journal. Alternatively get them to make lists of their ten favourite films, books, songs, paintings, plays, poems or people. After 15 minutes, try to delay for a further 15 minutes and so on. During such distraction the need to self-injure may subside and they may not need to cut or hurt themselves. In addition it will demonstrate that they can exert some control over their compulsion to self-injure.

ALTERNATIVE WAYS OF COMMUNICATION

Once your client has found ways to manage self-injury they can support these by finding alternative ways of communicating their distress. They could practise more effective communication skills to help them to talk and connect to others. In communicating with others, and sharing fears and vulnerabilities, your client will begin to release unexpressed feelings which will reduce their sense of shame and loneliness. This will lead to more effective emotional processing and thereby reduce the need to self-injure and self-medicate.

If your client has become dependent on alcohol or drugs to regulate their emotions they will need to seek specialist support to help them to reduce their dependency. This can be extremely difficult and painful especially as the feelings that have been suppressed through alcohol or drugs may re-emerge. It is vital to link self-medication and suppressed emotions to trauma so that your client can process these in a more healthy way.

Depending on the degree of self-medication your client may need to consider whether it would be beneficial to enter a residential detoxification or rehabilitation programme to help them on their road to recovery. Alternatively, your client may find the support and help available through 12 step fellowship programmes such as Alcohol Anonymous (AA) or Narcotics Anonymous (NA) more suitable for them. There are now a number of specialist 12 step fellowship programmes to help with a vast range of addictions including food, gambling, shopping as well as love and sex addiction.

GIVING UP SELF-INJURY

Finally, it helps for your client to recognise that reducing self-harm and self-injury can feel like a loss which needs to be mourned. Self-injury, alcohol, food or drugs will have become a reliable and predictable way of altering mood or avoiding feelings. To give up such behaviours can be terrifying and feel like the loss of a trusted companion or reliable friend.

This can lead to resistance as your client fears further loss of control. Before they can tackle giving up self-harm and self-injury they must make sure they have mastered alternative ways of regulating their emotions. Most importantly, they need to pace themselves to optimise their chances of success in replacing self-injury behaviours with more healthy alternatives.

SUICIDAL IDEATION

Self-injury and self-harm can also be ways of managing suicidal thoughts and suicide attempts. Your client may use self-injury as a way to ward off suicidal feelings, or as an alternative to suicide. Or they may use self-injury as a form of Russian roulette in which they risk self-injury leading to death. Here the motivation is not necessarily to die but the cessation of pain. If your client is preoccupied with thoughts of suicide or actively suicidal it is vital that you make a safety contract and contact their GP or psychiatrist if they have one.

 Warning
If your client's self-injury is out of control or they have persistent thoughts about suicide you will need to draw up a safety contract and contact their GP.

Their safety plan must include a list of their support network, both personal and professional, as well as their doctor's contact details and a list of specialist services such as the Samaritans. Your client could draw up a contract with a trusted friend that if suicidal thoughts threaten to overpower them, your client will contact them to discuss these. If your client has several trusted friends they might consider a rota system for extra support.

17

SETTING AND MANAGING HEALTHY PERSONAL BOUNDARIES

The nature and dynamics of complex trauma can prevent survivors from setting and managing healthy boundaries. This is due to the violation and invalidation of boundaries during the abuse and confusion around healthy boundaries. As a result many survivors lose contact with, or split off, basic needs for safety and boundaries making it hard to set appropriate boundaries. This is exacerbated if attempts to set boundaries, such as saying 'No' to the abuser are ignored, punished or ridiculed.

This chapter will look at the common boundary problems faced by survivors of complex trauma such as not being able to set boundaries, or alternatively setting rigid boundaries which lead to avoidance and distance from others. It will also look at the purpose and function of healthy boundaries and how survivors can learn to set these through the use of assertion skills.

COMMON BOUNDARY DIFFICULTIES

Many survivors struggle with boundaries and have considerable difficulties in setting, or managing them. The dynamics of complex trauma create a distorted view of boundaries in which abusers violate or impose boundaries in order to manipulate, punish or control others. This leaves a legacy for survivors who either become afraid to set boundaries for fear of the consequences such as rejection, abandonment or punishment, or set very rigid boundaries as an attempt to control others.

Survivors of complex trauma find it particularly difficult to set boundaries in personal relationships in terms of regulating closeness and distance, commonly becoming either enmeshed, distant or oscillating between the two. While optimal relational closeness is highly subjective, varying from individual to individual, there are some commonalities. Most relationships experience fluctuations in emotional and physical closeness and distance and tend to strive for a balance between not becoming too intrusive or smothering, or too distant or avoidant. This is not always easy to attain due to inevitable mismatches between partners of what is considered optimal, which can generate conflicts about closeness and distance from time to time. It is important for survivors to understand the importance of balancing closeness and distance and not to re-enact trauma related conflicts or misinterpret desire for closeness or distance. Many survivors believe that distance is a signal of disapproval, punishment or lack of caring and feel that they have to submit to whatever their partner demands of them.

 Top tip
Learning to set personal boundaries is most effective when the survivor has mastered the skills of identifying and expressing needs.

RANGE OF BOUNDARY DIFFICULTIES

Many survivors struggle with wanting to be close to others and yet fear connection. This is due to the betrayal of trust in which closeness and connection are transformed into opportunities to abuse. In addition, being visible is dangerous as it may prompt abuse leading to a need to be invisible. The confusion generated by such conflicting needs and fear of punishment or abandonment results in a high degree of dependency and constant need for reassurance from others. This in turn generates fear and shame and increases the survivor's vulnerability to being hurt and let down. In order to manage closeness and distance survivors either find it impossible to set boundaries and therefore experience a collapse of boundaries, set rigid boundaries in which they become walled off from others and become highly independent and obsessively self-sufficient, or oscillate between the two.

COLLAPSED OR RIGID BOUNDARIES

Lax or collapsed boundaries (Steele *et al.*, 2001) leave the survivor at the mercy or other people's desires and needs while rigid boundaries isolate the survivor and prevent people from becoming close. To identify the impact that boundary violations have had on the survivor it is helpful to explore with the survivor what personal boundaries mean to them and what purpose they serve. To facilitate this it might be useful to get them to look at some of the common difficulties and tick those that apply to them (see Box 17.1).

Box 17.1 List of common difficulties with boundaries (adapted from Steele *et al.*, 2001)

COLLAPSED BOUNDARIES

• You cannot say 'no', because you are afraid of rejection or abandonment or the anger or disappointment of others

• You are unclear about your own identity and let others define who you are and what you do

• You tend to be either overly responsible and controlling, or passive and dependant

• You take on other people's problems and feelings as your own

• You share too much personal information too soon in a relationship and do not know how to pace personal sharing

• You find it hard to say 'no' to unwanted sexual contact and find yourself in sexual relationships you do not really want and often agree to have sex if the other person wants it

• You have a high tolerance for, or ignore, being treated with disrespect or abused

• You have trouble identifying your needs, wants and feelings

• Your wants, needs and feelings (if you know them) are almost always secondary to those of other people

• You feel responsible for the happiness and well-being of others while ignoring your own

• You tend to rely on other people's boundaries instead of your own

• You compromise your values and beliefs to please others or to avoid conflict

• When setting boundaries, you back down if the other person pushes a little

RIGID BOUNDARIES

• You say 'no' far more often than 'yes', especially in close interactions

• You avoid intimacy by being unable or unwilling to communicate, picking fights, working too much and otherwise being unavailable

- You have a fear of getting too close (phobia of attachment) or being rejected or abandoned (attachment loss) which keep you at a distance
- You rarely share personal information and feel uncomfortable when you do
- You have difficulty identifying your wants, needs and feelings and distance yourself from others
- You have few or no close relationships and spend the majority of your free time alone
- You rarely ask for help
- You are not curious about or respectful of other people's boundaries if they do not fit with yours
- You do not want to get involved with other people's problems

One area that is of particular concern with survivors of abuse is how collapsed or rigid boundaries affect the setting of physical and sexual boundaries. This can lead to setting extremely rigid boundaries by excluding or avoiding any physical or sexual contact and becoming sexually anorexic or to seeking physical intimacy through sexual contact either as a re-enactment of the abuse or as a way to feel close to others. Confusion around personal space and sexual feelings can make it hard for survivors to discuss sexual feelings, needs or desires with their partner. This is exacerbated if they have no sexual feelings at all, or find sex frightening, disgusting or shameful. As a result they tend to either avoid sex, and thereby avoid confusing feelings, or they compulsively seek sex to prove to themselves that their sexuality has not been compromised, or to prove that they are desired by others. Some survivors oscillate between collapsed and rigid boundaries, which adds further confusion to self and others, especially partners.

IDENTIFYING PERSONAL SPACE

To facilitate the setting and maintaining of boundaries you will need to encourage the survivor to identify their own optimal personal space and to feel comfortable in setting boundaries that are respectful to self and others. The survivor will need to choose their optimal boundaries rather than have someone else impose these. To aid survivors to identify personal space and set their own boundaries of closeness and distance to others practitioners might find the following exercises useful.

Exercise
Drawing boundaries between self and significant others

1. Invite the survivor to draw a representation of themselves on a sheet of paper.

2. Remind the survivor this can be a simple stick figure or a symbol such as a circle.

3. Next ask the survivor to draw or represent the people who are important to them and label them by name.

4. Link these with the current boundaries between self and other by using a range of lines (thick, thin, absent, continuous, dotted, irregular, colour).

5. The survivor could also use symbolic representations of links or blockages through the use of walls, gates, waterways, bridges or hedges.

6. Once complete invite the survivor to express the degree of closeness or distance depicted in the drawing and discuss any conflicts and any changes they would like to make.

7. Invite the survivor to draw how they would ideally wish the boundaries between self and others to be.

8. This could also be used as an exercise to identify violation and enmeshment of boundaries during the abuse.

Exercise
Drawing optimal personal space

1. Invite the survivor to draw an imaginary circle around themselves based on the distance they feel it is comfortable to have other people at.

2. Remind them that this is their personal space.

3. Next invite the survivor to widen the circle to represent the part that needs space.

4. Then invite the survivor to draw the circle smaller until they reach what feels comfortable for when wanting to be closer.

5. Invite the survivor to notice the difference between the original circles and the wider and closer ones and explore this.

HEALTHY PERSONAL BOUNDARIES

Once the survivor has identified their optimal personal space in relation to distance and closeness they can begin the process of learning to set healthy boundaries. At this stage it might be helpful to spend some time exploring the role and function of healthy personal boundaries (see Box 17.2) to enable the survivor to feel validated in setting and maintain boundaries.

Box 17.2 The role and function of healthy boundaries

- Boundaries enable individuals to protect and take care of the self
- Boundaries help the individual to set limits
- Boundaries are about knowing our own needs and feelings and being able to communicate these clearly to others
- Boundaries are about respect for self and others and respecting the boundaries of other people and expecting them to respect yours
- Boundaries help individuals to stay connected to others (Linden, 2008) and be close to them
- Boundaries allow individuals to be separate from others when necessary
- Boundaries allow individuals to regulate degrees of intimacy and how close or distant they want to be with other people
- Boundaries help to share personal information gradually in a mutually sharing and trusting relationship
- Boundaries help to identify or be receptive to exploring mistakes in relational difficulties
- Boundaries are not about controlling or being controlled
- Boundaries are about being able to say 'yes' or 'no' to others without feeling guilty or fearful
- Boundaries are about being comfortable with someone saying 'no' without feeling rejected, punished or ashamed
- Boundaries are about not tolerating abuse or disrespect
- It is important to know our own physical and sexual boundaries and be able to keep them
- Boundaries aid individuals to take responsibility for their own life while allowing others to be responsible for theirs
- Boundaries are about valuing our own opinions and feelings and those of others and not compromising these, or our integrity, to avoid rejection
- Boundaries enable individuals to ask for help when needed and manage on their own when appropriate
- Boundaries help to follow through with consequences if someone continually crosses boundaries set
- Boundaries are about taking responsibility for choices and actions and facilitate shared responsibility and power in a relationship without controlling or being controlled

Once the role and function of boundaries has been explored and the survivor has a better sense of the value of boundaries they can begin to apply these to themselves and how they might start to set healthy boundaries. You will need to remind the survivor that in setting these boundaries they will be able to regulate more effectively how much time they wish to spend with others, how much they do for others, how much emotional energy they invest in others and the degree of intimacy they have with others. It is important to remember that this process needs to be paced by the client so that they do not feel rushed or pushed, and is most effective when the survivor has mastered the skills of identifying and expressing needs. Once the survivor is ready to set boundaries they may need to practise and rehearse these skills. Counsellors can facilitate this in session through role playing which the survivor can then practise outside with a trusted friend or partner.

Exercise
Setting healthy boundaries

1. Invite the survivor to make a list of current boundaries and limits and determine whether these are healthy, lax or rigid.

2. Explore what helps them to keep the healthy boundaries and what makes it difficult to keep certain boundaries.

3. Encourage the survivor to notice whether their boundaries are different to those of others.

4. Next invite them to make a list of boundaries they find especially hard to keep or would like to set but have not yet been able to.

5. Look at these and encourage the survivor to reflect on them and identify what makes it difficult to keep boundaries.

6. Help the survivor to understand any inner conflicts about boundaries such as wanting to be hugged and touched and fearing this. Explore these and how these inner conflicts may prevent setting healthy boundaries and how to resolve them.

7. Invite the survivor to challenge any dysfunctional core beliefs and thoughts that support a particular unhealthy boundary such as being too lax or too rigid.

8. Consider looking at assertiveness skills to prepare for setting boundaries.

9. Consider using imagined rehearsal to enable the survivor to visualise successfully setting healthy boundaries and the various responses of the other person.

10. Help prepare the survivor to deal with these through role play either in session, or with a trusted friend or partner.

ASSERTIVENESS

Assertiveness must not be confused with being selfish, insensitive or hostile. Remind your client that it is a sophisticated social skill in which there is a balance between respect for the self and respect for others. To be assertive means being respectful of the rights of others while keeping your own respect and rights in mind. It means communicating in a non-aggressive, non-manipulative and proactive way whereby you maintain respect for your own needs and balance this with what is fair, reasonable and respectful of others.

Assertiveness does not demand that needs are met but is a way of expressing these in the hope that they can be met in negotiation with the other person. This may mean reaching a compromise in which both parties feel respected. The important ingredients are honesty in stating needs and being respectful to ourselves and others. While it helps to be assertive when face to face with the person, this is not always possible. If this is the case, then writing a letter, email, phoning or contact through a trusted third party can be helpful instead.

Four stages of assertiveness

To be assertive your client needs to work through the four stages of assertiveness. First they have to decide precisely what it is they want or need. Second you will need to help them to decide what is reasonable and fair. This will help in stage three, which is to generate a reasonable proposal which includes room for compromise. Finally the survivor has to consider and state the consequences if their proposal is not properly considered or ignored.

Once your client has gone through these stages, they will need to practise and rehearse their newly acquired assertion skills until they come more naturally. It helps to rehearse these with a trusted friend or in front of a mirror to build confidence.

Opposition to assertiveness

While most people respond well to the communication of feelings and needs, it is worth advising your client that some people refuse to acknowledge assertion. Instead they choose to interpret this as opposition, or defiance, especially if it threatens the status quo or long established ways of interacting. It helps to be prepared for potential opposition no matter how assertive your client is, especially if they are currently in an abusive relationship. In this case you must assess their safety before they approaching their partner.

Top tip

Remind your client that just because others do not accept their feelings or needs, this does not invalidate them.

Some of this opposition may be direct and explicit, while some may be much more subtle in terms of disapproval, emotional manipulation or redirection of blame. To manage any opposition your client will need to stand their ground and restate their case assertively, sometimes several times. Remind your client that while it is understandable that others may not want to accept their feelings or needs, this does not invalidate them. It certainly shouldn't become a reason to stop your client from expressing themselves. Encourage them to stay calm, and repeat their feelings or needs. If the other person remains negative in their responses, your client may need to accept that that person is being unreasonable.

If they remain unfair or try to manipulate your client or end the discussion, don't let your client interpret this as failure. It clearly demonstrates that the person they are talking to is not able to respect them, their feelings or their needs. Remind your client that the point of assertion is not demanding that their needs be met, but that they are expressing themselves in the hope of being heard. If their request or need is met that is a bonus. However if it is not then your client can still feel proud that they at least respected themselves in expressing their needs.

Warning

Some people, especially those who have, or had, power over your client will not respond well to assertion. They may punish your client to bring them back in line. Advise them to be careful and remind them to stay safe.

It can be difficult and taxing for your client to assert themselves and can prompt losses, such as the loss of relationships that are no longer tenable. It is important that your client paces themselves in developing assertiveness and seeks extra support if necessary, or attends an assertiveness training course.

Assertiveness skills

Providing the survivor is ready to set boundaries and has practised the skills learned, they will be able to set boundaries with increasing ease. Those survivors who find setting and maintaining boundaries particularly challenging may benefit from learning more general assertion skills. Research (Paterson, 2000; Phelps and Austin, 2002) has shown that assertiveness is a necessary interpersonal skill to help individuals express their needs in a confident, non-aggressive way without violating the rights of others. Assertiveness is an active rather than passive way to communicate needs, feelings and thoughts in a clear and mutually respectful way. It is also about being able to set appropriate limits and boundaries without feeling guilty.

Not only do assertiveness skills help the survivor to identify their own values, beliefs and opinions it also helps them to understand those of others without subsuming or sacrificing their own needs. This can help them to strengthen self-identity, improve confidence and strengthen relationships with others. Assertiveness skills tend to facilitate stronger and more stable relationships, in which the survivor can get their needs met more consistently.

Prior to introducing assertiveness skills, you may need to help the survivor to identify non-assertive strategies that impede communication and the setting of boundaries. Box 17.3 lists typical non-assertive strategies that are commonly used. It is helpful to go through these and identify which strategies are used by the survivor and make links to how these arose, how effective or not they are, and how they can be changed.

Box 17.3 Non-assertive strategies: appeasement, avoidance and aggression

APPEASEMENT

- Afraid to express anger or needs for fear of burdening others
- Characterised by feelings of rejection or being harmed
- 'People pleasers'
- Invest a lot of energy into appeasing behaviours
- Other people's needs and happiness prioritised and fulfilled at the expense of self

- When others react strongly tend to back down and apologise even if they feel they have done nothing wrong
- Generally passive and submissive
- Out of contact with feelings of anger which cannot be expressed
- Feel taken advantage of and underappreciated which breeds unexpressed resentment
- Expect that others should 'know' what they need and want without having to say it

AVOIDANCE

- Internal confusion
- Phobia of inner experiencing
- Avoid knowing their own needs or wants
- Unable to articulate needs
- Appear to be appeasing by going along with what others want
- Not aware or conscious of fears
- Out of contact with their inner needs and signals and so cannot identify what they need

AGGRESSION

- Only way to get their needs met is to be forceful and aggressively fight for their rights
- Do not understand the difference between aggression and assertiveness
- Distrust the motives of others
- Fearful that others will hurt or take advantage of them; have little empathy for what others may need
- On the defensive
- Come across as being entitled or bullying

Basic assertiveness skills

When the survivor is ready to work on boundary issues, then you can begin to introduce some basic assertiveness skills to help them set and maintain boundaries. Box 17.4 summarises some of the basic assertiveness skills that can benefit survivors of complex trauma. These will need to be introduced gradually and practised so that they become second nature. You will probably have used many of these implicitly during the counselling process and it is worth making them more explicit so that the survivor is more aware of them. It is important to remind the survivor that they need to be aware of both verbal and non-verbal communication and their ability to listen non-defensively and non-judgementally, and to create an open stance when making a request or discussing a difference in opinion. The emphasis must be on maximising the outcome of the interaction and survivors must be reminded to choose the timing of the encounter not only in relation to when they are ready, but also to offer some choice to the other party.

To maximise the outcome of the interaction survivors need to ensure that they remain congruent throughout and avoid mixed messages that can lead to misinterpretation. You may need to remind the survivor that if they become overwhelmed during the interaction they can take 'time-out' to gather their thoughts and come back to the conversation when they are ready. They should not feel 'bulldozed' into a decision and can respond at a later point. Most importantly, the survivor needs to be encouraged to reflect on their use of assertiveness skills and monitor how they aid communication and the setting of boundaries. Once the survivor feels they have mastered some of the basic assertiveness skills they may wish to apply them to a specific situation. This can initially be practised in session and rehearsed prior to the actual interaction. Finally the survivor may find it helpful to visualise a positive outcome in order to maintain their resolve and confidence.

MANAGING BOUNDARIES

Once the survivor has learnt to identify needs and to set boundaries in an assertive way, they can start to explore ways in which to maintain boundaries. This will help in their relationships with partners, friends, children and work colleagues as well as professionals while decreasing their vulnerability to re-victimisation. As the survivor becomes more confident in setting boundaries they will be able to set and maintain boundaries, and manage any ruptures in relationships without fearing abandonment, rejection or punishment. Equipped with assertiveness skills survivors will be able to manage their relationships more effectively and harmoniously, which will be explored in the next chapter.

Box 17.4 Summary of basic assertiveness skills

INTERPERSONAL STANCE
LISTENING

- Listen carefully and with an open mind
- Listen to their perspective and needs
- Listen non-defensively
- Listen non-judgementally

NON-VERBAL

- Face the other person
- Maintain eye contact
- Stand or sit tall, not slumped down
- Tone of voice neutral, not angry or submissive
- Be congruent in ensuring the body language matches what is said
- Do not smile if angry or look afraid of trying to stick to a boundary

VERBAL STANCE

- 'Own' the message by using 'I' statements instead of 'you' statements
- Own what is being said and do not blame others
- Give and receive constructive criticism or feedback
- Be specific and respectful when giving feedback
- Set clear limits by saying 'no' or 'not now'
- Ask questions to clarify
- Choose a time that is mutually convenient
- Be respectful and try to understand the other person
- Give context for request or disagreement
- Be specific rather than vague or tentative to avoid misinterpretation
- Ask for feedback and listen carefully to this
- Use respectful humour to stay connected
- Be open to the other person's opinion and needs rather than demanding
- See both sides of an issue
- Be your own advocate
- Take 'time-out' to gather thoughts
- Reflect on what is said

18

MANAGING RELATIONSHIPS

Complex trauma and child sexual abuse (CSA) can make it extremely hard to trust others or get close to them. Fear of being hurt again or that closeness will be sexualised can lead to the avoidance of intimacy. While this strategy can aid survival, it usually comes at a cost such as traumatic loneliness and difficulties in relationships. This creates a paradox in which the survivor yearns for closeness and yet is compelled to avoid it.

This 'double bind' of desire for intimacy and fear of being suffocated can be damaging, especially if it is combined with fear of further betrayal or abuse. It will either lead the survivor to avoid intimacy, or propel them to be too trusting, or over-intimate too quickly, making them more vulnerable to further betrayal or abuse. Both avoidance of closeness, and being over-intimate can cause difficulties in relationships.

In helping survivors to manage relationships more effectively you will need to explore how early experiences shape how we relate to others and how we value relationships. Many survivors may not be consciously aware of this and yet it is often sensed, felt or known to them and can easily be triggered by subtle cues that give rise to shame, anxiety or lack of worth. The masquerade of abuse as love and affection seen in complex trauma makes it difficult for survivors to know genuine love and nurturing. If the survivor did not experience love, warmth or nurturing as a child, they will often not know how to respond when this is offered in adulthood, or in the therapeutic setting. It is worth remembering that for many survivors tenderness is associated with confusion, yearning or pain.

The message in complex trauma is that the only worth the survivor has in relationships is to satisfy the needs or desires of others, primarily through sex. This lack of value and respect for the person can lead to wariness in their relationships, whether family, friends, partners, children, or professionals and work colleagues.

POWER AND CONTROL DYNAMICS

One way to manage complex trauma is to re-enact the power and control dynamics experienced during the abuse in which current relationships become the arena to restore power and control or to reduce feelings of powerlessness. This commonly results in either becoming compliant or submissive to avoid conflict or controlling through aggression or dominance. Survivors who resort to control may do this in obvious ways through anger and hostility, or they may adopt more subtle controlling behaviour patterns such as never revealing themselves in their relationships, not allowing others to get close, always being the carer, or through obsessive-compulsive behaviours such as cleanliness, tidiness, being busy all the time or working excessively.

Survivors who are compliant tend to divert authority to external sources of control and seek sanctuary in dependency, which replicates their abuse experience. While this dependency can be overt in always deferring to their partner, it can also be seen in less obvious ways of behaving such as a constant need for reassurance, the inability to make any decisions, not being able to trust their instincts, or by leading highly chaotic lives that need others to sort them out. The risk of such high level dependency is that the survivor may attract controlling partners who are likely to abuse them, or re-victimise them. Some survivors constantly switch between dominance and submission, which can be confusing and exhausting for partners and friends.

The inability to set healthy boundaries around power and control can affect the survivor's parenting, which is not only frightening for the child but can also be experienced as abusive. Many survivors feel shocked and mortified that they may be doing harm to their children and fear not being able to control how they are with them. This needs to be carefully monitored in terms of safeguarding concerns and must be explored.

Warning

Practitioners need to assess safeguarding concerns in the case of survivors who are unable to set healthy boundaries with their children and find a way to explore these in a non-threatening way.

The need to control and dominate, or be submissive and compliant, can cause considerable relationship difficulties with friends and work colleagues. Survivors who are domineering, controlling or hostile are perceived negatively and actively avoided, whereas survivors who are submissive and compliant are often taken advantage of and exploited. This can lead to a sense of betrayal or resentment on the part of the survivor which prevents them from developing an equal or respectful relationship. When survivors switch between control and compliance, friends and work colleagues become confused making them wary of entering into a relationship. The lack of predictability and mood swings lead to avoidance and the survivor is left feeling isolated and rejected.

Whichever position is taken it must be understood within the context of the abuse experience. Both positions use denial, dissociation and cognitive distortions to ward off painful emotions as a way of managing the abuse. This rollercoaster way of managing emotions is also often accompanied by substance abuse or compulsive behaviours which can give a temporary sense of power and control during times of vulnerability and stress.

Remember

Power and control dynamics in relationships are a replay of the complex trauma in which the survivor re-enacts either being the abuser or the victim.

EXPERIENCING RELATIONSHIPS

Intimacy increases resilience and is a central part of healing. Your client's recovery will be improved through healthy relationships and a trusted support network. To help them achieve this you will need to make them more aware of their experience of relationships, and help them identify obstacles that prevent them from enjoying intimacy and closeness. To develop close relationships they will need to explore what is meant by trust, to identify their needs and find assertive ways of expressing these. To increase awareness of how the survivor experiences relationships and the meaning they derive from them you might invite them to try the following exercise.

Exercise

What does relationships mean to you?

- Ask the survivor the following questions and get them to record their feelings and thoughts in their journal. What does love mean to you? What does mutual respect mean to you? How do you show that you love someone? How does it feel to receive love? How does it feel to cooperate with someone else? To what degree do you have confidence in others? How do you know you can trust someone? What evidence do you need to be ready to trust? How does it feel to trust others? How does it feel to be appreciated by others? How does it feel when you are disappointed or let down by someone?

- Explore the answers to these questions and reflect on them with your client.

- Next ask your client the following: what will make you feel more comfortable, safe, secure or happy in your relationships? What would you like to change or heal in your relationships?

- From this exercise the survivor can begin to identify their experience of relationships, their fears and obstacles to intimacy, and negative thoughts or feelings behind these.

- To reduce obstacles, the survivor will need to challenge any negative beliefs, and replace these with more accurate ones. This will free them up to develop healthier relationships in which they enjoy greater intimacy. It will also allow them to relate more authentically in an atmosphere that is based on mutual respect and genuine care.

IDENTIFYING RELATIONSHIP PATTERNS

The above exercise will also help the survivor to identify other fears such as fear of showing vulnerability, fear of dependency or neediness, fear of reaching out in case they are rebuffed, or fear of saying 'no' or expressing needs. To understand relationship patterns you will need to help the survivor to explore their fears and assess how these manifest in their relationships. For example, do they always prioritise or anticipate the needs of others over their own needs? Do they constantly need to please others, or do they find themselves 'second guessing' or 'mind reading' others? In addition it is important to asses to what extent the survivor compartmentalises their feelings and appears to be cold and unfeeling, or fiercely self-sufficient in refusing all help.

Alternatively, some survivors veer between approaching their partner or avoiding them. The survivor might find that as soon as they open up they feel compelled to shutdown, or that they feel angry after feeling close and need to reject their partner. These patterns will have been conditioned by the abuse wherein the survivor learnt to prioritise their abuser's needs, and focused on pleasing them. They also highlight that closeness meant danger, and that saying 'no' or expressing needs was either punished or ignored.

TRUST

The repeated betrayal in complex trauma leads to a basic lack of trust in self and others. This is extremely difficult for survivors, who because of the abuse have a greater need to be liked, accepted and understood. This can lead them to trust too easily, even when there is no evidence of trustworthiness. Survivors who have difficulties around trust need to examine and challenge their thoughts and feelings about people in their lives and assess to what degree their trust is warranted. This is best done by plotting the degree of trust the survivor has on a scale or continuum.

Trust is not a static state, polarised between 'trust' and 'no trust'; rather it exists on a spectrum which can fluctuate depending upon the stability of the relationship and how ruptures are managed. To help assess the degree of trust your client has in others you could suggest the following exercise.

 Exercise
Spectrum of trust

- Encourage the survivor to make a list of all the significant people in their life.

- Reflect with your client on who they feel they can trust, those they are unsure about, and those they feel they cannot trust at all.

- Next suggest that they draw a line representing a continuum of trust with 0 per cent at one end and 100 per cent at the other.

- The survivor can then plot each person along this scale on the basis of the degree of trust they have in them.

- If they are scattered across the whole spectrum then the survivor has a range of trusting relationships in which they do not over or under invest. If however most of the people they know are concentrated around the 0 per cent end of the continuum then it is likely that the survivor fears intimacy. In contrast, if the highest concentration is towards the 100 per cent mark, then that indicates that the survivor trusts too easily and becomes intimate too easily.

- Remind your client that it can be dangerous to trust or mistrust too easily or without monitoring the evidence on which that trust is based.

- It might be helpful for the survivor to look at the names on the continuum and assess the evidence for their trust in them, and see if they can be moved along the continuum accordingly.

- Explore with the survivor how they know when to trust someone and what evidence helps them in making that decision. The more aware they are of the factors that support their trust the more they will be able to assess their degree of trust.

It is helpful to review your client's level of trust throughout the course of a relationship as this is rarely static and will fluctuate. This can be very useful especially when there has been a betrayal of trust or when there is evidence of trustworthiness.

 Top tip
Trust is not all or nothing but exists on a spectrum of degree of trust.

FLUCTUATIONS IN RELATIONSHIPS

Avoidance of relationships not only reduces opportunities to develop trust and practise relationship skills, but prevents survivors from experiencing the natural fluctuations in relationships. Relationships are dynamic and their quality changes over time, with periods of closeness and periods of distance. For instance the initial thrill and excitement of attraction usually progresses into deep affection, while passion may transform into compassion and increased security and emotional intimacy. Such changes can sometimes be experienced as 'boredom' or terror as the emotional closeness intensifies. It is essential that survivors are able to notice and monitor any changes, evaluate these and understand their significance. If the survivor is feeling bored ask them if this really is boredom, or is it that they are unfamiliar with security and close intimacy. Alternatively, if they start to experience fear get them to explore what this represents before ending the relationship prematurely. In addition they might find that what initially attracted them to their partner or friend may repel them when the relationship is under stress. Suddenly the very thing that they were initially attracted to, such independence, serenity or attentiveness, can begin to feel like distance, lack of emotion or fussing.

The more the survivor understands the rhythm of relationships the more they will be able to accept that all relationships, including healthy ones, are messy at times. Ruptures can occur even in healthy relationships, and more importantly can be repaired. This will help the survivor to be more tolerant and realistic in their expectations of others and themselves in relationships.

RELATIONSHIP SKILLS

The survivor's lack of experience in relationships can also lead to a lack of confidence and the necessary social skills needed to get close to people. Developing social skills through use of body language, eye contact and smiling can all help the survivor to interact more easily with others. To help them acquire these try to get them to observe people who are socially skilled and are good at initiating relationships. These could be friends or colleagues or fictional characters on television, in films or in books. Survivors may benefit from exploring how they interact with others by looking at their body language, their facial expressions, how often they smile, and how long they hold eye contact. To help the survivor feel more comfortable when talking to others they could record friendly phrases in their journal which will help them to start and sustain conversations.

It is a good idea for survivors to practise these skills first with you or a trusted friend or colleague so that these become easier and more automatic when tested in public. Constructive feedback is also useful before entering more difficult social situations. The survivor may also find the assertiveness skills introduced in Chapter 17 useful in a managing relationships.

IDENTIFYING NEEDS

Before survivors can be assertive they will need to feel comfortable about expressing their feelings and needs in relationships. This can be hard if these were consistently ignored, or if they were punished for expressing them in the past. Many survivors are not in contact with their needs, or feel that they are not entitled to have any. Before survivors can express their needs they will have to identify them.

 Exercise
Identifying needs

- Get the survivor to think about their needs and make a list of these.

- If they are stuck, they should consider some of the following: the need to feel safe, to feel loved, to feel respected, to feel comfortable about showing vulnerability without fear or shame, to be able to say 'no' without being rejected or humiliated, and the need to be listened to.

- Invite the survivor to add any other needs that are important to them.

- Explore the list and ask the survivors to think about how they could meet these needs.

EXPRESSING NEEDS

Once the survivor has identified their needs they will need to find a way of expressing them. This is best achieved using assertiveness skills and developing relationship ground rules. Once the survivor feels comfortable expressing their feelings and needs they can begin to work on setting ground rules for their relationships. To facilitate this the survivor needs to make a list of the ground rules and boundaries that ensure that their needs are met. As they do this they may experience internal resistance and objections about expressing these such as 'People won't like me', 'I will be rejected', 'I am being selfish', or 'I will feel guilty'. Such objections, while common, need to be challenged so that the survivor can overcome them and feel more confident about setting boundaries (see Chapter 17, pp.227–8).

It is worth reminding the survivor that boundaries and ground rules help to build or rebuild trust, which will allow them to relate more authentically. With healthy boundaries in place the survivor can stop anticipating the needs of others, curb their tendency to mind-read others, and resist taking responsibility for the feelings, thoughts and behaviour of others. This will help them to stop prioritising others over their own needs. Healthy boundaries will also enable the survivor to distinguish between genuinely nurturing and nourishing relationships and those that are forceful and controlling. They will empower them to monitor the quality of their relationships and manage any difficulties more effectively rather than avoiding intimacy.

Most importantly, in expressing feelings and needs and communicating these more effectively, the survivor will be able to develop intimacy without feeling threatened or suffocated. This will help them to listen to others and talk honestly and openly with mutual respect. In this climate they will be able to build trust and reconnect to self and others. If the survivor needs additional support in their relationship you could consider advising them to contact Relate (see p.299) who offer counselling to couples.

Remind your client
To balance memories of abuse it is helpful to recall positive memories.

Exercise
Recalling Positive memories
Invite your client to write down ten positive memories. If these cannot be recalled from childhood then encourage them to think of more recent

experiences. To facilitate full recall, the survivor will need to write these down making sure they include as many sensory cues as possible. Once these have been recorded you can encourage the survivor to recall some of these positive memories whenever they feel low or to counteract overwhelming negative memories.

19

MANAGING SEXUALITY

Complex trauma, sexual violence and CSA can give rise to a range of sexual difficulties which can be distressing and affect sexual relationships. While some survivors experience few or no difficulties, others feel that their sexual lives have been forever damaged. The spectrum of sexual difficulties can range from avoidance of all sexual activities through to indiscriminate sexual encounters.

Your client might avoid sexual intimacy because of fear or mistrust, or because sexual experiences are physically or emotionally painful. Or they might experience phobic reactions to certain parts of the body or specific sexual acts. They might also experience physical complications such as pain on penetration or erectile difficulties, which can fuel a fear of failure and sense of inadequacy.

Alternatively your client may suffer from flashbacks or intrusive memories during sex, even when in a loving relationship. Sex might also be so tainted by shame or guilt that they cannot experience any pleasure. Or they might avoid sex altogether and only engage in compulsive masturbation in which they experience neither pleasure or satisfaction.

In the case of indiscriminate sexual behaviour, your client may have had numerous sexual partners yet experience little or no sexual pleasure. This may be due to a need to prove that they have not been sexually damaged, or a way of getting their need for affection met. Your client could also be trying to empower themselves by being predatory or in control of their sexual encounters. Sometimes, such behaviour is simply due to not being able to say 'no' to someone who wants to have sex. This can make them vulnerable to sexually abusive relationships in which love and hurt become intertwined and confused.

To manage sexual difficulties your client will need to rebuild a safe sexual foundation and learn to take sensual pleasure in their body. To help them achieve this identify with your client any myths about sex they may have and challenge these. From here they can develop a greater understanding and knowledge of sex and sexual arousal. This will help your client to recognise the importance of a safe and healthy relationship in which to develop sexual trust.

The quality of your client's sexual relationship will be enhanced if they can communicate sexual fears as well as their sexual desires without shame or fear of rejection. This can help them to break old associations to sexual abuse. As your client begins to feel more comfortable about intimacy you can help them reclaim their body and their sexuality.

 Remind your client
To reclaim their body and sexuality it is critical to go at their pace.

SEXUAL MYTHS

Sexual myths influence beliefs around sex and sexuality, and direct sexual behaviour. Some of these myths may have been conditioned during the sexual abuse or imposed by the abuser to distort reality and obtain power and control over your client. The first step in reclaiming sexuality is to help them become more conscious and aware of the myths that influence their beliefs about sex.

 Exercise
Sexual myths
Below is a list of common myths as reported by survivors. Look at these with your client and have them identify those that apply and those that have affected their sexual relationships. Discuss them with your client or have them talk to a friend or trusted advisor and try to challenge them with alternative or more accurate beliefs.

- Any physical contact inevitably leads to sex.

- All cuddles are a prelude to sex.

- If you are aroused you must want to have sex.

- Men always want and must be ready for sex, and if not they are inadequate.

- If your partner does not have sex with you then they don't love you or find you unattractive.

- To have sex necessitates an erection.

- Sex is only sex when penetration takes place.

- Once you are sexually aroused you lose control and have to have sex.

- Men and women have to have orgasms to enjoy sex.

- Sex is only satisfying if both partners orgasm at the same time.

- Once orgasm or ejaculation occurs sex is over.

- Lots of sex is the only way to a healthy relationship.

- You must agree to sex whenever your partner wants to.

- You are not allowed to say 'no' to sex.

- To be sexual you must be young, beautiful or have a good body.

- Sexual abuse and sexual violence make you gay or lesbian.

For your client to reclaim their sexuality they will to need challenge these myths and replace them with more accurate knowledge. Such knowledge will improve their understanding of sex and sexuality and the quality of their sexual relationships. Your client will be able to reverse the sexual naivety imposed by their abuser and take more control over their sexual responses. CSA denied your client the natural discovery of sexual likes and dislikes, wants or desires. It also distorted their image of the role of love and care in sexual relationships, by entwining hurt and pain with pleasure. In essence it dictated what your client should and should not feel, and created a pattern for all future sexual relationships.

UNDERSTANDING THE IMPACT OF SEXUAL VIOLENCE AND SEXUAL ABUSE

The pleasure of physical contact through hugs has become confused and tainted with the demands of being sexual and to satisfy someone else's needs. Sexual violence and CSA also distort understanding of the nature of sexual relationships, and the ebb and flow of feeling sexual attractive or attracted to a partner. It also affects your client's ability to regulate sexual behaviour, being able to say 'no' without feeling guilty or ashamed, and the frequency with which they should have sex.

The betrayal of the body

Your client may have felt betrayed by their body if they felt pleasure during the sexual abuse. Yet they may not realise that the abuser most likely performed specific sexual acts on your client to deliberately arouse. By feeling pleasure they will blame themselves, believing that they wanted the sexual contact. This is a clever way for the abuser to shift responsibility for the abuse onto your client, thereby reducing the risk of disclosure. The shame of being sexually aroused or having an orgasm further reduces the likelihood of disclosure.

Bodily responses

It is important for your client to realise that if they had an erection, or became lubricated, these are natural responses in the presence of sexual touch. Remind them that erections can be involuntary and happen in a variety of situations, including fear and stress. Similarly, vaginal lubrication in females is an automatic biological reaction which acts as a natural form of protection from tissue damage. Neither of these necessarily indicate sexual desire or arousal. Such reactions can occur for non-sexual reasons much like nipples that become erect not just during sexual arousal but also due to fear or cold.

The sexual arousal cycle

Once the sexual arousal system has been activated, and in the presence of continued stimulation, it will naturally tend to lead to orgasm. If your client experienced involuntary orgasms or ejaculation during sexual abuse this does not mean that they wanted, or encouraged the sexual encounter. It certainly does not mean that they are responsible or to blame for the assault(s) or sexual abuse.

 Remind your client
Their body is biologically programmed to become aroused, experience pleasure and orgasm in the presence of sexual stimulation.

Emphasise to your client that they are not dirty, sinful or a whore. Remind them that their body responded to the sexual stimulation and not the person. These normal physical responses were exploited by the abuser to make them feel bad and ashamed in order to reduce the risk of disclosure.

 Remind your client
Their body responded to the sexual stimulation and not the person.

SEXUAL AROUSAL AND SEXUAL DESIRE

It is vital that you help your client to distinguish between sexual arousal and sexual desire. Sexual arousal and sexual desire are two quite separate things; we can be sexually aroused without the desire to be sexual or engage in a sexual experience. Thus sexual arousal is an appropriate response to sexual stimulation. It is the abuser's sexual activity with your client as a child that is inappropriate.

Physical pain during sex may be fear related as your client involuntarily can tense up to protect themselves, which can lead to further anxiety and sexual difficulties. They may believe that such pain is as a result of physical damage to external or internal sexual organs. If your client has such fears they might be able to allay these by having a medical examination with a sensitive specialist. In addition, if they have anatomical concerns such as the shape or size of their penis, breasts, clitoris or vagina, suggest that they talk these through too. While most survivors do not sustain physical damage or deformities due to abuse it is important they take their concerns seriously and seek medical advice.

 Top tip
If your client is concerned about physical or sexual damage it is worth them seeking advice from a sensitive medical practitioner.

A reflex reaction to fear is muscular tension which can lead to pain when attempting sexual intercourse. This is called vaginismus whereby the muscles contract upon attempting penetration, making it virtually impossible to insert a penis. While lubricants can help, it is more beneficial in the long term if your client can learn to reduce their fears and learn to relax. You should also advise men who have extremely tight foreskins which make erections and sexual intercourse painful to seek medical advice.

EMOTIONAL REACTIONS DURING SEXUAL INTIMACY

Fear can also affect the emotional temperature of sexual relationships. Your client may feel overwhelmed by powerful feelings during sex such as terror, shame, humiliation or anger that they fear they cannot contain. They may experience flashbacks or intrusive memories during sexual stimulation which can lead to 'tuning out', or dissociation. This is because sexual intimacy triggers the same bodily sensations as during the abuse which propel them back to the abuse experience.

Your client's terror, anxiety or anger in turn triggers a range of defensive reactions such as detachment, withdrawal or aggression. This can be frightening to both your client and their partner especially if the link to sexual abuse has not been made. It does not mean that your client does not love and care for their partner; it is a conditioned response as a result of sexual abuse. In linking such responses to sexual abuse, and identifying the triggers that induce fear, anger or dissociation, you can help your client to begin to take control of them.

Exercise

Identifying triggers and sensory cues

Get your client to think about all the cues that were present during the abuse and make a list of these. Ask them to include as many of the sensory cues as possible. They should list all the smells they associate with the abuse such as body odours or breath, the smell of tobacco or alcohol, semen or any others. Next identify with your client as many sounds as they can remember, such as the abuser's voice or any other voices, the radio, TV or music. Then have your client list all that they could see during the abuse and the quality of the light or darkness. They also need to identify any tactile sensation such as how the abuser touched them. Was it tender and gentle or rough and aggressive? Were the abuser's hands soft or abrasive? What body parts did they touch? Which parts did your client have to touch and how did that feel to them? Also list with your client any tastes associated with the abuse such as semen or other bodily secretions. Lastly, help your client identify positions their body was placed in and the preferred position of the abuser.

CHANGING SENSORY CUES

Once your client has identified these sensory cues they can begin to erase or replace them with new sensory cues that are associated with their present loving relationship. Have your client talk to their partner and explore how they can make changes. If possible your client should vary their sexual positions and introduce pleasant smells such as body oil or lotions to offset the unpleasant smells and to change the experience of being touched. They should try to find new ways to experience pleasure that do not repeat the sexual stimulation used by the abuser.

Advise your client to vary the light by using candles, and the sound by talking in a loving way, or by being silent, or by involving other sounds such as music. If the abuse always took place in the bedroom, suggest that your client experiments by having sex in different settings to see if that makes a difference. They could also experiment with who initiates sexual contact, or by taking more control of the process to offset the abuse experience.

The more your client experiments with different sensory cues the more they will be able to erase the old associations that reduce any defence mechanisms. As they feel more pleasure in their body, your client may want to experiment more. Suggest that they might increase their sexual pleasure through fantasy, looking at or reading erotic material, or using sexual aids. Your client should not do this if they were forced to do this during the sexual abuse. Changing sensory cues can really help your client to reclaim their sexuality and allow them to feel pleasure for pleasure's sake without feeling guilty, dirty or ashamed.

WHAT IT MEANS TO BE SEXUAL

To further reclaim sexuality your need to help your client work out what being sexual means to them. Sexual abuse prevented your client from exploring their sexuality and as a result they will know how to perform without necessarily feeling sexual. To discover what being sexual means to them, your client will need to explore feelings about their body, and identify what gives them pleasure.

Exercise

What being sexual means

Take time to reflect with your client on what being sexual means to them. What do they enjoy the most about being sexual? What do they like the least? What makes them feel comfortable, or uncomfortable? What are your client's fears around sex and sexual relationships? What is the purpose of sex? Help them answer these, and any other questions they have and get them to list the responses in their journal. Reflect on these with your client and record what they would like to change and what would help them to make those changes.

Your client's feelings about their body can have considerable effect on their feelings about being sexual. If your client hates their body or the body parts that have been fetishised by the abuser, this will impact significantly on their sexuality. Negative feelings, confusion about the body or lack of control over bodily responses can lead to shame and guilt.

BODY SHAME

If your client feels ashamed of their body they will tend to want to hide their body covering up or disguising their appearance. This includes wearing dull or baggy clothing, putting on excess weight, or disfigurement to ward off sexual advances. Your client may also neglect personal hygiene to repel others and to avoid physical closeness. Alternatively your client may wear layers of makeup to compensate for feeling unattractive, or dress in an overtly sexual manner. This is an attempt to hide feeling asexual or to achieve a sexual identity through dress. Your client might also diet to excess, or starve themselves to reduce breast size or curves that remind them of sexuality. Be wary of this as to achieve it they might binge and purge food as a way of recreating the bodily conflict of pleasure and pain of sexual abuse.

If your client is a male survivor they may bodybuild to excess to compensate for feeling vulnerable and to protect against any future abuse. Females may also exercise to excess to gain control over a body they feel betrayed them during the sexual abuse. To enable your client to enjoy and take pleasure in their body, get them to try the following exercise.

 Exercise

Exploring how to enjoy the body

Examine with your client what could give them pleasure. This can be through affection from being held, cuddled or stroked in a non-sexual way. Or it could be being wrapped in a warm, fluffy towel, splashing in water, feeling air on their skin, or being naked without being sexualised. Your client could also find pleasure through running, swimming, dancing, skipping or any physical activity which allows them to feel in control of their body and develop bodily trust. Further sources of pleasure include dressing up, wearing soft, sensual clothing, taking pride in their appearance, and receiving compliments without feeling shame or fear of sexual abuse.

Reflect with your client on how they could start to take pleasure in their body by allowing themselves to engage in some of these things on a regular basis. Your client can also gain pleasure from nourishing their body in taking care of it by eating healthily and exercising regularly. Your client could also take more pleasure in their appearance by wearing soft, sensual clothing and wearing scent. Suggest that your client can nourish their skin by applying scented oil or lotion after bathing, or by having a regular relaxing massage.

SENSATE FOCUS

A powerful way to reclaim sexuality is to explore their body and its responses through specific exercises as used in sensate focus. This can be done individually or with a partner. Sensate focus is designed to get to know the body through self-exploration or mutual exploration with a trusted partner. Your client can start by looking at themselves in the mirror and noting down what they like and dislike about their body.

Tell your client to follow this by stroking themselves and noticing how that feels. Initially this involves your client stroking their head, hands and feet and noting down any feelings or bodily sensations. Once they feel comfortable stroking these areas they can start to stroke their legs, arms, neck and upper body. Gradually they should work up to stroking the breast and genital area, remembering to write down their feelings and sensations. When they feel comfortable with this they can stimulate the genitals by rhythmically stroking their penis or clitoris, or by inserting a finger into the vagina.

It is essential that your client takes their time to explore their body at a pace that is comfortable for them. If your client feels in any way uncomfortable, anxious or upset, they need to stop and try again another day. It is best that your client practises sensate focus over several weeks rather than rushing through it. It is also important that they reflect on their feelings and note which sensations are pleasurable and which are uncomfortable as this will help your client to identify what gives them pleasure.

Sensate focus with a partner

This can improve the communication between your client and their partner so that they know how to please each other. When practising sensate focus with a partner they each need to take turns to touch and stroke each other. While doing this it is helpful for them to tell each other how the touch feels and what is pleasurable and what is not. It is essential when doing this that your client and their partner agree that either of them can stop at any point.

To get the most benefit from sensate focus your client will also need to agree not to have sex throughout the period of exploration, no matter how aroused. This ensures safety and increases communication of the full range of sensations. Giving each other pleasure without sex can help your client and their partner to know how to please each other non-sexually, to know how to talk to each other and to discover more creative ways of expressing their sensuality as well as their sexuality.

Warning

Advise your client that if they practise sensate focus with a partner, they need to make sure that the partner is truly willing and committed to this and that they agree to the boundaries.

MOOD AND SEXUAL INTIMACY

Your client's sexual relationship is also influenced by their mood. Stress and unresolved anger can reduce libido, which can impact on the desire to have sex as well as arousal and erectile difficulties. For women, the monthly hormonal cycle plays a significant role in enhancing or reducing libido. Unresolved anger, conflicts and arguments all pose considerable obstacles to a healthy sexual relationship.

Lack of control and unpredictability can also become a problem as these are reminiscent of the abuse. Your client may prefer to have a sense of advance warning of when to have sex so that they can mentally prepare themselves and get in the right mood. A degree of advance warning may feel more comfortable rather than feeling it is imposed. While this reduces spontaneity it does mean that your client will have some of control over when to have sex.

Alternatively you might find that your client may resort to alcohol to reduce sexual fears and anxiety as alcohol can reduce any inhibitions they may have. While a small amount of alcohol can help to relax remind your client to be wary that too much alcohol can affect both performance and the experience of pleasure.

To enhance sexual mood, desire and arousal your client will need to feel safe and be free of any interruptions. This is necessary especially if they feared and yet desired interruption when they were being abused. If they cannot fully relax they will find it difficult to enjoy the sexual experience. Sexual trust is another necessary component of a healthy sexual relationship. In order to enable sexual trust you need to help your client have clear boundaries and ground rules. This ensures their safety and reduces feeling demeaned or humiliated. This can only be achieved with good communication wherein they are free to express their needs to feel safe.

 Exercise

Safety needs

Your client needs to take some time to think about their needs to feel safe in their sexual relationship. If this is difficult it may be easier to help them think of what needs were not met during the abuse as this can highlight what they do need. The most common needs include the need to feel loved, to feel equally in control, to feel able to say 'no' or stop having sex if uncomfortable, and the need to feel fine with not always wanting penetrative sex. Male survivors need to feel accepted and valued despite occasional erectile difficulties, premature ejaculation or inability to perform. Most importantly, your client needs to feel that they are valued for who they are and not just as a sexual object. Remind your client to add any other specific needs to this list. Once they have compiled their list of needs they can express and discuss them with their partner, to establish mutually agreed ground rules.

CONCLUSION

The more your client can talk to their partner and express their sexual needs without fear of upsetting their partner, being hurtful, or rejecting, the more they will experience sexual trust. This will also allow your client to set limits, boundaries and ground rules in which they can express their desire, or say 'no' without fearing negative consequences.

Ground rules are necessary for a healthy sexual relationship and must include regularly telling each other 'I love you', paying each other compliments, and permitting each other to initiate or stop sex. It is vital that either partner can say 'no' without feeling hurt, rejected or humiliated. A particularly important ground rule is that hugs or cuddles do not always need to lead to sex but are merely an expression of affection. In discussing and establishing mutually agreed ground rules your client will significantly improve the quality of their sexual relationship.

If your client finds it too terrifying to have sex with another person they may need to put sexual intimacy on hold. Explain that they may find it easier to engage in sexual fantasy through the use of the internet, or by watching or reading erotic material and masturbation. This must always be a choice and should not be judged by your client or anyone else. Your client must not let themselves be pressurised to enter a sexual relationship if they are not ready for it. While many sexual difficulties can be worked though themselves, or with a partner, your client can always seek extra support through specific psychosexual therapy. If they have concerns about being addicted to sex or pornography they may benefit from joining a group that specialises in sex and love addiction (SLA).

20

MANAGING LOSS
AND MOURNING

Sexual violence, CSA and trauma are inextricably linked to loss, both in the past and present. You may find however that your client does not feel entitled to grieve due to self-blame, shame and negative self-beliefs. The losses sustained in complex trauma occur across all dimensions including the physical, psychological and spiritual. In order to mourn losses first help your client to identify theirs.

Common losses associated with complex trauma and CSA include actual and symbolic losses such as loss of childhood, loss of protective parent(s) and loss of a nurturing family, as well as the loss of self, self-esteem and self-worth, and loss of control and autonomy. Loss of trust in self and others and loss of belief that the world can be a benign place are also common.

Complex trauma also results in the loss of well-being, of control over the body, of continuity or belongingness, of healthy relationships and of the belief in a better future. Spiritual losses cluster around loss of faith and hope, and in the case of clerical abuse, of religious beliefs. Current and future losses include loss of hope in restoring damaged family relationships or the yearned for relationship with the abuser or non-abusing parent(s). These losses will also need to be mourned.

OBSTACLES TO GRIEVING
You may find that your client is haunted by self-blame and negative self-thoughts which will present a major obstacle to grieving as they prevent them from legitimising their trauma. Before starting the grieving process your client will need to work through shame, self-blame and negative self-beliefs to fully acknowledge the impact trauma has had on them. This needs to be supported by self-compassion and empathy in order to

permit the grieving process. This may present a number of challenges as the grief process is rarely straightforward or continuous.

PHASES OF GRIEF

As your client begins to grieve they will find themselves weaving in and out of various phases of grief. These tend to include periods of numbness, yearning for what is lost, and preoccupation with loss. In addition loss and grieving give rise to many feelings, not just sadness. Your client might also experience feelings of guilt, anger, shame and jealousy. These are all normal and need to be worked through before they will be able to accept the loss and recover.

Built-up grief forms a reservoir which when grieving starts can feel overwhelming. For this reason it is vital that your client paces themselves and makes sure that they nurture themselves throughout the process. They need to take their time to work through the range of losses and increase self-nurturing activities. Over time the aching pain of loss subsides but there may always be a nub of sadness.

TRAUMATIC GRIEF

If built-up grief is not released it can turn into what is called traumatic grief. Traumatic grief is grief that has been prolonged over many years. This is usually accompanied by chronic clinical depression, persistent sadness and a deep sense of hopelessness. This can severely undermine the capacity to function and engage in life. If your client experiences persistent traumatic grief that overwhelms and incapacitates them, they need to seek additional support through counselling.

Warning

If your client experiences persistent traumatic grief that overwhelms and incapacitates they may need to seek additional support from their support network.

EXERCISES TO HELP GRIEVING

There are a number of exercises that can help grieving and your client may find some of these helpful. Remind your client to only attempt those that they feel could be useful and to pace themselves. Before starting the grieving process they will need to identify the range of losses they have experienced.

Exercise
Identifying the range of losses

Encourage your client to think about and make a list of all the losses they have experienced. They could record these in two lists. One list can represent losses in the past while the other represents losses in the present, or that they face during their recovery. Remind your client that many of the losses associated with abuse are symbolic such as the loss of innocence, loss of childhood, or loss of self-discovery of sexuality. Some are still present now such as loss of control over body, loss of well-being, or loss of belief in a future without pain or abuse. Examine your client's lists with them and reflect on what feelings emerge and note these. Next explore with them how they have managed feelings of loss in the past. Did your client avoid their feelings or did they try to connect with them? Did they reach out to others or did they withdraw from them? How would they like to be in the future?

Remind your client

They should give themselves space to grieve and to really acknowledge their losses and sadness.

Understanding the impact of loss

As your client identifies each loss they should try to notice their thoughts and feelings and link these to the loss. This will give them a deeper understanding of how the loss affected them in the past, and how it continues to affect them in the present.

Exercise
Things missed and things not missed

Look at your client's list of losses with them and ask them to make two columns in their journal, one headed 'Things I miss' and one 'Things I don't miss'. Ask them to enter losses under these headings to help them identify those losses that still hurt and those losses that they have let go of and do not miss. It is also important that your client considers any losses they might sustain whilst making changes during their recovery and to grieve these. These can also be divided into those things that your client will miss and those they will not miss.

Memorial rituals

To help your client in the grieving process, advise them to mark their losses by performing a memorial ritual to honour the loss and their grief. This can be performed for each loss individually or suggest they devote a specific period of time to honour a number of losses. Present them with the exercises below.

Exercise
Memory book or box

Ask your client to gather together photographs or clippings of both sad and pleasant memories. They then need to place the photographs in their memory book or album and write or make notes alongside these. If your client is making a memory box advise them to put in things that remind them of their losses. This could include images of childhood, a favourite childhood book or film, a stuffed toy, or reminders of a childhood hobby or collection. Ask them to write down any associated thoughts or feelings in their memory book and put it into their memory box.

Your client needs to keep their memory book or box in a place where they can easily find it and look at it whenever they feel sad and are in contact with their losses. They can also make specific time to grieve such as in the following exercise.

Exercise
A night to remember

Tell your client to set aside a specific time such as a 'night to remember' away from any distractions to grieve. They should light some scented candles or spray their favourite scent or aftershave to ground them. They might use an aromatic scent that is commonly used in commemoration ceremonies such as sage, sandalwood or rosemary, or burn incense to create the right atmosphere. This is not a good idea if such scents are associated with the abuse, such as in clerical abuse. Your client might also put on some celebratory music to accompany the ceremony. Ask them to take out and look at their memory book or box and add things to these. They might consider writing a special letter to the source of the loss such as the young child, the innocent self or the lost parts of the self. This letter can then be 'sent' by burying or burning it and scattering the ashes.

Memorial ceremonies can be very healing in encouraging the survivor to say goodbye to their losses, hurt and pain. Alternatively you could suggest your client writes a message on a balloon and releases this. As they watch the balloon rise and drift away, they should recognise their acceptance and letting go of the loss. A variation on this is the 'River of Life' ceremony in which survivors make a small paper boat in which to place their message regarding the loss. They place a tealight into the boat and light the candle. Then they set the boat afloat in a small river or stream and watch it float away. They could also put a flower or other significant, symbolic object into the boat with their message.

Expressing grief

Whichever ritual or ceremony is used, remind your client to record their grief journey by writing about their experiences. Remind them to express the full range of their feelings including anger and tears. If your client has difficulty releasing either anger or tears, explore their beliefs with them around the expression of emotions and how much that has been shaped by the trauma.

Often tears are seen as a weakness, especially in males, or were ignored or not permitted when a child. Similarly, your client may fear expressing their anger or vulnerability because they were punished or humiliated for that in childhood. It will help to explore with your client any negative beliefs around crying or expressing anger or vulnerability and to reassess these so they can be expressed. Remind them that while these messages originated in childhood they do not have to persist in adulthood as they can sabotage recovery.

Exercise

Exploring beliefs around crying

Your client will need to reflect on what messages shaped their beliefs about crying. What were the messages in their family around crying? How was your client made to feel when they cried – weak, pathetic, vulnerable or contemptuous? Were they punished when they cried, or did it increase the level of cruelty? Perhaps not crying and detaching took the pain away? If your client is male were they taught that boys or men should not cry no matter how much pain they feel? Alternatively, are they afraid that if they cry they will lose control, or not be able to stop?

Ask your client to list whichever messages apply to them and check the evidence for these messages. They will also need to consider the benefits of crying such as the release of sadness, hurt and pain and how it aids healing. Crying is known to improve well-being and reduce blood pressure and heart rate. If your client is comfortable with crying, they could do the same exercise to identify beliefs about the expression of anger and vulnerability.

Remind your client

They cannot force tears so they must allow themselves to cry naturally and allow themselves to reclaim this human response to sadness and loss.

Reclaiming losses

Once your client has identified their losses you can begin to explore with them what was missing in their childhood and is still absent in adulthood.

While they can never replace these losses they can begin to compensate for any deficits by ensuring that these no longer persist in their current everyday life. For instance if your client was too terrified to play or not allowed to have fun, encourage them to give themselves permission to have fun or to play now. If they lacked nurturing, make sure that they are nurtured now.

Exercise
Reclaiming losses

Examine their list of losses and highlight those losses that your client can replace. In identifying those things that were missing in childhood they will be able to consider how they can balance them now. Ask your client to make a list of the losses that can be reclaimed and how they can introduce these into their life now. For example, if their losses include lack of security it is important they find sources of safety and security in the present. If your client avoided people in the past they could develop friendships now. If they never felt 'special' they could ensure that they do things now that make them feel special.

If your client felt psychologically orphaned as a child they can rebalance this by building a good support network now. This will reinstate a sense of belongingness by creating a new 'family' in which they are respected, nurtured and loved. While these can never make up for the actual losses incurred, they can go some way to improving the quality of your client's life in the present and future.

READJUSTING TO THE WORLD

Recognising and mourning losses will help your client to relegate the trauma to the past and allow them to readjust to the world now and move forward. Although their abuse experiences will always remain a part of their life history, the experiences will no longer dominate or control who they are. They will merely be a part of your client's life experiences rather than identifying the whole them. In this your client will become freer to move forward and embrace their future without being haunted by the terror, pain and fear of abuse.

To celebrate moving forward your client could honour their losses by making something that symbolises their journey of recovery. This could be a painting, a sculpture, a poem or song. You could also advise them to paint a painting or a commemorative plate, plaque or a memory tile which symbolises their journey of recovery.

Part 4

POST-TRAUMATIC GROWTH

21

RESTORING REALITY AND TRUST IN SELF

To restore reality means learning to trust oneself again. In trusting ourselves we can begin to trust others. The more your client understands how their traumatic experiences have affected them the better they will be able to see how this prevented them from listening to themselves. This will help your client to get in touch with how they feel. Once they are no longer on red alert, and avoiding their inner experiencing, your client will be able to gauge how they feel and think. Then your client can stop being influenced by the expectations of others. This will allow them to reject other people's judgements of them and to value their own judgement.

INNER EXPERIENCING

A useful way to restore trust in intuition is to encourage your client to listen to their inner experiencing, or gut instinct. Do not let them be forced into making any instant decisions and advise them to take time to reflect on what they truly feel or think. Remind your client it is okay to say 'I don't know but will get back to you'. Anyone who rushes them into instant answers or decisions is not respecting your client's right to reflect in their own time. If they have any doubts this means they are not sure and need to think about what is being said or requested. It is essential that you get your client to listen to their doubts and take them seriously. The following exercise will help them to be more skilled in this and you can help them develop their internal gauge.

 Exercise
Developing an internal gauge
To develop your client's internal gauge, encourage them to imagine it as ruler with a scale of 1 to 10, with 1 being very unsure and 10 being very sure.

Whenever they have doubts about something, get them to plot the degree of doubt on the scale. If they are unsure make sure they listen to the doubts before making any decision. Get them to make a list of the doubts and reflect on them by asking themselves what the evidence is for or against them. This will allow your client to move the doubts along the scale and help them to decide what is best.

Remind your client
Doubts are inner signals that they are not sure. They need to listen to them before making any decision.

INNER WISDOM

The more your client listens to themselves the more they will be able to develop their own inner value system and inner wisdom. Using their own inner wisdom, or internal locus of evaluation, will restore your client's trust in themselves rather than being influenced by others. This will help rebuild their self-esteem and help them make more positive choices that are right for them.

As your client starts to listen to and trust themselves more they will find that they are more able to be in contact with their needs, rather than focusing on the needs of others. This will free your client up to express their needs and find ways of meeting these. In this they will find it easier to distinguish what feels right for them and will allow them to establish internal locus of evaluation and control in which they feel they are in control of their thoughts, feelings and actions.

In trusting themselves more your client will be able to accept and value themselves more, including their personal qualities. This will help to repair their self-esteem and develop a self-image that is based on a realistic evaluation of themselves rather than that imposed by others. The exercise below can help with this.

Exercise
Personal qualities

Encourage your client to make a list in their journal of which personal qualities they admire in others. Examine this list with your client and note how many of these also apply to them. Make sure they add others that they know they have. Get them to talk to a trusted friend who may also have some qualities to add to their list. As your client reflects on their personal qualities try to gauge with them to what extent they accept or reject these in their daily life. Make sure your client regularly reminds themselves of these qualities and thereby changes their self-image. They could do this by including their personal qualities in their cookie jar (see p.132).

RESTORING SELF-RELIANCE

Restoring trust in themselves will allow your client to become more self-reliant. This will reduce their dependency on others who may let them down or betray their trust. Such self-reliance must not be confused with fierce self-sufficiency which is really a protection from others. This self-reliance is based on knowing that they can trust themselves in identifying, expressing and meeting their needs without depending on others to decide for them. It also means that they can choose when to ask for help or feedback from others and when to be independent. Ultimately, this provides your client with more choices rather than feeling controlled by others.

Initially it might be hard for your client to become more self-reliant as it means making changes that can produce anxiety and fears. To help them manage these remind them to pace themselves and monitor their progress. Keeping a record of situations in which they have shown increased trust in themselves can act as a powerful reminder of their recovery. Remind them to include both positive and negative things that have happened, and how they managed these to give them direct evidence of their accomplishments.

It also helps for your client to record what they have learnt about themselves and how this has increased their self-confidence. With practice and regular monitoring your client will be able to balance their internal and external reality based on their own judgement and evaluation. In addition, as they trust themselves more they will be able to begin to trust others and trust in a better future.

22

RELAPSE PREVENTION AND MAINTAINING SELF-CARE

As the survivor starts to recover and begins to rebuild their life, it is important that they continue to practise everything they have learnt. It might help them to review their progress so far.

REVIEWING PROGRESS

 Exercise

Reviewing self-care

Encourage your client to make a list in their journal of all the things they do now to look after themselves. Determine with your client which ones give them the most pleasure or satisfaction. Which are they most proud of accomplishing? Which have been the most helpful to them? Which have been most inspirational? Are there any that your client has not been able to maintain? In reflecting on these with them, are there any skills or activities they would like to develop more? Or are there some other self-care activities they would like to add? You could help your client develop these and add them to their current self-care plan.

If there are any self-care strategies that your client has not been able to maintain, you might suggest that they try some alternative ones, or recommend that they adapt those they have tried to suit them more. Encourage your client to be creative. The aim is to have a balance of regular exercise, rest, work and play that suits them and their needs. The focus also has to be on improving the quality of their everyday life.

Remind your client to regularly engage in activities that they can enjoy for pleasure's sake. It is really important to find time just to play. Play is a very good way of staying in the present and enjoying the moment. This stops survivors from over-focusing on the past or constantly worrying about the future. Remind your client that they cannot change the past and they cannot know the future, but they can be in and know the present. Now that there is greater safety in their life, they can allow themselves to become absorbed in the present and enjoy time to play. To be in the present can help your client to feel more grounded and bring more peace and tranquillity into their life.

As your client becomes more conscious of how it feels to be more contented encourage them to start enjoying life more. Remind them to be realistic though. There may be periods of time when their life is more difficult or stressful and it becomes harder to maintain a self-care programme. Rather than letting your client become discouraged during these times, try to remind them of what they can and cannot do and do not put too much pressure on them, or allow them to pressure themselves. Even if they can just do one of the things on their self-care list that is enough to stay on track. If they are too overwhelmed to do any, then help them accept that for the moment it is not possible. Once things become easier then your client can start again. If they find that they are starting to revert to old, harmful patterns of coping advise them to consider seeking additional help from their support network.

Exercise

Worry box

Encourage your client to make a worry box. Get them to write their worries down on strips of paper and put them into their worry box. This allows them to clear their mind to continue whatever else they need to do without becoming overwhelmed by the weight of all their worries. It can also help your client to contain the worries so that they do not become overwhelmed. When you find they feel stronger and more able to cope, tell them to take out one of the strips of paper and spend some time exploring that worry. It helps to limit the amount of time they spend on worrying to about ten minutes. If they come to a solution then they should discard the strip of paper, if not tell them to return it to the worry box. If your client feels the worries are piling up, suggest they commit to spending 20 minutes a day looking at some of the worries and begin to problem solve at least one of them.

Top tip

Advise your client to make a 'worry box' in which to place their worries until they feel strong enough to deal with them.

It is important that your client continues writing in their journal and checks that they are moving in the right direction to reach their goals.

Remind your client to record all their achievements and to reward themselves for accomplishments. A good way for your client to reward themselves is to make a 'reward box'.

Exercise

Reward box

Encourage your client to make reward box in which they place small treats to celebrate their achievements. The reward box can include things that give pleasure such as small chocolate treats, a scented candle, a new bath product, a new music CD, DVD, book or favourite magazine. It can also include handwritten vouchers to trade in such as treating themselves to a nice bath or a massage, having a meal out with friends, or going to the cinema or a special day out.

Top tip

Get your client to make a 'reward box' in which they place small treats to celebrate their accomplishments.

MAINTAINING RELATIONSHIPS AND FRIENDSHIPS

To support your client's self-care it is important they maintain their relationships and friendships. Regular contact with friends is crucial as it helps your client to share their experiences, to have fun and to feel connected to others. Encourage them to have regular face to face contact, but if this is not possible encourage them to try to stay in touch by email or telephone. Ensure they vary their contact with friends so that the focus is not always on talking about their recovery, but that it includes other activities that are enjoyable and fun. To maintain your client's recovery it helps if they give themselves permission to enjoy life's pleasures.

In remaining connected to others your client will find that they will be more connected to themselves which will help them to maintain their self-care in making positive choices. This will include being able to say 'I want' and 'I can' rather that 'I am not allowed' or 'I can't'. Freeing themselves up from such restrictions will help them to embrace their new life and continue to flourish. Maintaining their self-care will also help your client to manage any setbacks they encounter in moving forward.

MANAGING SETBACKS

Assisting your client to maintain their self-care can help to manage any potential setbacks and prevent any relapse in their recovery. It is important that they acknowledge that setbacks are inevitable and that these represent moments of vulnerability. It is also important that your client views these as opportunities to use all the skills they have learnt throughout their recovery, rather than feeling discouraged. As some setbacks are predictable suggest they examine how they might manage these in advance.

Remind your client
Setbacks are inevitable and mark a time of vulnerability. They are an opportunity to use newly learnt coping skills.

It helps to focus your client's thinking in advance of any setbacks so that they are prepared and can manage them more easily. Once the setback has taken hold your client may become too distressed or overwhelmed to manage it as effectively. When setbacks occur it is best for them to go back to the basic skills they have learnt. Remind your client to make sure they are safe and if they are not, advise them to put in place whatever is necessary to restore safety. Next they should use the grounding skills that work best for them so that they can calm themselves before tackling the setback. Suggest they talk to a trusted friend, or seek out additional professional help for extra support.

To help your client plan in advance for any setbacks and to make a realistic and effective action plan they may find the following exercise helpful.

Exercise
Developing an action plan

Ask your client to make a record in their journal of risky situations and any potential setbacks. Examine these with your client in turn and try to help them predict typical automatic or negative thoughts in that situation. Encourage them to challenge these by checking the evidence for and against such thoughts. Next get them to consider the behaviours which usually occur alongside such negative thoughts or situations of stress. Evaluate with them the effectiveness of these behaviours and think of some alternative ways of managing the situation. Ask your client what would make them feel better, and develop their action plan from this. Remind your client to be realistic in their action plan so that this does not create more pressure.

It also helps to look at potential setbacks in terms of how difficult they are to manage. Ask your client to rate them in terms of those they can manage with little difficulty, those they would struggle to manage, those that represent a minor lapse and those that they consider to be a major relapse. This will help your client to gauge the severity of the setback and what action plan needs to be put into place.

You may find that your client needs to make more than one action plan depending on the situation. Once you have helped them devise their action plan(s) get them to record these onto a bright coloured sticky note and put it in an accessible place in their journal so that they can find it quickly in an emergency. When setbacks occur they should follow the instructions of their action plan to help them through it.

When your client has managed the setback and feels more in control, it is really important that they reflect on why the setback happened and what they can learn from this. Often setbacks signal areas of vulnerability and outstanding work that needs to be done to continue recovery. Ask your client to take note of these and try to work on that particular area so that they can feel more in control or be better prepared in the future. Also explore with your client what they would like to do in the future and add these to their goals for recovery.

Another way to prevent relapse is for the client to continue to measure their recovery and check that their goals are realistic and achievable. Remind your client to break down their goals into small measurable stages and to reward themselves from their reward box as they reach each of these stages. It may be necessary for your client to revise their goals as they progress through their recovery. Their goals should be dynamic and flexible. You may find that your client is happy to have achieved as much as they have without reaching their ultimate goal, or that their goal changes slightly as they begin to achieve each stage. The most important thing is for your client to remain realistic and to be open to experiment in reaching goals. If they are not reaching their goals, rather than see this as a setback you may need to help them evaluate those goals to check how realistic they are. Alternatively they might need to revise the stages for reaching that goal in the light of their achievements so far.

 Top tip

Your client must be realistic in their goals and then they can achieve them. Setbacks may be due to unrealistic goals rather than failure on their part.

If your client does relapse encourage them to reduce any other pressures in their life. The aim of your client's recovery is to reduce pressure not to increase it. It may be necessary for your client to reduce their commitments in other areas of their life until the setback is resolved. You may need to remind your client to say 'no' and to take more time for themselves. They may also need to ask for help from others without feeling a failure. Encourage them to seek out people in their support network who can support them through this. It is important for your client to access as much support as they can during crises until things return to a more manageable level. Their focus has to be on reducing areas of stress and maximising stabilisation.

To help your client assess the impact of the setback measure their level of distress by using the Subjective Units of Distress Scale (SUDS) (see Box 22.1). They can add to this scale by adding any other signs of distress such as number of hours spent sleeping, increase in work hours, or temptation to resort to self-harming behaviours.

Box 22.1 Subjective Units of Distress Scale

Ask your client the following and get them to rate answers on a 10 point scale.

1. How alert are you? (1 being asleep and 10 wide awake)

2. How calm are you? (1 being most calm and 10 highly anxious)

3. How well are you able to focus on tasks such as conversation, reading a book or watching TV? (1 being very focused and 10 not able to focus at all)

4. How regulated is your mood? (1 being totally normal and 10 being extreme mood swings. Try to include the frequency and severity of the mood swings)

5. How long does it take you to get back to normal? (1 being very quickly and 10 a long time)

It is also useful to compare your client's scores with their level of distress prior to the setback. As the scale helps you to assess your client's levels of distress, it is worth using the scale on a weekly basis. Not only will this help you to monitor their level of distress but it will also alert them to a reduction in their stability. This can help to forewarn your client of changes in their well-being in advance so that they can take action before their distress level reaches a critical point. This can help in predicting setbacks and prevent major relapses.

While there will always be setbacks what is critical in measuring emotional well-being is how your client handles stressors and setbacks. It is unrealistic to expect to be 100 per cent free of trauma reminders or distress and you need to encourage your client to accept this. The most important factor in measuring recovery is not the number of setbacks but how your client is able to bounce back from distress and trauma reminders.

Remind your client

Setbacks are an opportunity to measure progress in how quickly they can rebalance their emotional state and restore stability.

While your client may fear that setbacks mean that they are regressing, this is rarely the case as long as they listen to the signals and take appropriate action. In addition, do not let them assume that setbacks will mean a return to the same intense levels of distress. This is a result of fear and does not mean that will become reality. The skills you have given them during their recovery will come into play and help them to manage their reactions.

Remind your client to trust themselves and the skills they have to cope with any setback or threatened relapse. Also encourage them to be patient with themselves. Recovery from abuse takes time and your client needs to pace their recovery.

Warning

If your client does relapse and feels that they are in danger of harming themselves or being harmed by others, consider contacting additional professional support.

23

MAINTAINING POST-TRAUMATIC GROWTH

In working through this handbook you have helped you client take control of their recovery. Take a moment with your client to reflect on their accomplishments. Your client may wish to look through their journal entries to see how much they have achieved. Check to see if your client feels that they have more control of their emotions, are able to face memories without being overwhelmed, or being plagued by flashbacks or intrusive memories or nightmares. Your client may feel more in touch with their feelings and more able to enjoy life's pleasures and may have a stronger bond with others. Whatever their recovery has brought to their life, remind your client to celebrate the changes and continue to embrace their future.

At this point in your client's recovery they can begin to experience what professionals call post-traumatic growth. While some survivors may only ever experience abuse as destructive, research has shown that many survivors find that they begin to open up to further potential growth. This growth is not necessarily directly linked to the trauma but may be as a result of what they have learnt through their struggle to cope with the aftermath of abuse.

Survivors have reported that post-traumatic growth can be seen in six significant areas of their lives. The first is in a sense of personal strength. This is because when vulnerability coexists with an increased capacity to survive, they can become stronger. While your client may experience their vulnerability as dangerous or an obstacle it is in reality an opportunity for growth. The second thing that survivors report is a greater appreciation of life, especially the more ordinary, everyday things in life. This appreciation is seen in refining priorities and spending more time doing things that are personally meaningful such as spending time with friends and family. By remaining in the present time slows down so that they will notice the small details of life such as the wind rustling in the trees, the sunlight dappling through the leaves, and the warmth of the sun on their skin. This allows your client to be more in touch with their bodily sensations and make them feel a part of something bigger than themselves.

Third, post-traumatic growth is seen in getting closer to other people especially friends and family in which your client values relationships more than material things or work. This is supported by being more comfortable with intimacy, maybe for the first time ever. In reconnecting to themselves and others they feel less like an island but part of the wider world. The process of recovery promotes the fourth area of post-traumatic growth, that of greater self-understanding. Your client's journey of healing is a journey of self-discovery which allows them to reconnect with their real self and strengthen their self-identity.

The fifth area of post-traumatic growth is spiritual development. When people experience life-threatening events such as trauma, they are faced with fundamental questions about the meaning of life and death. While trauma challenges all previous assumptions about life it also raises deep questions about beliefs, values and the purpose of life. Such questions are as a result of surviving powerful experiences rather than some abstract or intellectual exercise. In some cases, abuse, especially if it occurred within a religious or faith context, will result in spiritual injury. This can lead either to a loss of faith or a deepening of faith. Ultimately, recovery from complex trauma can be transforming in which resolving painful trauma can lead to experiencing life at a much deeper level of awareness. Lastly, post-traumatic growth can result in the opening up of new possibilities which can be life changing. A new and changed perspective on life can be the beginning of changing the direction of their path. This could be a career change, moving to a new environment or country, going back to college, or a change in their priorities.

Overall, post-traumatic growth can lead to a greater sense of control and purpose in life which will help your client to appreciate life even more. In embracing life they can finally move from merely surviving to thriving and flourishing.

Part 5

PROFESSIONAL ISSUES

24

PRACTITIONER SELF-CARE

Working with survivors of complex trauma can be extremely challenging and demanding. Bearing witness to brutality and dehumanisation can impact on well-being and shatter assumptions about the nature of human beings and the world as a safe and benign place (Janoff-Bulman, 1985). Practitioners need to be mindful that repeated exposure to trauma narratives can lead to vicarious traumatisation (VT), or secondary traumatic stress (STS). To minimise the risk of STS it is essential that practitioners understand the impact of working with complex trauma and professional self-care.

This chapter will look at what is meant by VT and STS and how these impact on professional and personal functioning. It will highlight how it can affect practitioners on a range of dimensions including physical, emotional, cognitive, behavioural and spiritual well-being and how to manage these most effectively through self-care. Practitioners are urged to ensure that they look after themselves to build resilience in order to provide a safe and secure base for both survivors and themselves.

VICARIOUS TRAUMATISATION, COMPASSION FATIGUE AND BURNOUT

There is considerable research on how working with trauma impacts on professionals and mental health practitioners (Figley, 1995; Sanderson, 2010a). Witnessing trauma through survivor narratives is bound to affect practitioners in that 'if you gaze into an abyss, the abyss gazes also into you' (Nietzsche, 1886, p.146). This can impact on how practitioners view the world and how they view human nature, and undermine their sense of safety. More importantly it is necessary and human to be affected by the suffering and pain of others. However, repeated exposure over time can become so overwhelming that compassion is eroded and the practitioner begins to feel powerless and helpless. That witnessing and listening to trauma can impact on professionals is now recognised and validated by inclusion in DSM-V (APA, 2013) in their criteria for developing PTSD.

 Remember

It is human and natural to be affected by the suffering of others. Practitioners need to make sure they are not overwhelmed and do not feel powerless and helpless.

Box 24.1 Definitions of vicarious traumatisation, compassion fatigue, burnout and secondary traumatic stress

Vicarious traumatisation: VT is 'the negative transformation in the self of the helper that comes about as a result of empathic engagement with survivors' trauma material and a sense of responsibility or commitment to help' (McCann and Pearlman, 1990, p.132).

Compassion fatigue: 'A state of tension and preoccupation with the traumatized patients by re-experiencing traumatic events, avoidance/numbing of reminders, and persistent arousal (e.g. anxiety) associated with the patient' (Figley, 2002, p.1435).

Burnout: '[A] state of physical, emotional and mental exhaustion caused by long term involvement in emotionally demanding situations. It is marked by physical depletion and chronic fatigue, by feelings of hopelessness, and by the development of negative self-concept and negative attitudes toward work, life and other people' (Maslach et al., 1996, p.4).

Secondary traumatic stress: 'The natural consequent behaviours resulting from knowledge about a traumatizing event experienced by a significant other. It is the stress resulting from wanting to help a traumatized or suffering person' (Figley and Kleber, 1995, p.79).

While there are a number of terms (see Box 24.1) used to describe the impact of trauma on professionals they are all characterised by PTSD symptoms which mirror many of the symptoms seen in survivors. Practitioners frequently report strong reactions of disbelief, terror and rage, as well as an erosion of well-being as manifested in feelings of helplessness, powerlessness and loss of faith in humanity (Herman, 1992b). These symptoms frequently co-exist with an increase in self-sacrificing behaviours in which the clinician becomes over-involved with clients and neglects to look after themselves, which further exacerbates the PTSD symptoms. Alternatively, some practitioners feel so overwhelmed that they actively disengage from clients and colleagues and begin to withdraw. Overtime this can lead to the development of STS (Figley and Kleber, 1995).

To reduce the development of STS practitioners need to consistently monitor their reactions to ensure that they manage any negative impact. One way of achieving this is through reflecting on their reactions to trauma narratives and through supervision. A simple checklist (see Box 24.2, below) for phases of the burnout process has been complied by Freudenberger and North (2006) and can be used as a guide to whether you are in danger of developing burnout. In addition there are a number of scales that measure a range of symptoms that indicate burnout such as the Maslach Burnout Inventory (Maslach *et al.*, 1996) or STS such as the The Traumatic Stress Scale (Bride, Robinson, Yegedis and Figley, 2004).

Box 24.2 Common phases in the burnout process (adapted from Freudenberger and North, 2006)

- Compulsion to prove oneself
- Working harder
- Neglecting one's needs
- Displacement of conflicts
- Changes in value systems
- Denial of emerging problems
- Withdrawal and isolation
- Changes in behaviour
- Depersonalisation
- Inner emptiness
- Depression
- Burnout syndrome

To assess to what degree you are being affected on a somatic, emotional, psychological and cognitive level it might be helpful to look at the Maslach Burnout Inventory (see Box 24.3) and answer the questions. If your answer is 'yes' to most of the questions it might be worth filling out the full version of the inventory and seeking supervision or some psychological support. This is particularly important to avoid any further deterioration or the development of STS.

Box 24.3 The Maslach Burnout Inventory: Manual (adapted from Maslach *et al.,* 1996)

1. Do you feel run down and drained of physical or emotional energy?

2. Do you find that you are prone to negative thinking about your job?

3. Do you find that you are harder and less sympathetic with people than perhaps they deserve?

4. Do you find yourself getting easily irritated by small problems, or by your co-workers and team?

5. Do you feel misunderstood or unappreciated by your co-workers?

6. Do you feel that you have no one to talk to?

7. Do you feel that you are achieving less than you should?

8. Do you feel under an unpleasant level of pressure to succeed?

9. Do you feel that you are not getting what you want out of your job?

10. Do you feel that you are in the wrong profession?

11. Are you becoming frustrated with parts of your job?

12. Do you feel that bureaucracy frustrates your ability to do a good job?

13. Do you feel that there is more work to do than you practically have the ability to do?

14. Do you feel that you do not have time to do many of the things that are important to doing a good quality job?

15. Do you find that you do not have time to plan as much as you would like to?

SECONDARY TRAUMATIC STRESS

Secondary traumatic stress is characterised by symptoms which closely mirror those of PTSD, in particular symptoms of intrusion, avoidance and arousal. DSM-V now includes professionals 'experiencing repeated or extreme exposure to aversive details of (the) traumatic event(s)' in its criteria for developing acute stress disorder and PTSD. While many of the effects are natural reactions they have to be monitored as they can have a negative impact on professional and personal functioning (see Box 24.4).

Box 24.4 Common reactions in secondary traumatic stress

- Trauma like reactions – hypervigilance, heightened physiological arousal, numbness
- Somatic reactions – irritability, exhaustion, apathy, restlessness, changes in appetitive behaviours, nightmares
- Cognitive changes – distorted perceptions, intrusive thoughts, ruminating over cases, preoccupation with abuse, uncertainty, impaired concentration, loss of meaning, shattered assumptions about the world
- Behavioural – avoidance, disconnecting from others, adversarial, over/under protectiveness towards own children, self-medication
- Emotional – anxious, sense of powerlessness, helplessness, despair, loss of trust

---

As can be seen from Box 24.4, the impact of working with trauma can evoke behaviours and emotions that are not dissimilar to the trauma responses of the survivor. For counsellors who are exposed to many accounts of trauma on a daily basis this can have a cumulative impact which can threaten their health and well-being. This is further exacerbated as practitioners have to be containers not only for the survivor but also their own responses and reactions. This can lead to classic PTSD symptoms of hyper-arousal, intrusion, avoidance and numbing. If left unattended, these symptoms can prompt an avoidance of trauma material, withdrawal, diminished interest in activities, and a sense of detachment and estrangement from others (Sanderson, 2010a). In addition, practitioners can experience hyper-reactivity and a decrease in the ability to focus and concentrate. Alternatively, some practitioners become numb and desensitised to suffering as they habituate to repeated accounts of trauma making it harder to feel compassion or empathy.

Secondary traumatic stress can also lead to shattered assumptions about the self, others and the world as a meaningful place (Janoff-Bulman, 1985). This can evoke a pervasive sense of uncertainty and increased levels of anxiety leaving the practitioner feeling paralysed and helpless (just as the client does) which further impacts on professional and personal functioning (Sanderson, 2010a). To monitor or assess to what degree working with survivors of complex trauma is impacting, practitioners will find it helpful to look at the list of symptoms included on Bride *et al.*, (2004) Secondary Traumatic Stress Scale (see Box 24.5).

This measures intrusion, avoidance and arousal symptoms on a scale of 1–5 with a range of questions on symptoms experienced within the last seven days on a scale of 1 to 5.

Box 24.5 Sample questions from Secondary Traumatic Stress Scale (adapted from Bride *et al.*, 2004)

I feel emotionally numb

My heart starts pounding when if think about my work with clients

It seems as if I am reliving the trauma(s) experienced by my client(s)

I have trouble sleeping

I feel discouraged about the future

Reminders about my work with clients upset me

I have little interest in being around others

I feel jumpy

I am less active than usual

I think about work with my clients when I don't intend to

I have trouble concentrating

I avoid people, places, or things that remind me of my work with clients

I have disturbing dreams about my work with clients

I want to avoid working with some clients

I am easily annoyed

I expect something bad to happen

I notice gaps in my memory

IMPACT OF STS ON PROFESSIONAL FUNCTIONING

The symptoms associated with STS can affect both professional and personal functioning. In terms of its impact on professional functioning counsellors will need to be aware how STS symptoms can affect their work in the therapeutic setting. To manage overwhelming states of arousal counsellors may become distanced and detached with an accompanying reduction in empathy and compassion, which can lead to ruptures in the therapeutic relationship. Some practitioners find that they habituate to trauma accounts and become desensitised to the pain and suffering of survivors resulting in compassion fatigue. Becoming too detached can also affect the ability to assess risk accurately and erode self-efficacy. To compensate for this the counsellor may take on more and more trauma work in order to test their ability to cope (Sanderson, 2010a) and to prove that they can manage. All feelings of vulnerability tend to be denied in striving to prove that they are not being affected leading to an avoidance of seeking help or support, including supervision. As the counsellor withdraws they feel increasingly powerless, helpless and isolated (Sanderson, 2010a). This sense of isolation will be particularly exacerbated for those counsellors in private practice.

As can be seen in Table 24.1 the STS symptoms can impact on a range of dimensions including the emotional, cognitive and behavioural. This can lead to an increase in mistakes, poor decision making and an avoidance of work related tasks, which further impact on professional functioning. Some counsellors will become over-responsible in attempting to rescue the survivor, or become resentful, blaming the survivor for their symptoms. This can lead to increased conflicts, therapeutic ruptures and open hostility which further exacerbates their sense of helplessness. Rather than take breaks the counsellor will increase their workload risking even further exhaustion and general dissatisfaction.

Table 24.1 Impact on professional functioning		
Emotional	Cognitive	Behavioural
• Burnout • Exhaustion • Dissatisfaction • Overwhelmed • Lack of motivation • Desensitisation and habituation • Helplessness and powerlessness	• Negative attitude to work • Poor concentration • Inattentiveness • Inoculation to trauma and abuse • Impaired risk assessment • Impaired decision making	• Impaired communication • Increased mistakes • Increased absences • Avoidance of co-workers • Avoidance of supervision • Adversarial stance • Increasing workload • Taking on more clients • Not taking regular breaks

Impairments in professional functioning are often also reflected in STS symptoms in organisations which expect staff to manage extremely high workloads while failing to recognise the impact the work has (Sanderson, 2010a; Wastell, 2005; Yassen, 1995). Practitioners who work in statutory or voluntary agencies may see the impact of STS in low retention rates and high turnover of staff and in increased illness and absenteeism. This may be accompanied by widespread cynicism, staff dissatisfaction, disillusionment and increased boundary violations. To manage these, staff may project their STS symptoms onto the organisation leading to increased levels of criticisms of management structure, procedures and systems (Sanderson, 2010a). Over time both staff and the organisation feel beleaguered and assaulted on all fronts as they seek to survive. If this is not addressed the organisation will fail in their duty of care to staff which will impact on the practitioners duty of care to the survivor.

 Warning
STS impacts on professional function and on organisations. To minimise STS organisations must ensure they invest in staff self-care and offer appropriate psychological support to ensure duty of care.

To minimise STS in organisations it is critical that senior management and clinical managers are aware of the impact of the work on staff and the possibility of developing STS. This will need to be accompanied by assessment of the needs, limits, emotional resources and resilience of individual members of staff. In addition they need to ensure that they provide regular supervision and encourage a climate of open and honest communication between staff and organisation. To facilitate this, organisations must endeavour to identify and deal with practices that lead to an increase in STS. In the long term organisations need to invest in building staff resilience by actively encouraging staff self-care and providing appropriate psychological support.

IMPACT OF STS ON PERSONAL FUNCTIONING
The pervasive effects of STS also affects personal functioning (see Table 24.2) in eroding general well-being, elevated stress reactions and impaired immune functioning. This can put counsellors at risk of developing PTSD, depression or other mental health problems. In the same way that survivors may resort to self-medication, practitioners may seek to manage their anxiety by resorting to alcohol, food or drugs to

regulate their mood. Some counsellors may find that they disconnect from partners, family or friends in attempts to avoid intimacy, or become over-protective of loved ones (Sanderson, 2010a). This is especially the case if there is a re-activation of their own painful childhood experiences that have remained unprocessed.

Table 24.2 Impact on personal functioning				
Emotional	**Cognitive**	**Physical**	**Behavioural**	**Spiritual**
• Anger and rage • Sadness • Depression • Hyper-arousal • Hyper-vigilance • Anxiety • Apathy • Numbness • Terror • Frustation	• Impaired concentration • Confusion and disorientation • Dissociation • Forgetfulness • Rumination • Guilt • Impaired trust • Disbelief	• Somatic reactions • Impaired immune functioning • Changes in cortisol levels • Self-medication • Changes in appetitive behaviours – sleep, rest, eating, sex, activity	• Withdrawal • Isolation • Avoidance • Irritability • Impatience • Increased neediness	• Loss of meaning and purpose • Hopelessness • Disconnection from others • Loss of vitality • Loss of spirituality • Loss of faith in humanity • Loss of joy

It is critical that if you feel that you are suffering from burnout or STS you seek appropriate support. This can be through supervision, mentoring or a return to personal therapy. It is also essential to ensure that you have a good personal support network among family and friends with whom you can enjoy experiences that are not trauma related. In addition it is important to take regular breaks from work and ensure that you make time to invest in your own self-care to minimise the risk of STS. To help you assess your work-life balance you might find the following exercise useful.

 **Exercise**
Work/life balance

- On a blank piece of paper, draw a large circle to represent your life.

- Place a smaller circle in the centre to represent you and label it with your name.

- Divide the large circle into slices as in a pie to show the various activities that you are engaged in on a regular basis, e.g. work, family, leisure, physical exercise, emotional self-care, spiritual well-being.

- Reflect on this and ask yourself to what extent you are living a balanced life. Are your values reflected in how you spend your time? Are you spreading yourself too thinly? If you had only one month to live how would you divide your time? Are there things that you are avoiding or putting aside? What changes would you like to make?

- On a new sheet of paper, draw a circle and divide it up into how you would like to balance your life.

 Remember

To minimise STS you need to have a good professional and personal network and access emotional and psychological support.

THE PREVENTION OF SECONDARY TRAUMATIC STRESS

To prevent or minimise STS, counsellors need to ensure that they have a strong personal and professional support network and understand the importance of self-care. Regular supervision, preferably with a supervisor who is experienced in trauma work, is essential and a prerequisite when working with complex trauma. This can be supported with regular peer supervision, or in complex cases by consulting a specialist in the field. Continuous professional development is an ideal way to enhance knowledge and awareness of complex trauma and provides an opportunity to network and keep up to date with new techniques. Reflexivity, or self-supervision, (Casement, 1990) in which to mentalise your experience of working with survivors of complex trauma is a valuable way to remain connected to self and enhance understanding of your reactions. Self-reflection allows you to become a more sentient practitioner and to remain in contact with your internal responses and stay connected and attuned to the survivor.

To assess to what extent working with survivors of complex trauma impacts on you and to identify signals that indicate that you are under stress try the following exercise.

Exercise
Exploring signs of stress

- On a sheet of paper list in what ways your work impacts on you.

- Next reflect on how you know that you are becoming stressed and list any signs or symptoms. Look at these and make a list of what you commonly do to manage these.

- Next list some of the triggers that cause you to become particularly stressed.

- Reflect on what you have written and consider what would help you most to manage triggers and stress reactions.

COUNSELLOR SELF-CARE

To remain connected you need to ensure that you are attuned to your needs, which will allow you to maintain a balance between personally meaningful life activities and work. Yassen (1995) proposes that counsellors balance client work with other activities that support the prevention of trauma, as well as extending their support network beyond their immediate work. This will enable you to ensure access to self-support both professionally and personally. In seeking support you are acknowledging your vulnerability and compassion for self as well as permitting the expression of a full range of emotions (Sanderson, 2010a).

Salzer (2002) has identified four sources of support: emotional; informational; instrumental and companion. Emotional support is the kind you might get from a partner, family member or a close and trusted friend who offers care, love, care, empathy, acceptance and understanding. Informational support consists of access to knowledge, information and skills. This is typically sought from peers, colleagues or a mentor, manager or supervisor. Instrumental support is the kind of support that helps you to get things done, especially stressful or unpleasant tasks that require assistance. Alongside this, companion support consists of the companionship that is gained from feeling connected to others especially through recreational activities such as a sport, hobby or passionate interest. To ensure you have access to a good support network, and go to the person who can offer the support needed, it might help to identify your sources of support through the following exercise.

Exercise
Mapping your support network

- On a blank sheet of paper, draw a large circle.

- Divide the circle into slices as in a pie and place headings such as emotional support, informational support, instrumental support, companion support and any other category of your choice.

- Next write the names of those people in your personal, professional and social world that can offer you support in the categories (you can put the same person in more than one slice).

- Reflect on this and identify how you feel about your social support network. Do you have enough people in your network? Do they provide you with the support you need? Do you seek support from the person who can offer it? Would you like more support and in which areas? How might you be able to seek such support?

- Reflect on how frequently you have accessed members in your support network in the last month and the last seven days.

- Look at this and think about whether there are things you would like to change.

- It is also worth reflecting on how many people you support in your social network, and how comfortable you are with that.

It is critical that you are able to recognise and acknowledge strengths as well as limitations and that you are able to seek support without feeling ashamed. You must feel comfortable around asking for help without feeling embarrassed or that you have failed. Not to do so is unprofessional and puts you and your clients at risk. In the same way that survivors need a trusted support network so does the practitioner. Remember support is an opportunity to explore your thoughts and feelings, share concerns and reflect on the work. Through this you can explore and learn to set limits and boundaries, balance trauma work with other work, and make sure that you take regular breaks.

Self-care incorporates the ability to allow others to care and to be able to accept companionable support (de Zulueta, 2008; Sinason, 2008). It is critical that counsellors can permit the expression of their own vulnerabilities and dependency needs to avoid defensive feelings of invincibility or self-sufficiency (Sanderson, 2010a).

Remember

With appropriate support counsellors can minimise STS and remain empathically attuned to the survivor and enhance the therapeutic relationship.

Alongside seeking support, counsellors must also allow themselves to pursue personal pleasures that provide 'avocational avenues for creative and relaxing self expression in order to regenerate' (Danieli, 1994, p.385), and have fun. Some clinicians argue that 'feeling free to have fun and joy is not frivolity in this field but a necessity without which one cannot fulfil one's professional obligations…' (Danieli, 1994, p.664). Many counsellors feel that they do not deserve to take time out to enjoy life and can become self-sacrificing not realising that this is not healthy for them or their clients. Counsellors must take responsibility for taking care of themselves so that they can fully extend their duty of care. To this effect, they need to incorporate physical and creative activities that induce relaxation and spiritual well-being. Many trauma professionals have found physical activities such as martial arts, tai chi, yoga and meditation which stimulate the right hemisphere activity in the brain particularly beneficial in helping them stay embodied (van der Kolk, 2004).

Box 24.6 Counsellor self-care (Sanderson, 2010a)

- Work – supervision, consultation, mentoring, peer support, CPD, balance trauma work, regular breaks, set limits and boundaries
- Body – physical health, diet, rest, relaxation, yoga, martial arts, play
- Mind – reflection, sense of control and agency, recreational activities that stimulate, reading for fun
- Emotion – respect and nurture self, listen to music, watch films, see plays, laughter, humour
- Creativity – allow for inspiration, write, draw, paint, sculpt, make music
- Spirituality – beauty, nature, tranquillity, hope, optimism, passion

---

To ensure self-care on all dimensions (see Box 24.6) you will need to explore and identify activities that bring a sense of peace or contentment whether it be love, friendship, children, play, laughter, being in contact with nature, writing or visiting museums or galleries (Sinason, 2008). Once you have identified which activities inspire passion, facilitate creativity, enhance well-being or allow for spiritual connection, it is essential to commit to these. Ideally regular times or breaks to engage in your chosen activity are better than long, infrequent breaks. To this effect, it is helpful to engage in some of the activities on a weekly basis and to incorporate them into your weekly schedule. That way you are more likely to reap the benefits. You may already have a number of self-care strategies that you use to manage work. It is useful to identify these and make a commitment to pursuing them on a regular basis (see Box 24.7).

Box 24.7 Self-care strategies

- Take a sheet of paper and list as many activities and self-care strategies as you can, especially those that you enjoy and which are a source of pleasure, contentment or fun

- Take another sheet of paper and divide this into four or more columns with the following headings – physical self-care, emotional and psychological self-care, spiritual self-care, work place self-care and any other sources

- Next place the activities on your first list under each heading and highlight those that you already engage in regularly

- Look at the lists again and put a star next to those that you would like to incorporate into your life

- Make a commitment to incorporate these in the future

- NB: you might find the counsellor self-care checklist in Box 24.8 useful

---

To counterbalance the impact of bearing witness to complex trauma and any accompanying loss of meaning, you need to pursue a range of personally meaningful activities that inspire and allow for passion and joy to predominate, such as time with family and friends and engaging in activities unconnected to work to ensure a more grounded and balanced lifestyle. To enjoy and take pleasure in life through play, humour and love can have a hugely restorative effect which allows for post-traumatic growth. Balancing trauma by connecting to self, others and the world allows for renewed vitality and appreciation of life and the resilience of the human spirit.

Box 24.8 Counsellor self-care checklist (adapted
from Saakvitne and Pearlman, 1996)

Rate the following by scoring 2 for Frequently; 1 Sometimes; and 0 for Never

In your work how often do you take time for...

- Stepping back and assessing priorities
- Social interaction
- Giving attention to your bodily needs: proper meal breaks, comfort breaks, fresh air, temperature
- Finding opportunities for consultation and peer support
- Reviewing your terms and conditions of employment
- Ensuring professional development time
- Having quiet time for uninterrupted work
- Balancing clients – number and type of presenting symptoms
- Being clear with yourself and colleagues/family about the limits of your work role and what you can and cannot take on
- Making your work space right for you and your work
- Taking as much autonomy and control of your own work and decisions as you can

In your body and bodily well-being how often do you...

- Eat healthily and regularly
- Take exercise and other physical activities (but not excessively)
- Do things that help you sleep well
- Avoid ingesting harmful substances, as well as control levels of potentially harmful ones, such as nicotine, alcohol, recreational drugs
- Take time for satisfying sex, alone or with a partner
- Take time off from everyday routines for relaxing activities
- Do any relaxation yoga, tai chi, or similar exercises or massage
- Act in a timely way about heath concerns and routine health checks
- Get away from the computer early enough at night and often enough; get off the sofa and away from TV often enough

In your mind and psychological well-being how often do you…

- Have quiet times for rest and reflection/contemplation
- Have times when you share your emotions with people you trust, being yourself and talking about things that concern or make you happy
- Enjoy close, loving times with a particular person or animal
- Take part in recreational activities that stimulate you and take your mind off work and stretch you in a new direction
- Spend time with a supportive social group/network such as friends, church, clubs, etc.
- Have times when other people can be in the 'driving seat' or caring for you rather than you caring for them
- Have people around you who you can let your guard down with and show the real you
- Take enough control over your working and personal life
- Take time for holidays and short breaks, away from telephones and responsibilities
- Put aside time to reflect on your thoughts, feelings and beliefs, through a personal diary, reading, studying, counselling, psychotherapy, mentoring, life coaching

In your emotions and emotional well-being how often do you…

- Keep in touch with people who are important to you
- Take time to be with people whose company you enjoy
- Allow yourself to acknowledge when you have done well
- Like yourself and treat yourself with respect
- Allow yourself to experience all your emotions – happiness, anger, sadness, laughter, etc.
- Have time with young people or animals, especially in play
- Make time for listening to music, reading, watching films
- Appreciate nature or creative activities
- Laugh or giggle

In your spirit and creativity how often do you…

- Notice things that inspire you
- Notice beauty in everyday surroundings

- Have awareness of what is meaningful to you and take time to acknowledge and celebrate it
- Meditate, pray, or contemplate, formally or informally
- Find time to be tranquil, maybe in quiet, peaceful surroundings, but also sometimes in making that 'space' in crowded or busy times or places
- Engage in, or observe, creative or artistic activities such as music, art or poetry
- Develop ways to encourage your hope, optimism and energy for life
- Engage in something where you allow yourself to experience overwhelming joy and passion and peak experiences or to be transported
- Engage in spiritual community or partnership/friendship or something you believe in deeply
- Take part in celebrations with your family, friends, community, etc.

RESOURCES

SOURCES OF HELP

A GP, health visitor, social worker or other professional can assist you in getting help from a clinical psychologist or other therapist. Do not be afraid to ask to see a woman if you feel uncomfortable talking to a man (or vice versa).

The national addresses, phone numbers or website addresses for various organisations are listed below. For information on local sources of help contact the national office or try your local telephone directory. Please include a stamped self-addressed envelope for written replies.

TELEPHONE HELPLINES

The organisations listed below offer someone to talk to, advice and sometimes face-to-face counselling.

One in Four

One in Four offers a voice to, and support for, people who have experienced sexual abuse and sexual violence.

219 Bromley Road, Bellingham, Catford SE6 2PG
Helpline: 020 8697 2112; Monday to Friday 6–9pm, Saturday 1–5pm
Email: admin@oneinfour.org.uk
Website: www.oneinfour.org.uk

Childline

Children can phone or write if they are in trouble or are being abused. There is also an NSPCC 24-hour helpline for parents, children, abusers and professionals.

Freepost NATN1111, London, E1 6BR
Helpline (children): 0800 1111 (free)
Helpline (NSPCC): 0808 800 500

Family Matters

Counselling service for children and adult survivors of sexual abuse and rape.

13 Wrotham Road, Gravesend, Kent DA11 0PA
Tel: 01474 536 661; Monday to Friday 9–5 pm
Helpline: 01474 537 392

Rape and Sexual Abuse Support Centre
Helpline for women and men, staffed by trained female volunteers.

Helpline: 01483 546 400 (women)
01483 568000 (men); Sunday to Friday 7.30–9.30 pm

NAPAC (National Association of People Abused in Childhood)
NAPAC is a registered charity based in the UK, providing support and information for people abused in childhood.

42 Curtain Road, London EC2A 3NH
Support line: 0800 085 3330
Website: http://www.napac.org.uk

Survivors UK
For male survivors of rape and sexual abuse.

Helpline: 08451 221 201
Website: www.survivorsuk.org/

SAFE: Supporting Survivors of Satanic Abuse
Helpline for survivors of ritual and satanic abuse. Offers counselling, listening, advice and referrals.

PO Box 1557, Salisbury SP1 2TP
Helpline: 01722 410 889; Wednesday 6.30–8.30 pm, Thursday 7–9pm

Samaritans
24-hour listening and befriending service for the lonely, suicidal or depressed.

Helpline: 08457 90 90 90

Victim Supportline
Supportline offers emotional support and information to callers.

Helpline: 0845 30 30 900; Monday to Friday 9 am–9 pm,
weekends 9 am–7 pm, bank holidays 9 am–5 pm

PREVENTING ABUSE
Phone one of the helplines listed above or contact the following agencies if you suspect a child is being abused or is at risk of abuse, or you know of an abuser who has any contact with children.

Police
Many districts now have a special police unit that works with sexual abuse. Phone your local police station and ask to speak to the officer who deals with sexual abuse.

Social services
Phone your local office and ask for the Child Protection Officer or the Duty Officer.

If you are abusing children or have urges to abuse children phone the NSPCC or contact social services or the police.

THERAPY/COUNSELLING AND SUPPORT

Action for Children
Provides national network of child sexual abuse treatment centres providing support and counselling for children and their families. Adult survivors also.

Chesham House, Church Lane, Berkhamstead, Herts HP4 2AX
Tel: 0300 123 2112
Website: www.actionforchildren.org.uk

British Association for Counselling and Psychotherapy
BACP House, 15 St John's Business Park, Lutterworth LE17 4HB
Tel: 0870 443 5252 or 01455 883 300; Monday to Friday 8.45 am to 5 pm, both numbers
Email: bacp@bacp.co.uk
Website: www.bacp.co.uk

Children 1st
83 Whitehouse Loan, Edinburgh EH9 1AT
Headquarters: 0131 446 2300
ParentLine Scotland: 0808 800 2222
Website: www.children1st.org.uk

Citizens Advice Bureau
This is part of the overall grouping Citizens Advice and can direct you to local groups who can help. Find the number of your nearest office in the phone book or visit www.citizensadvice.org.uk.

Clinical psychologists
Your GP can refer you to a clinical psychologist or you can ask another professional for advice on how to get to see a psychologist; or visit www.bps.org.uk, the website of the British Psychological Society.

DABS (Directory and Book Services)
DABS collate information and produce a national directory for resources for survivors. They also provide an excellent mail order service for books.

4 New Hill, Conisbrough, Doncaster DN12 3HA
Tel: 01709 860 023; Monday to Friday 10 am–6 pm
Website: www.dabsbooks.co.uk

EMDR (Eye Movement Desensitisation and Reprocessing)
The website will provide you with information about EMDR and will help you to find an accredited EMDR therapist in the UK.

Website: www.emdrassociation.org.uk

MIND
Offers individual counselling and group work.

Helpline: 08457 660 163; Monday to Friday, 9 am–5 pm
Email: info@mind.org.uk
Website: www.mind.org.uk

Relate
Can help with relationship difficulties and sexual problems. Provides couple counselling, face to face or by phone.

Premier House, Carolina Court, Lakeside, Doncaster, South Yorkshire DN4 5RA
Tel: 0300 100 1234
Email: enquiries@relate.org.uk
Website: www.relate.org.uk

SEREN
SEREN is a specialised counselling service in Wales for adults who have been sexually abused as children.

2nd Floor, NatWest Chambers, Sycamore Street, Newcastle Emlyn SA38 9AJ
Tel: 01239 711 772
Website: www.seren-wales.org.uk

Victim Support
Coordinates nationwide victim support schemes. Trained volunteers offer practical and emotional help to the victims of crime including rape and sexual assault.

Hallam House, 56–60 Hallam Street, London N1W 6JL
Tel: 020 7268 0200
Website: www.victimsupport.org.uk

Women's Therapy Centre
Offers group and individual therapy by women for women.

10 Manor Gardens, London N7 6JS
Psychotherapy enquiries: 020 7263 6200; Monday to Thursday 2–4 pm
General enquiries: 020 7263 7860
Email: info@womenstherapycentre.co.uk; appointments@womenstherapycentre.co.uk
Website: www.womenstherapycentre.co.uk

SPECIAL AGENCIES

ACT (Ann Craft Trust)

Provides an information and networking service to adult and child survivors with learning disabilities and workers involved in this area.

Centre for Social Work, University Park, Nottingham NG7 2RD
Tel: 0115 951 5400; Monday to Thursday 8.30 am–5 pm, Friday 8.30 am–2 pm
Email: ann-craft-trust@nottingham.ac.uk
Website: ww.anncrafttrust.org

Accuracy About Abuse

Information service providing background to media controversies.

Website: www.accuracyaboutabuse.org

Beacon Foundation

Services for survivors of satanic/ritualistic abuse and their carers and support for professionals.

3 Grosvenor Avenue, Rhyl, Clwyd LL18 4HA
Helpline: 01745 343 600; Monday to Friday 10 am–4 pm

Kidscape

Information on protecting children.

Tel: 020 7730 3300
Website: www.kidscape.org.uk

London Lesbian and Gay Switchboard

Tel: 020 7837 7324; Monday to Sunday 10 am–11 pm
Website: www.llgs.org.uk

National Deaf Children's Society

Agency catering for deaf children and their families. Can offer books/information to professionals.

15 Dufferin Street, London EC1Y 8UR
Tel: 020 7490 8656
Helpline: 0808 800 8880 (also minicom); Monday to Friday 9.30 am–5 pm
Email: ndcs@ndcs.org.uk
Website: www.ndcs.org.uk

Solace Women's Aid

An independent charity providing a comprehensive range of services for women and children affected by domestic and sexual violence.

Website: www.solacewomensaid.org

The Survivors Trust
A national umbrella agency for 130 specialist voluntary sector agencies providing a range of counselling, therapy and support.

Website: www.thesurvivorstrust.org

ABUSE BY CLERGY

National Association of Christian Survivors of Sexual Abuse
An international organisation run by survivors for survivors.

CSSA (National), P.O. Box 951, Northampton, NN7 9AS
Website: www.ncssa.org.uk

MACSAS (Ministry and Clergy Sexual Abuse Survivors)
BM MACSAS, London WC1N 3XX
Helpline: 0808 801 0340
Email: macsas@hotmail.com
Website: www.macsas.org.uk

Lantern Project
Tel: 0151 638 7015
Website: www.lanternproject.org.uk

Innocent Voices UK
Website: www.innocentvoicesuk.com

SNAP Survivors Network for those Abused by Priests
Website: www.snapnetwork.org

DISSOCIATION

Pottergate Centre for Trauma and Dissociation
26 Princes Street, Norwich NR3 1AE
Tel: 01603 660 029/633 115
Email: remyaquarone@btconnect.com (Director)
Website: www.dissociation.co.uk

Clinic for Dissociative Studies
Valerie Sinason (Director)
London

Tel: 0207 794 1655
Email: vsinason@aol.com
Website: www.clinicds.com

PODS (Positive Outcomes for Dissociative Survivors)
83a High Street, Huntingdon PE29 3DP
Tel: 01480 878 409
07746 799 221
Website: www.pods-online.org.uk

TAG (Trauma and Abuse Group)
The Willows Centre, 11 Prospect Place, Swindon SN1 3LQ
Email: chairman@tag-uk.net
Website: www.tag-uk.net

FPP (First Person Plural)
PO Box 2537, Wolverhampton WV4 4ZL
Email: fpp@firstpersonplural.org.uk
Website: www.firstpersonplural.org.uk

RAINS (Ritual Abuse Information Network and Support)
PO BOX 458, Godalming, Surrey GU7 2YT
Tel: 01483 898 600

BIBLIOGRAPHY

Ainsworth, M.D.S., Blehar, M.C., Waters, E. and Wall, S. (1978) *Patterns of Attachment: A Psychological Study of the Strange Situation.* Hillsdale, NJ: Lawrence Erlbaum.

Alexander, P.C. and Anderson, C.L. (1994) 'An attachment approach to psychotherapy with the incest survivor.' *Psychotherapy 31*, 665–673.

Allen, J.G. (2001) *Traumatic Relationships and Serious Mental Disorders.* Chichester: Wiley.

Allen, J.G. (2006) *Coping with Trauma: Hope through Understanding,* 2nd edition. Washington, DC: American Psychiatric Publishing.

Allen, J.G., Bleiberg, E. and Haslam-Hopwood, T. (2003) *Mentalizing as a Compass for Treatment.* Houston, TX: Menninger Clinic.

Allen, J.G. and Fonagy, P. (eds) (2006) *Handbook of Mentalization Based Treatment.* Chichester: Wiley.

Allen, J.G., Fonagy, P. and Bateman, A.W. (2008) *Mentalizing in Clinical Practice.* Arlington, VA: American Psychiatric Publishing.

Allez, G.H. (2010) *Infant Losses, Adult Searches: A Neural Developmental Perspective on Psychopathology and Sexual Offending.* London: Karnac Books.

American Psychiatric Association (2013*) Diagnostic and Statistical Manual of Mental Disorders (DSM) V.* Washington, DC: American Psychiatric Association.

Anderson, C.L. and Alexander, P.C. (1996) 'The relationships between attachment and dissociation in adult survivors of incest.' *Psychiatry 59*, 240–254.

APA DSM-V Task Force (2010) *Proposed Draft Revisions to Disorders and Criteria, Diagnostic and Statistical Manual of Mental Disorders (DSM-V).* Arlington, VA: American Psychiatric Association.

Arnsten, A.F. (1998) 'The biology of being frazzled.' *Science 280*, 1711–1721.

Bartholomew, K. (1990) 'Avoidance of intimacy: An attachment perspective.' *Journal of Social and Personal Relationships 7*, 147–148.

Bartholomew, K. and Horowitz, L.M. (1991) 'Attachment styles among young adults: A test of a four-category model.' *Journal of Personality and Social Psychology 61*, 226–244.

Beck, A.T. (1976) *Cognitive Therapy and Emotional Disorders.* New York: New American Library.

Berger, H. (2001) 'Trauma and the Therapist.' In T. Spiers (ed.) *Trauma: A Practitioner's Guide to Counselling.* Hove: Brunner-Routledge.

Bergin, A.E. and Garfield, S.C. (eds) (1994) *Handbook of Psychotherapy and Behaviour Change,* 4th edition. Chichester: Wiley.

Bateman, A. and Fonagy, P. (2004) *Psychotherapy for Borderline Personality Disorder: Mentalization-based treatment.* New York: Oxford University Press.

Bernstein, E.M. and Putman, F.W. (1986) 'Development, reliability, and validity of a dissociation scale.' *Journal of Nervous Mental Diseases 174*, 12, 786–788.

Blizard, R.A. (2003) 'Disorganised attachment, development of dissociated self states, and a relational approach to treatment.' *Journal of Trauma and Dissociation 4*, 3, 27–50.

Bomstein, R.F. (1995) 'Active dependency.' *Journal of Nervous and Mental Disease 183*, 64–77.

Boon, S., Steele, K. and van der Hart, O. (2011) *Coping with Trauma Related Dissociation: A Skills Training for Patients and Therapists.* New York: W.W. Norton.

Bowlby, J. (1965) *Child Care and the Growth of Love*, 2nd edition. London: Penguin Books.

Bowlby, J. (1969) *Attachment and Loss: Attachment.* London: Penguin.

Bowlby, J. (1973) *Attachment and Loss: Separation.* London: Penguin.

Bowlby, J. (1977) 'The making and breaking of affectional bonds.' *British Journal of Psychiatry 130*, 201–210.

Bowlby, J. (1980) *Attachment and Loss: Loss, Sadness and Depression,* Vol. III. New York: Basic Books.

Bowlby, J. (1988) *A Secure Base: Parent-Child Attachment and Healthy Human Development.* New York: Basic Books.

Braun, B. (1998) 'The BASK Model of Dissociation.' *Dissociation 1*, 2, 16–23.

Bride, B.E., Robinson, M.R., Yegedis, B. and Figley, C.R. (2004) 'Development and validation of the Secondary Traumatic Stress Scale.' *Research on Social Work Practice 14*, 27–35.

Briere, J. (1995) *Trauma Symptom Inventory (TSI).* Odessa, FL: Psychological Assessment Resources.

Briere, J. (2000) *Inventory of Altered Self Capacities (IASC).* Odessa, FL: Psychological Assessment Resources.

Briere, J. (2004) *Psychological Assessment of Adult Posttraumatic Stress: Phenomenology Diagnosis and Measurement,* 2nd edition. Washington, DC: American Psychological Resources.

Briere, J. and Scott, C. (2006) *Principles of Trauma Therapy: A Guide to Symptoms, Evaluation and Treatment.* Thousand Oaks, CA: Sage.

Briere, J., Scott, C. and Weather, F.W. (2005) 'Peritraumatic and persistent dissociation in the presumed etiology of PTSD.' *American Journal of Psychiatry 162*, 2295–2301.

Briere, J. and Spinazzola, J. (2005) 'Phenomenology and psychological assessment of complex posttraumatic states.' *Journal of Traumatic Stress 18*, 401–412.

Briere, L. and Gil, E. (1988) 'Self-mutilation in clinical and general population samples. Prevalence, correlates and functions.' *American Journal of Orthopsychiatry 68*, 609–620.

Bromberg, P.M. (1994) 'Speak! that I may see you: Some reflections on dissociation, reality, and psychoanalytic listening.' *Psychoanalytic Dialogue 4*, 517–547.

Bromberg, P. (1993) 'Shadow and substance: A relational perspective on clinical process.' *Psychoanalytic Psychology 10*, 147–168.

Bromberg, P. (1998) *Standing in the Spaces: Essays on Clinical Process, Trauma and Dissociation.* Hillsdale, NJ: Analytic Press.

Bromberg, P. (2011) *The Shadow of the Tsunami and the Growth of The Relational Mind.* London: Routledge.

Bryant-Davis, T. (2005) *Thriving in the Wake of Trauma: A Multicultural Guide.* Westport, CT: Praeger.

Brown, R. and Stobart, K. (2008) *Understanding Boundaries and Containment in Clinical Practice*. London: Karnac Books.

Cairns, K. (2002) *Attachment, Trauma and Resilience: Therapeutic Caring for Children*. British Association for Adoption and Fostering (BAAF).

Calof, D.L. (1995) 'Dissociation: Nature's tincture of numbing and forgetting.' *Treating Abuse Today 5*, 3, 5–8.

Carlson, B.E. (1991) 'Domestic Violence.' In A. Gitterman (ed.) *Handbook of Social Work Practice with Vulnerable Populations*. New York: Columbia University Press.

Carlson, V., Cicchetti, D., Barnett, D. and Braunwald, K. (1989) 'Finding Order in Disorganization: Lessons from Research in Maltreated Infants' Attachments to their Caregivers.' In D. Cicchetti and V. Carlson (eds) *Child Maltreatment: Theory and Research on the Causes and Consequences of Child Abuse and Neglect*. New York: Cambridge University Press.

Carlson, P.J., Singh, J.B., Zarate, C.A., Drevets, W.C. and Manji, H.K. (2005) 'Neural circuitry and neuroplasticity in mood disorders.' *Insight for Novel Therapeutics 3*, 22–41.

Casement, P. (1990) *Further Learning from the Patient. The Analytic Space and Process*. London: Tavistock/Routledge, 1990.

Chu, J.A. (1991) 'The repetition compulsion revisited: Reliving dissociated trauma.' *Psychotherapy 28*, 327–332.

Chu, J.A. (2011) *Rebuilding Shattered Lives: The Responsible Treatment of Complex Post-traumatic and Dissociative Disorders*, 2nd edition. New York: Wiley.

Clarkson, P. (1993) *On Psychotherapy*. London: Whurr.

Clarkson, P. (2003) *The Therapeutic Relationship, second edition*. Bognor Regis, West Sussex: Wiley Blackwell.

Cloitre, M., Cohen, L.R. and Koenen, K.C. (2006) *Treating Survivors of Childhood Abuse: Psychotherapy for the Interrupted Life*. New York: Guilford.

Cloitre, M., Koenen, K.C., Cohen, L.R. and Han, H. (2002) 'Skills in affective interpersonal regulation followed by exposure: A phase-based treatment for PTSD related to childhood abuse.' *Journal of Consulting and Clinical Psychology 70*, 1067–1074.

Cloitre, M., Stovell-McClough, K.C., Miranda, R. and Chemtob, C.M. (2004) 'Therapeutic alliance; negative mood regulation, and treatment outcome in child abuse related posttraumatic stress disorder.' *Journal of Consulting and Clinical Psychology 72*, 411–416.

Cohen, J. (1985) 'Trauma and repression.' *Psychoanlaytic Inquiry 5*, 164–189.

Courtois, C.A. (1999) *Recollections of Sexual Abuse: Treatment Principles and Guidelines*. New York: Norton.

Courtois, C.A. (2010) *Healing the Incest Wound: Adult Survivors in Therapy*, 2nd edition. New York: Norton.

Courtois, C.A. and Ford, J. (eds) (2009) *Treating Complex Traumatic Stress Disorders: An Evidence Based Guide*. New York: Guilford.

Cohen, A.P. (1985) *The Symbolic Construction of Community*. London: Tavistock.

Cozzolino, L. (2010) *The Neuropsychology of Psychotherapy: Healing the Social Brain*. New York: Norton.

Dale, P. (1997) 'Stress in Child Psychotherapists.' In V.P. Varma (ed.) *Stress in Psychotherapists.* London: Routledge.

Dale, P. (1999) *Adults Abused as Children: Experiences in Counselling and Psychotherapy.* London: Sage.

Dalenberg, C.J. (2000) *Counter-Transference and the Treatment of Trauma.* Washington, DC: American Psychological Association.

Danieli, Y. (1994) 'Countertransference in the Treatment of PTSD.' In J.P. Wilson and J.D. Lindy (eds) *Countertransference in the Treatment of PTS.* New York: Guilford.

Davies, J.M. and Frawley, M.G. (1994) *Treating the Adult Survivor of Childhood Sexual Abuse: A Psychoanalytic Perspective.* New York: Basic Books.

Dedcovic, K., Duchesne, A., Andrews, J., Engers, V. and Pruessner, J.C. (2009) 'The brain and the stress axis: The neural correlates of cortisol regulation in response to stress.' *Neuro Image 47,* 864–871.

Dell, P.F. (2006) 'A new model of dissociative identity disorder.' *Psychiatric Clinics North America 29,* 1–26.

De Zulueta, F. (2008) 'Developmental Trauma in Adults: A Response to Bessel van der Kolk.' In S. Benamer and K. White (eds) *Trauma and Attachment. The John Bowlby Memorial Conference Monograph.* London: Karnac.

Dozier, M. and Tyrrell, C. (1998) 'The Role of Attachment in Therapeutic Relationships.' In J. Simpson and W. Rholes (eds) *Attachment Theory and Close Relationships.* New York: Guilford.

Dutton, D.G. (1985) 'An ecologically nested theory of male violence towards intimates.' *International Journal of Women's Studies 8,* 4, 404–413.

Dutton, D.G. (2007) *The Abusive Personality: Violence and Control in Intimate Relationships,* 2nd edition. New York: Guilford.

Dutton, D.G. and Painter, S.L. (1981) 'Traumatic bonding: The development of emotional attachment in battered women and other relationships of intermittent abuse.' *Victimology: An International Journal 6,* 139–155.

Dutton, D.G. and Painter, S.L. (1993) 'Emotional attachment in abusive relationships: A test of traumatic bonding theory.' *Violence and Victims 8,* 105–120.

Engel, G.L. and Schmale, A.H. (1972) 'Conservation-Withdrawal: A Primary Regulatory Process for Organismic Homeostasis.' In *Ciba Foundation Symposium: Physiology, Emotion and Psychosomatic Illness.* New York: Elsevier.

Field, N. (1989) 'Listening with the body: An exploration in the countertransference.' *British Journal of Psychotherapy 5,* 4, 512–522.

Field, T. (1985) 'Attachment as Psychobiological Attunement: Being on the Same Wavelength.' In M. Reite and T. Field (eds) *The Psychobiology of Attachment and Separation.* New York: Academic Press.

Figley, C.R. (1995) 'Compassion Fatigue as Secondary Traumatic Stress Disorder: An Overview.' In C.R. Figley (ed.) *Compassion Fatigue: Coping with Secondary Stress Disorder in those who Treat the Traumatized.* New York: Brunner/Mazel.

Figley, C.R. (2002a) *Treating Compassion Fatigue.* New York: Brunner/Mazel.

Figley, C.R. (2002b) 'Compassion fatigue: psychotherapists' chronic lack of self care.' JCLP/In Session, *Psychotherapy in Practice 58* 11, 1433–1441.

Figley, C.R. (2004) 'Foreword.' In J.P. Wilson and R.B. Thomas (eds) *Empathy in the Treatment of Trauma and PTSD*. New York: Brunner-Routledge.

Figley, C.R. and Kleber, R.J. (1995) 'Beyond the 'Victim': Secondary Traumatic Stress.' In R.J. Kleber, C.R. Figley and B.P.R. Gersons (eds) *Beyond Trauma: Cultural and Societal Dynamics*. New York: Plenum.

Foa, F.B. and Rothbaum, B. (1998) *Treating the Trauma of Rape: Cognitive Behavioural Therapy for PTSD*. New York: Guilford.

Foa, F.B., Zinbarg, R. and Rothbaum, B.O. (1992) 'Uncontrollability and unpredictability in posttraumatic stress disorder: An animal model.' *Psychological Bulletin 112*, 218–238.

Fonagy, P. (1999) 'Pathological Attachments and Therapeutic Action.' Paper presented at the Annual Meeting of the California Branch of the American Academy of Child and Adolescent Psychiatry, Yosemite Valley, CA, January.

Fonagy, P. (2001) *Attachment Theory and Psychoanalysis*. New York: Other Press.

Fonagy, P. (2002) 'Multiple Voices versus Metacognition: An Attachment Theory Perspective.' In V. Sinason (ed.) *Trauma and Multiplicity: Working with Dissociative Identity Disorder*. London: Routledge.

Fonagy, P., Gergely, G., Jurist, E.L. and Target, M. (2002) *Affect Regulation, Mentalization and the Development of the Self*. New York: Other Press.

Fonagy, P., Leigh, I., Steele, M., Steele, H., *et al.* (1996) 'The relation of attachment status, psychiatric classification, and response to psychotherapy.' *Journal of Consulting and Clinical Psychology 64*, 24–31.

Fonagy, P., Steele, M., Steele, H., Leigh, T., *et al.* (1995) 'Attachment, the Reflective Self, and Borderline States.' In S. Goldberg, R. Muir and J. Kerr (eds) *Attachment Theory: Social, Developmental and Clinical Perspectives*. Hillsdale, NJ: Analytic Press.

Fonagy, P. and Target, M. (1997) 'Perspectives on Recovered Memories Debate.' In J. Sandler and P. Fonagy (eds) *Recovered Memories of Abuse: True or False*. Madison, CT: International Universities Press.

Fonagy, P., Target, M. and Gergely, G. (2003) 'Attachment and borderline personality disorder.' *Psychiatric Clinics of North America 23*, 91, 103–123.

Ford, J.D. (2007) 'Trauma, posttraumatic stress disorder and ethnoracial minorities: Toward diversity and cultural competence in principles and practices.' *Clinical Psychology: Science and Practice 15*, 62–67.

Ford, J.D., Courtois, C.A., Steele, K., Van der Hart, O. and Nijenhuis, E.R.S. (2005) 'Treatment of complex posttraumatic self regulation.' *Journal of Traumatic Stress 18*, 437–447.

Ford, J.D. and Kidd, P. (1998) 'Early childhood trauma and disorders of extreme stress to predictors of treatment outcome with chronic PTSD.' *Journal of Traumatic Stress 11*, 743–761.

Freudenberger, H.J. and North, G. (2006) 'The Burnout Cycle.' *Scientific American Mind 3*, 17, 31.

Fuchs, T. (2004) 'Neurobiology and psychotherapy: an emerging dialogue.' *Current Opinions in Psychiatry 17*, 479–485.

Gabbard, G. and Wilkinson, S. (1994) *Management of Counter-transference with Borderline Patients*. Washington, DC: American Psychiatric Press.

George, C. and West, M. (2001) 'The development and preliminary validation of a new measure of adult attachment: The adult attachment projective.' *Attachment and Human Development 3*, 30–61.

Gerbode, F. (1989) *Beyond Psychology: An Introduction to Meta Psychology,* 2nd edition. Palo Alto, CA: IRM Press.

Gerdhardt, S. (2004) *Why Love Matters: How Affection Shapes a Baby's Brain*. Hove and New York: Brunner-Routledge.

Glaser, D. (2008) 'Child Sexual Abuse.' In M. Rutter, D. Bishop, D. Pine, D. Scott *et al.* (eds) *Rutter's Child and Adolescent Psychiatry*. Oxford: Blackwell Publishing Ltd.

Harlow, H.F. and Harlow, M. (1971) 'Psychopathology in Monkeys.' In H.D. Kinnel (ed.) *Experimental Psychopathology*. New York: Academic Press.

Harter, S. (1999) *The Construction of the Self: A Developmental Perspective*. New York: Guilford.

Hartman, D. and Zimberoff, M.A. (2004) 'Corrective emotional experience in the therapeutic process.' *Journal of Heart-Centered Therapies 7*, 2, 3–84.

Hazan, C. and Shaver, P. (1987) 'Romantic love conceptualized as an attachment process.' *Journal of Personality and Social Psychology 52*, 3, 511–524.

Herbert, C. (1995/2007) *Understanding your Reactions to Trauma: A Guide for Survivors of Trauma and their Families*, 3rd edition. Gloucester: Blue Stallion.

Herbert, C. (2002) 'A CBT-based therapeutic alternative to working with complex client problems.' *European Journal of Psychotherapy Counselling and Health 5*, 2, 135–144.

Herbert, C. (2005) 'Healing from Complex Trauma: An Integrated 3 Systems' Approach.' In J. Congal, H. Payne and H. Wilkinson (eds) *About a Body: Working with the Embodied Mind in Psychotherapy*. London: Taylor and Francis.

Herbert, C. and Wetmore, A. (1999/2006) *Overcoming Traumatic Stress: A Self Help Guide using Cognitive Behavioural Techniques*, 2nd edition. London: Constable and Robinson.

Herman, J.L. (1992a) *Trauma and Recovery*. New York: Basic Books.

Herman, J.L. (1992b) 'Complex PTSD: A syndrome in survivors of prolonged and repeated trauma.' *Journal of Traumatic Stress 5*, 377–392.

Herman, J.L. (2001) *Trauma and Recovery*, 2nd edition. London: Pandora.

Herman, J.L. (2002) 'Evolution of Trauma Therapy.' Paper presented at Trauma Conference: 'Psychological Trauma: Maturational Processes and Therapeutic Interventions', Boston University School of Medicine and Trauma Center, Boston, MA, 31 May – 1 June.

Herman, J.L. (2005) 'Justice from the victim's perspective.' *Violence Against Women 11*, 571–602.

Herman, J.L. (2006) 'My Life and Work.' In C.R. Figley (ed.) *Mapping Trauma and its Wake: Autobiographical Essays by Pioneer Trauma Scholars*. New York: Routledge.

Herman, J.L. (2007) 'Shattered States and their Repair: An Exploration of Trauma and Shame.' The John Bowlby Memorial Lecture presented at the Centenary John Bowlby Memorial Conference 1907–2007, Shattered States: Disorganised Attachment and its Repair, London, 9–10 March.

Herman, J.L., Perry, C. and van der Kolk, B.A. (1989) 'Childhood trauma in border line personality disorder.' *American Journal of Psychiatry 146*, 490–494.

Hesse, E., Main, M., Abrams, K.Y. and Rifkin, A. (2003) 'Unresolved states regarding loss or abuse can have 'second-generation' effects: Disorganised, role-inversion and frightening ideation in the offspring of traumatised non-maltreating parents'. In D.J. Siegel and M.F. Solomon (eds) *Healing Trauma: Attachment, Mind Body and Brain.* New York: Norton.

Hesse, E. (1999) 'The adult attachment interview: historical and current perspectives.' In J. Cassidy and P. Shaver (eds) *Handbook of Attachment: Theory, Research and Clinical Applications.* New York: Guilford.

Holmes, J. (2010) *The Search for the Secure Base: Attachment Theory and Psychotherapy.* London: Routledge.

Howe, D. (2005) *Child Abuse and Neglect: Attachment Development and Interventions.* Basingstoke: Palgrave MacMillan.

Howell, E. (2005) *The Dissociative Mind.* Hillsdale, NJ: Analytic Press.

Hunter, M. and Struwe, J. (1998) *The ethical use of touch in psychotherapy.* London: Sage.

Janoff-Bulman, R. (1985) 'The Aftermath of Victimisation: Rebuilding Shattered Assumptions.' In C.R. Figley (ed.) *Trauma and its Wake: The Study and Treatment of Post Traumatic Stress Disorder.* New York: Brunner/Mazel.

Janoff-Bulman, R. (1992) *Shattered Assumptions: Towards a New Psychology of Trauma.* New York: Free Press.

International Society for the Study of Trauma and Dissociation (2011) 'Guidelines for Treating Dissociative Identity Disorder in Adults.' Third Revision. *Journal of Trauma and Dissociation 12*, 2 188–212.

Johnson, L.D., Miller, S.D. and Duncan, B.L. (2000) *The Session Rating Scale 3.00.* Chicago, Il: Authors.

Kohut, H. (1971) *The Analysis of the Self.* New York: International Universities Press.

Kohut, H. (1972) 'Thoughts on Narcissism and Narcissistic Rage.' In P. Ornstein (ed.) *The Search for Self: Selected Writings of Heinz Kohut, vol. 2.* New York: International Universities Press.

Kohut, H. (1977) *The Restoration of the Self.* New York: International Universities Press.

Krystal, J.H. (1988) *Integration and Self Healing: Affect, Trauma and Alexithymia.* Hillsdale, NJ: Analytic Press.

Krystal, N. (2007) 'Neuroplasticity as a target for pharmacotherapy of psychiatric disorders. New opportunities for synergy with psychotherapy.' *Biological Psychiatry 62*, 834.

Kubler-Ross, E. (1969) *On Death and Dying.* New York: Macmillan.

Kahn, M. (1997) *Between Therapist and Client: The New Relationship.* New York: Freeman and Company.

Kluft, R.P. (1992) 'Dissociative disorders in childhood and adolescence: New frontiers.' *Dissociation 5*, 1, 2–3.

Lambert, M.J. and Ogles, B.M. (2004) 'The efficacy and effectiveness of psychotherapy.' In M.J. Lambert (ed.) *Bergin and Garfield's handbook of Psychotherapy and Behavior change, 5th edition.* New York: Wiley.

Lanius, R., Lanius, U., Fisher, J. and Ogden, P. (2006) 'Psychological Trauma and the Brain: Toward a Neurobiological Treatment Model.' In P. Ogden, K. Minton and C. Pain (eds) *Trauma and the Body*. New York. Norton.

Levine, P. (1992) *The Body as Healer: Transforming Trauma and Anxiety*. Boulder, CO: Lyons.

Levine, P. (1997) *Waking the Tiger: Healing Trauma*. Berkeley, CA: North Atlantic.

Levine, P. (200) *Healing Trauma: A Pioneering Program for Restoring Wisdom of your Body*. Boulder, CO: Sounds True.

Lichtenberg, J.D. (1989) *Psychoanalysis and Motivation*. Hillsdale, NJ: Analytic Press.

Lifton, R.J. (1979) *The Broken Connection: On Death and the Continuity of Life*. New York: Simon and Schuster.

Lilienfeld, Scott O., Lynn, S.J., Kirsch, I., Chaves, J. *et al.* 'Dissociative identity disorder and the sociocognitive model: Recalling the lessons of the past.' *Psychological Bulletin 125*, 5, 507–523.

Linden, A. (2008) *Boundaries in Human Relationships: How to Be Separate and Connected*. Bancyfelin, Carmarthen: Crown House Publishing.

Linden, D.E.J. (2006) 'How psychotherapy changes the brain: the contribution of functional neuroimaging.' *Molecular Psychiatry 11*, 528–538.

Linehan, M.M. (1993) *Cognitive-Behavioural Treatment of Borderline Personality Disorder*. New York: Guilford.

Liotti, G. (1992) 'Disorganised/disoriented attachment in the etiology of the dissociative disorders.' *Dissociation 5*, 196–204.

Liotti, G. (1999). 'Disorganization of attachment as a model for understanding dissociative psychopathology.' In J. Solomon and C. George (eds) *Disorganization of attachment*. New York: Guilford Press.

MacLean, P.D. (1990) *The Triune Brain in Evolution: Role in Paleocerebral Functions*. New York: Plenum.

Main, M. and Soloman, J. (1986) 'Discovery of an insecure disorganized/disoriented attachment pattern: procedures, findings and implications for the classification of behavior.' In T. Braxelton and M.Yogman (eds) *Affective development in infancy*. Norwood, NJ: Ablex.

Main, M. (1995) 'Recent studies in attachment: Overview with selected implications for clinical social work.' In S. Goldberg, R. Muir, and J. Kerr (eds) *Attachment theory*. Hillsdale, NJ: The Analytic Press.

Main, M. (1999) 'Attachment Theory: Eighteen Points with Suggestions for Future Studies.' In J. Cassidy and P.R. Shaver (eds) *Handbook of Attachment: Theory, Research and Clinical Applications*. New York: Guilford.

Main, M. and Morgan, H. (1996) 'Disorganization and disorientation in infant Strange Situation behavior: Phenotypic resemblance to dissociative states?' In L. Michelson and W. Ray (eds), *Handbook of dissociation*. New York: Plenum Press.

Maltsberg, J.T. and Buie, O.H. (1974) 'Countertransference: Hate in the treatment of suicidal patients.' *Archives of General Psychiatry 30*, 625–633.

Maslach, C., Jackson, S.E. and Leiter, M.P. (1996) *MBI: The Maslach Burnout Inventory: Manual*. Palo Alto, CA: Consulting Psychologists Press.

Mattley, C. (1998) 'Field Research With Phone Fantasy Workers: Managing The Researcher's Emotions.' In M.D. Schwartz (ed.) *Researching Sexual Violence Against Women: Methodological and Personal Considerations.* Thousand Oaks, CA: Sage Publications.

McCann, I.L. and Pearlman, L.A. (1989) 'Vicarious traumatisation: A framework for understanding the psychological effects of working with victims.' *Traumatic Stress 3*, 131–149.

McCann, I.L. and Pearlman, L.A. (1990) *Psychological Trauma and the Adult Survivor: Theory, Therapy and Transformation.* New York: Brunner/Mazel.

McCann, I.L., Sakheim, D.K. and Abrahamson, D.J. (1988) 'Trauma and victimisation: A model of psychological adaptation.' *Counselling Psychologist 16*, 4, 531–594.

Meins, E. (1997) *Security of Attachment and the Social Development of Cognition.* Hove: Psychology Press.

Mendelson, M., Herman, J., Scharsaw, E., Coco, M., Kallivayalil, C. and Leviran, J. (2011) *The Trauma Recovery Group: A Practical Guide.* New York: Guilford.

Millon, T. (1977) *Millon Clinical Multiaxial Inventory Manual.* Minneapolis, MN: National Computer Inventory and Computer Systems.

Mollon, P. (1993) *The Fragile Self: The Structure of Narcissistic Disturbance.* London, Whurr Publishers.

Mollon, P. (2000) 'Is Human Nature Intrinsically Evil?' In U. McCluskey and C. Hooper (eds) *Psychodynamic Perspectives on Abuse: The Cost of Fear.* London: Jessica Kingsley Publishers.

Mollon, P. (2002a) 'Dark Dimensions of Multiple Personality.' In V. Sinason (ed.) *Attachment, Trauma and Multiplicity: Working with Dissociative Identity Disorder.* London: Brunner-Routledge.

Mollon, P. (2002b) *Remembering Trauma: A Psychotherapist's Guide to Memory and Illusion,* 2nd edition. London: Whurr.

Mollon, P. (2008) Psychoanalytic *Energy Psychotherapy: Inspired by Thought Field Therapy, EFT, TAT, and Seemorg Matrix.* London: Karnac Books.

Myers, C.S. (1940). *Shell Shock in France 1914-18.* Cambridge: Cambridge University Press.

Najavits, L.M. (2000) *Seeking Safety: A Treatment Manual for PTSD and Substance Abuse.* New York: Guilford.

Najavits, L.M., Sullivan, T.P., Scmitz, M., Weiss, R.D. and Lee, C.S.N. (2004) 'Treatment utilization of women with PTSD and substance dependence.' *American Journal of Addictions 13*, 215–224.

National Institute for Clinical Excellence (2005) *Post Traumatic Stress Disorder: The Management of PTSD in Adults and Children in Primary and Secondary Care.* National Clinical Practice Guideline Number 26. London: Gaskell and the British Psychological Society.

Nathanson, D.L. (1992) *Shame and Pride: Affect, Sex, and the Birth of the Self.* New York: W.W. Norton.

Nietzsche, F. (1886) *Beyond Good and Evil.* Penguin Books, 1973.

Nijenhuis, E.R.S., Spinhoven, P., Van Dyck, R., Van der Hart, O., and Vanderlinden, J. (1996) 'The development and the psychometric characteristics of the Somatoform Dissociation Questionnaire (SDQ-20).' *Journal of Nervous and Mental Disease 184*, 688–694.

Nijenhuis, E.R.S. and van der Hart, O. (1999) 'Forgetting and Re-experiencing Trauma.' In J. Goodwin and R. Attais (eds) *Splintered Reflections: Images of the Body in Treatment.* New York: Basic Books.

Nijenhuis, E.R.S., Vanderlinden, J. and Spinhoven, P. (1998) 'Animal defensive reactions as a model for trauma induced dissociative reactions.' *Journal of Traumatic Stress 11*, 243–260.

Nijenhuis, E.R.S., Van Engen, A., Kusters, I. and Van der Hart, O. (2001) 'Peritraumatic somatoform and psychological dissociation in relation to recall of childhood sexual abuse.' *Journal of Trauma and Dissociation 2*, 3, 49–68.

Ogden, P. and Minton, K. (2000) 'Sensorimotor psychotherapy: one method for processing traumatic memory.' *Traumatology 6*, 1–21.

Ogden, P. (2006) *Trauma and the Body: A Sensorimotor Approach to Psychotherapy.* New York: Norton.

Ogden, P., Minton, K. and Pain, C. (2006) Trauma and the Body: A Sensorimotor Approach to Psychotherapy. New York: Norton.

Parkes, C.M. (2001) *Bereavement: Studies of Grief in Adult Life,* 3rd edition. Philadelphia, PA: Taylor & Francis.

Parkes, C.M., Relf, M. and Couldrick, A. (1996) *Counselling in Terminal Care and Bereavement.* Baltimore, MD: BPS Books.

Paterson, R.J. (2000) *The Assertiveness Workbook.* Oakland, CA: New Harbinger.

Pearlman, L.A. (1998) 'Trauma and the self: A theoretical and clinical perspective.' *Journal of Emotional Abuse 1*, 7–25.

Pearlman, L.A. (2001) 'The Treatment of Persons with Complex PTSD and other Trauma-related Disruptions to the Self.' In M.F. Friedman, J.P.Wilson and J.D. Lindy (eds) *Treating Psychological Trauma and PTSD.* New York: Guilford.

Pearlman, L.A. (2003) *Trauma Attachment Belief Scale (TABS) Manual.* Los Angeles, CA: Western Psychological Services.

Pearlman, L.A. and Courtois, C.A. (2005) 'Clinical applications of the attachment framework: Relational treatment of complex trauma.' *Journal of Traumatic Stress 18*, 449–459.

Pearlman, L.A. and Saakvitne, K.W. (1995a) *Trauma and the Therapist: Counter-transference and Vicarious Traumatization in Psychotherapy with Incest Survivors.* New York: Norton.

Pearlman, L.A. and Saakvitne, K.W. (1995b) 'Treating Therapists with Vicarious Traumatization and Secondary Traumatic Stress Disorders.' In C.R. Figley (ed.) *Compassion Fatigue: Coping with Secondary Traumatic Stress Disorder in Those who Treat the Traumatized.* New York: Brunner/Mazel.

Phelps, S. and Austin, N. (2002) *The Assertive Woman,* 4th edition. Atascadero, CA: Impact Publishers Inc.

Pines, M. and Aronson, E. (1988) *Career Burnout: Causes and Cures.* New York: Free Press.

Pistole, C.M. and Tarrant, N. (1993) 'Attachment style and aggression in male batterers.' *Family Therapy 20*, 3, 165–174.

Putnam, F.W. (1989) *Diagnosis and Treatment of Multiple Personality Disorder.* New York: Guilford.

Putnam, F.W. (1997) *Dissociation in Children and Adolescents: A Developmental Perspective.* New York: Guilford.

Renzetti, C. (1992) *Violent Betrayal Partner Abuse in Lesbian Relationships.* Newbury Park, CA: Sage.

Resick, B.A. and Schnick, M.K. (1993) *Cognitive Processing Therapy for Rape Victims: A Treatment Manual.* Newbury Park, CA: Sage.

Ross, C.A. (1997) *Dissociative Identity Disorder: Diagnosis, Clinical Features and Treatment of Multiple Personality.* New York: Wiley.

Ross, C.A. (2009) *Trauma Model Therapy: A Treatment Approach to Trauma, Dissociation and Complex Co-Morbidity.* Richardson, TX: Manitou Communications Ltd.

Ross, C.A., Heber, S., Norton, G.R., Anderson, D., Anderson, G. and Barchet, P. (1989) 'The Dissociative Disorders Interview Schedule: a structured interview.' *Dissociation 2*, 169–189.

Ross, C.A., Joshi, S. and Currie, R. (1990) 'Dissociative experiences in the general population.' *American Journal of Psychiatry 147*, 1547–1552.

Rothschild, B. (2000) *The Body Remembers: The Psychology of Trauma and Trauma Treatment.* New York: Norton.

Rothschild, B. (2003) *The Body Remembers Casebook: Unifying Methods and Models in the Treatment of Trauma and PTSD.* New York: Norton.

Rothschild, B. (2010) *8 Keys to Safe Trauma Recovery: Take Charge Strategies to Empower Your Healing.* New York: Norton.

Rothschild, L. (2003) 'A taxometric study of personality disorder.' *Journal of Abnormal Psychology 112*, 4, 657–666.

Saakvitne, K.W., Gamble, S.G., Pearlman, L.A. and Lev, B. (2000) *Risking Connection: A Training Curriculum for Working with Survivors of Childhood Abuse.* Lutherville, MD: Sidran Foundation Press.

Saakvitne, K.W. and Pearlman, L.A. (1996) *Transforming the Pain: A Workbook on Vicarious Traumatization.* New York: Norton.

Salter, A.C. (1995) *Transforming Trauma: A Guide to Understanding and Treating Adult Survivors of Child Sexual Abuse.* Thousand Oaks, CA: Sage.

Salzer, M. (2002) 'Consumer-delivered services as a best practice in mental health care delivery and the development of practice guidelines.' *Psychiatric Rehabilitation 6*, 3, 355–382.

Samuels, A. (1985) 'Countertransference: The 'mundus imaginalis' and a research project.' *Journal of Analytical Psychology 30*, 47–71.

Sanderson, C. (2004) *The Seduction of Children: Empowering Parents and Teachers to Protect Children from Child Sexual Abuse.* London: Jessica Kingsley Publishers.

Sanderson, C. (2006) *Counselling Adult Survivors of Child Sexual Abuse*, 3rd edition. London: Jessica Kingsley Publishers.

Sanderson, C. (2008) *Counselling Survivors of Domestic Abuse.* London: Jessica Kingsley Publishers.

Sanderson, C. (2010a) *Introduction to Counselling Survivors of Interpersonal Trauma.* London: Jessica Kingsley Publishers.

Sanderson, C. (2010b) 'Managing sexually harmful behaviour in young children.' *Protecting Children Update 68,* May.

Sanderson, C. (2010c) *The Warrior Within: A One in Four Handbook to Aid Recovery from Childhood Sexual Abuse and Violence.* London: One in Four.

Sanderson, C. (2010d) 'Working with young survivors of childhood sexual abuse.' *Protecting Children Update 73,* November.

Sanderson, C. (2011) *The Spirit Within: A One in Four handbook to Aid Recovery from Religious Sexual Abuse Across All Faiths.* London: One in Four.

Sanderson, C. (2012) 'Working with Survivors of Rape and Domestic Violence.' In C. Feltham and I. Horton (eds) *Sage Handbook of Counselling & Psychotherapy,* 3rd edition. London: Sage.

Schore, A.N. (2001) 'The effects of early relational trauma on right brain development, affect regulation and infant mental health.' *Infant Mental Health Journal 22,* 201–269.

Schore, A.N. (2003a) *Affect Dysregulation and Disorders of the Self.* New York: Norton.

Schore, A.N. (2003b) *Affect Dysregulation and the Repair of the Self.* New York: Norton.

Schore, A.N. (2011) 'The Human Unconscious: The Development of the Right Brain and its role in Early Emotional Life.' In V. Green (2011) (ed.) *Emotional Development in Psychoanalysis, Attachment Theory and Neuroscience: Creating Connections.* London: Routledge.

Schore, A.N. (2012) *The Science of the Art of Psychotherapy.* New York: Norton.

Schwartz, H.L. (2000) *Dialogues with Forgotten Voices: Relational Perspectives on Child Abuse Trauma and Treatment of Dissociative Disorders.* New York: Basic Books.

Scott, J.P. (1987) 'The Emotional Basis of Attachment and Separation.' In J.L. Sacksteder, D.P. Schwartz and Y. Akabane (eds) *Attachment and the Therapeutic Process: Essays in Honor of Otto Allen Will Jr., MD.* Madison, CT: International Universities Press.

Secretary of State for the Home Department (2003) *Safety and Justice: The Government's Proposals on Domestic Violence.* London: The Stationery Office.

Seligman, M.E.P. (1975) *Helplessness: On Depression, Development and Death.* San Francisco, CA: W.H. Freeman.

Shapiro, F. (1989) 'Eye Movement Desensitisation: a new treatment for post-traumatic stress disorder.' *Journal of Behavior Therapy and Experimental Psychiatry 20,* 211–217.

Shapiro, F. (1995) *Eye Movement Desensitisation and Reprocessing: Basic: Principles, Protocols and Procedures.* New York: Guilford Press.

Shapiro, F. (2002a) *EMDR as an Integrative Psychotherapy Approach: Experts of Diverse Orientations Explore the Paradigm Prism.* Washington, DC: American Psychological Association Press.

Shapiro, F. (2002b) 'EMDR twelve years after introduction: a review of past, present and future directions.' *Journal of Clinical Psychology 58,* 1–22.

1a

Shaver, P., Hazan, C. and Bradshaw, D. (1988) 'Love as Attachment: The Integration of Three Behavioural Systems.' In R.J. Sternberg and M. Barnes (eds) *The Psychology of Love*. New Haven, CT: Yale University Press.

Shaw, R. (2003) *The Embodied Therapist: The Therapist's Body Story*. Hove: Brunner-Routledge.

Shaw, R. (2004) 'The embodied psychotherapist: An exploration of the therapist's somatic phenomena within the therapeutic encounter.' *Psychotherapy Research 14*, 3, 271–288.

Siegel, D.J. (1996) 'Dissociation, Psychotherapy and Cognitive Sciences.' In J. Spira (ed.) *The Treatment of Dissociative Identity Disorder*. San Francisco, CA: Jossey-Bass.

Siegel, D. (1999) *The Developing Mind*. New York: Guilford.

Siegel, D.J. (2002) 'An Interpersonal Neurobiology of Psychotherapy: The Developing Mind and the Resolution of Trauma.' In M. Solomon and D.J. Siegel (eds) *Healing Trauma*. New York: Norton.

Sinason, V. (2008) 'How do we help ourselves?' In S. Benamer and K. White (eds) *Trauma and Attachment. The John Bowlby Memorial Conference Monograph 2006*. London: Karnac.

Solomon, R.C. (2002) *Spirituality for the Skeptic: The Thoughtful Love of Life*. New York: Oxford University Press.

Spanos, N.P. (1996) *Multiple Identities and False Memories: A Sociocognitive Perspective*. Washington, DC: American Psychological Association.

Steele, K., van der Hart, O. and Nijenhuis, E.R.S. (2001) 'Dependency in the Treatment of Complex Posttraumatic Stress Disorder and Dissociative Disorders.' *Journal of Trauma and Dissociation 2*, 4, 79–116.

Steele, K., Van der Hart, O., Ellert, R.S. and Nijenhuis, E.R.S. (2005) 'Phase-Oriented Treatment of Structural Dissociation in Complex Traumatization: Overcoming Trauma-Related Phobias.' *Journal of Trauma and Dissociation 6*, 3.

Steele, K. and Van der Hart, O. (2009) 'Treating dissociation.' In J.D. Ford and C. Courtois (eds) *Treating Complex Traumatic Stress Disorders (Adults): An Evidence-based Guide*. New York: Guilford.

Steinberg, M. (1994) *The Structured Clinical Interview for DSM-IV Dissociative Disorders-Revised (SCID-D)*. Washington, DC: American Psychiatric Press.

Steinberg, M. (1995) *Handbook for the Assessment of Dissociation: A Clinical Guide*. Washington, DC: American Psychiatric Press.

Stein, H., Allen, J.G. and Hill, J. (2003) 'Roles and relationships: A psychoeducational approach to reviewing strengths and difficulties in adulthood functioning.' *Bulletin of the Menninger Clinic 67*, 281–313.

Stern, D.N. (1985) *The Interpersonal World of the Infant: A View from Psychoanalysis and Developmental Psychology*. New York: Basic Books.

Stien, P.T. and Kendall, J. (2004) *Psychological Trauma and the Developing Brain: Neurologically Based Interventions for Troubled Children*. New York: Haworth Maltreatment and Trauma Press.

Teicher, M.H. (2000) 'Wounds that time won't heal: the neurobiology of child abuse'. *Cerebrum 2*, 4, 50–67.

Terr, L.C. (1991) 'Childhood traumas: An outline and overview.' *American Journal of Psychiatry 148*, 1, 10–20.

Terr, L.C. (1994) *Unchained Memories.* New York: Basic Books.

Thornhill, R. and Palmer, C.T. (2000) *A Natural History of Rape: Biological Basis of Sexual Coercion.* Cambridge, MA: MIT Press.

Tronick, E.Z. (1998) 'Dyadically expanded states of consciousness and the process of therapeutic change.' *Infant Mental Health Journal 19,* 3, 290– 299.

Tronick, E.Z., Als, H., Adamson, I., Wise, S. and Braelton, T.B. (1978) 'The infant's response to entrapment between contradictory messages in face-to face interaction.' *Journal of American Academy of Child Psychiatry 17,* 1–13.

Trujillo, L., Lewis, D.O., Yeager, C.A. and Gidlow, B. (1996) 'Imaginary companions of school boys and boys with dissociative disorder/multiple personality disorder.' *Child and Adolescent Psychiatric Clinics of North America 5,* 1, 2–3.

Van der Hart, O., Nijenhuis, E.R.S. and Steele, K. (2006) *The Haunted Self: Structural Dissociation and the Treatment of Chronic Traumatization.* New York: W.W. Norton.

Van der Hart, O., Steele, K., Boon, S. and Brown, P. (1993) 'The Treatment of Traumatic Memories: synthesis, realization, and integration.' *Dissociation 6,* 2/3, 162–180.

Van der Kolk, B.A. (1987) *Psychological Trauma.* Washington, DC: American Psychiatric Press.

Van der Kolk, B.A. (1989) 'The compulsion to repeat the trauma: Re-enactment, revictimisation, and masochism.' *Psychiatric Clinics of North America 12,* 2, 389–411.

Van der Kolk, B.A. (1994) 'The body keeps the score: Memory and evolving psychobiology of posttraumatic stress.' *Harvard Review of Psychiatry 1,* 253–265.

Van der Kolk, B.A. (1997) 'Trauma, Memory and Self-Regulation: Clinical Applications of Current Research.' Paper presented at Harvard Medical School Summer Seminars, Nantucket, MA, September.

Van der Kolk, B. (2004) 'The future of trauma work.' *Counselling and Psychotherapy Journal 15,* 4, 10–13.

Van der Kolk, B.A. (2005) 'Developmental Trauma Disorder: Toward a rational diagnosis for children with complex trauma histories.' *Psychiatric Annals 35,* 401–408.

Van der Kolk, B.A., Burbridge J.A. and Suzuki, J. (1997) 'The psychology of traumatic memory: clinical implications of neuroimaging studies.' In R. Yehuda and A.C. McFarlane (eds) *Psychobiology of Posttraumatic Stress Disorder (Annals of the New York Academy of Sciences)* 82, 99–113.

Van der Kolk, B.A. and Fisher, R. (1995) 'Dissociation and the fragmentary nature of traumatic memories: overview and exploratory study.' *Journal of Traumatic Stress 8,* 4, 505–25.

Van der Kolk, B.A., Roth, S., Pelcovitz, D., Sunday, S. and Spinazzola, J. (2005) 'Disorders of extreme stress: The empirical foundation of complex adaptation to trauma.' *Journal of Traumatic Stress 18,* 389–399.

Vanderlinden, J., Van Dyck, R., Vandereycken, W. and Vertommen, H. (1993) 'Dissociation and traumatic experiences in the general population of The Netherlands.' *Hospital and Community Psychiatry 44,* 8, 786–788.

Wastell, C. (2005) *Understanding Trauma and Emotion: Dealing with Trauma – An Emotion Focussed Approach.* Maidenhead: Open University Press.

Welldon, E.V. (2004) *Mother, Madonna, Whore: The Idealisation and Denigration of Motherhood*. London: Karnac.

Wilson, J.P. (2002) 'The Abyss Experience and Catastrophic Stress.' Paper presented at St Joseph's University, Philadelphia, PA, 11 October.

Wilson, J.P. (2003) *Empathic Strain and Posttraumatic Therapy*. New York: Guilford.

Wilson, J.P. (2004) 'Broken Spirits.' In J.P. Wilson and B. Drozdek (eds) *Broken Spirits: The Treatment of Traumatized Asylum Seekers, Refugees, and War and Torture Victims*. New York: Brunner-Routledge.

Wilson, J.P. (2006) 'The Posttraumatic Self.' In J.P. Wilson (ed.) *The Posttraumatic Self: Restoring Meaning and Wholeness to Personality*. New York: Routledge.

Wilson, J.P., Friedman, M.J. and Lindy, J.D. (2001) *Treating Psychological Trauma and PTSD*. New York: Guilford.

Wilson, J.P. and Lindy, J.D. (eds) (1994) *Countertransference in the Treatment of PTSD*. New York: Guilford.

Winnicott, D.W. (1958) *Collected Papers: Through Paediatrics to Psychoanalysis*. London: Tavistock.

Winnicott, D.W. (1965) *The Maturational Process and the Facilitating Environment: Studies in the Theory of Emotional Development*. New York: International Universities Press.

Winnicott, D.W. (1966) *The Family and Individual Development*. New York: Basic Books.

Winnicott, D. (2008) *Play and Reality*. London: Routledge.

Worden, J.W. (2003) *Grief Counselling and Grief Therapy: A Handbook for the Mental Health Practitioner*, 3rd edition. London: Brunner-Routledge.

World Health Organisation. (2007) *The ICD-10 Classification of Mental and Behavioural Disorders: Clinical Descriptions and Diagnostic Guidelines*. Geneva: WHO.

Yalom, I. (2008) *Staring at the Sun: Overcoming the Dread of Death*. London: Piatkus Books.

Yassen, J. (1995) 'Preventing Secondary Traumatic Stress Disorder.' In C.R. Figley (ed.) *Compassion Fatigue: Coping with Secondary Stress Disorder in Those who Treat the Traumatized*. New York: Brunner/Mazel.

Young, B.H., Ruzick, J.I. and Ford, J.D. (1999) 'Cognitive-behavioural group for disaster-related PTSD.' In B.H. Young and D.D. Blake (eds) *Group Treatments for Posttraumatic Stress Disorder*. Philadelphia: Brunner-Mazel.

Young, J.E., Klosko, J.S. and Weishaar, M. (2003) *Schema Therapy*. New York: Guilford Press.

Zak, P.J. (2008) 'The Neurobiology of Trust'. Scientific American June 2008, 99–95.

FURTHER READING

SELF-HELP BOOKS FOR SURVIVORS

Ainscough, C. and Toon, K. (2000) *Breaking Free: Help for Survivors of Child Sexual Abuse.* London: Sheldon Press.

Davis, L. (2002) *The Courage to Heal: A Guide for Women Survivors of Child Sexual Abuse.* New Edition, London: Vermilion.

Gil, E. (1983) *Outgrowing the Pain: A Book for and about Adults Abused as Children.* Rockville, MD: Launch.

Mines, S. (1996) *Sexual Abuse, Sacred Wound: Transforming Deep Trauma.* Station Hill Openings. (The role of expressive and creative work in healing from sexual abuse.) Barrytow, NY:

Parkes, P. (1989) *Rescuing the Inner Child: Therapy for Adults Sexually Abused as Children.* London: Souvenir Press (E&A) Ltd.

Sanford, L.T. (1990) *Strong at the Broken Places: Overcoming the Trauma of Childhood Abuse.* London: Virago.

Sanderson, C. (2010) *The Warrior Within: A One in Four Handbook to Aid Recovery from Sexual Violence.* London: One in Four.

Wood, W. and Hatton, L. (1988) *Triumph over Darkness: Understanding and Healing the Trauma of Childhood Sexual Abuse.* Hillsboro, OR: Beyond Words Publishing Inc.

FOR SURVIVORS ABUSED BY WOMEN

Elliot, M. (ed.) (1993) *Female Sexual Abuse of Children: The Ultimate Taboo.* London: Longman.

FOR BLACK WOMEN SURVIVORS

Wilson, M. (1993) *Crossing the Boundary: Black Women Survive Incest.* London: Virago.

FOR MALE SURVIVORS

Etherington, K. (1995) *Adult Male Survivors of Sexual Abuse.* London: Pitman Publishing.

Grubman-Black, S.D. (1990) *Broken Boys/Mending Men: Recovery from Childhood Sexual Abuse.* Blue Ridge Summit, PA: Tab Books.

Hunter, M. (1990) *Abused Boys: The Neglected Victims of Sexual Abuse.* Lexington, MA: Lexington.

Lew, M. (1988) *Victims No Longer: Men Recovering from Incest and Other Sexual Child Abuse.* New York: Neuramount Publishers.

FOR SURVIVORS WITH LEARNING DISABILITIES

Hollins, S. and Sinason, V. (1992) *Bob Tells All*. St. George's Hospital Mental Health Library. London: Beyond Words Publishing Inc.

Hollins, S. and Sinason, V. (1992) *Jenny Speaks Out*. St George's Hospital Mental Health Library. London: Beyond Words Publishing Inc.

WRITINGS FOR SURVIVORS

Farthing, L., Malone, C. and Marce, L. (eds) (1996) *The Memory Bird: Survivors of Sexual Abuse*. London: Virago. (More than 200 male and female contributors.)

AUTOBIOGRAPHY

Angelou, M. (1983) *I Know Why the Caged Bird Sings*. London: Virago.

Chase, T. (1998) *When Rabbit Howls*. London: Sidgwick and Jackson. (The story of a woman who developed multiple personalities to survive her abuse.)

Fraser, S. (1989) *My Father's House: A Memoir of Incest and of Healing*. London: Virago.

Smart, P.D. (2006) *Who's Afraid of the Teddy bear's Picnic: A Story of Sexual Abuse and Recovery Through Psychotherapy*. Brentwood: Chipmunka Publishing.

Spring, J. (1987) *Cry Hard and Swim*. London: Virago.

FICTION

Walker, A. (1983) *The Colour Purple*. London: Women's Press.

FOR PARTNERS AND FAMILIES OF SURVIVORS

Davis, L. (1991) *Allies in Healing: When the Person you Love was Sexually Abused as a Child*. New York: Harper Perennial.

Graber, K. (1988) *Ghosts in the Bedroom: A Guide for Partners of Incest Survivors*. Deerfield Beach, FL: Health Communication.

Messages from Parents whose Children have been Sexually Abused. The Child and Family Resource Group, Leeds Community and Mental Health Trust, Belmont House, 3/5 Belmont Grove, Leeds LS2 9NP.

From Discovery to Recovery: A Parent's Survival Guide to Child Sexual Abuse. Warwickshire Social Services department, PO Box 48, Shire Hall, Warwick CV34 4RD. Audiotape and booklet.

HELP WITH RELATIONSHIPS

Litvinoff, S. (1991) *The Relate Guide to Better Relationships*. London: Ebury Press.

Secunda, V. (1992) *When you and your Mother can't be Friends*. Romsey, Hampshire: Cedar.

FOR THERAPISTS

Hall, L. and Lloyd, S. (1989) *Surviving Child Sexual Abuse: A Handbook for Helping Women Challenge their Past*. Lewes: Falmer Press.

Sanderson, C. (2004) *The Seduction of Children: Empowering Parents and Teachers to Protect Children from Child Sexual Abuse*. London: Jessica Kingsley Publishers.

Sanderson, C. (2006) *Counselling Adult Survivors of Child Sexual Abuse*, 3rd edition. London: Jessica Kingsley Publishers.

Sanderson, C. (2010) *Introduction to Counselling Survivors of Interpersonal Trauma*. London: Jessica Kingsley Publishers.

FUTURE ONE IN FOUR HANDBOOKS

Workbook for Survivors of Childhood Sexual Abuse
Surviving Rape and Sexual Violence
Surviving Clerical Abuse
Films on Childhood Sexual Abuse
Capturing the Friedman's
Hard Candy
London To Brighton
Precious
War Zone
The Woodsman

SUBJECT INDEX

AUTHOR INDEX